Advance praise

The letters of Slippery Elm are the plumage of a nightingale who soars high, singing the lyrical anarchism of Spain. Language is the means of struggle, of subversion, satire and celebration, in a voice that turns from ecstatic to erotic. As they lift the groaning bones of Franco from his grave, the fascist myth that elides the history of Al-Andalus crumbles to dust. Slippery Elm plays his part, sings the hidden song of lost Lorca, whose duende weeps as a spring more precious than gold, evokes a world that was and is, and is yet to come. An adventurer, whose path has all the light stepping and emphatic stamp of the flamenco dancer, whose dancing ground is strewn with poetry, a lover who writes with candour and beauty. It is a rare and precious thing to find a book which talks to the heart, and it takes a troubadour to perform such a miracle.

Peter Grey, author of *Apocalyptic Witchcraft* (Scarlet Imprint)

The Dead Hermes Epistolary

Slippery Elm

The Dead Hermes Epistolary

ISBN
978-1-7325523-5-7

First Printed
by Gods&Radicals Press 2019

Cover Design by Li Pallas
likeanarch.com

Layout by Casandra Johns
houseofhands.net

Editing Team
Rhyd Wildermuth
Casandra Johns

Gods&Radical Press
PO Box 11850
Olympia Washington 98508

Solidarity, bulk discount, and wholesale copies available.
Contact the editors or author, or for distro:
distro@abeautifulresistance.com

Gods&Radicals Press is a not-for-profit anti-capitalist Pagan publisher.
View our other works and online journal at
abeautifulresistance.org

Ἑρμοῦ Χθονίου, θυμίαμα, στύρακα.

Κωκυτοῦ ναίων ἀνυπόστροφον οἶμον ἀνάγκης,
ὃς ψυχὰς θνητῶν κατάγεις ὑπὸ νέρτερα γαίης,
Ἑρμῆ, βακχεχόροιο Διωνύσοιο γένεθλον,
καὶ Παφίης κούρης, ἑλικοβλεφάρου Ἀφροδίτης,
ὃς παρὰ Περσεφόνης ἱερὸν δόμον ἀμφιπολεύεις,
αἰνομόροις ψυχαῖς πομπὸς κατὰ γαῖαν ὑπάρχων·
ἃς κατάγεις, ὁπόταν μοίρης χρόνος εἰσαφίκηται,
εὐϊέρῳ ῥάβδῳ θέλγων ὑπνοδώτιδι πάντα,
καὶ πάλιν ὑπνώοντας ἐγείρεις. σοὶ γὰρ ἔδωκεν
τιμὴν Φερσεφόνεια θεά, κατὰ Τάρταρον εὐρὺν
ψυχαῖς ἀενάοις θνητῶν ὁδὸν ἡγεμονεύειν.
ἀλλά, μάκαρ, πέμποις μύσταις τέλος ἐσθλὸν ἐπ᾽ ἔργοις.

Table of Contents

Madkhal
[Introduction] ... 9
Risāla fī sh-sharq wa l-gharb
[Risāla on the East and West] ... 19
Risālat al-ʿandalīb
[Risāla of the Violet Smile] ... 33
Risāla fī l-bāṭin wa ẓ-ẓāhir
[Risāla on the Inner and the Outer] ... 49
Risāla fī l-hīrmīs aṣ-ṣāmat
[Risāla of the Dead Hermes] ... 63
Risālat as-sahm fī l-qalb
[Risāla of the Arrow in the Heart] ... 81
Risālat al-filāḥa
[Risāla on Agriculture] ... 101
Risāla fī jannat al-janān
[Risāla of the Closed Garden] ... 145
Risāla fī l-kawkaba taḥta l-arḍ
[Risāla of the Anti-Court] ... 187
Risālat al-kahf
[Risāla of the Cave] ... 213
Bibliography ... 223
Index ... 235

Mad<u>kh</u>al

[Introduction]

☿

It is the great hour of the night and you are sleeping. The air is voiceless and still: the polished mirror of a lake void of ripples. A moonbeam falls across your breathing chest and lingers on for a count of three heartbeats. Suddenly, you are thrown to vigil, and your eyes are a peacock's fan that snaps open as you feel a thin needle in your heart. While slightly unsettling, this first seed of high-pitched pain blossoms into a cold fire that spreads down your arms and legs and fills you to the finger tips with an old nocturnal ecstasy.

You feel like a bowstring drawn and shot.

Outside, there is a sound between the deed of an archer and a harpist followed by a sharp thud. You rise up and pass through the door to the garden. There are wingbeats and the same sad harp before the garden regains its voiceless calm. You look about and almost turn back until you notice a gaunt feather of smoke rising from the rose bushes and move closer to spread the foliage.

That's when you see it.

Still smoking, the thing glows black like meteoritic stone, like a fruit fallen from the arboretum of the sky. Yet it also possesses the quality of having been devoured by loam, boiled in the crucible of the earth's mantle and shot to the surface per volcanic eruption. Like a diamond. Like a black diamond. There, hanging a few feet above the ground, is a dark envelope pierced through by a rose's thorn. An errant cloud quits the moon's face, whose naked light now rouses the silver ink inscribed thereon, and you realize with a gasp the envelope is addressed to you...

Whether secreted into a pocket, hidden beneath a pillow, or pinned to a front door, there is a certain magical quality about receiving a letter or message. Where did it come from? Who is it for? What distances did it traverse?

What hands did it pass through? What dangers braved? What ill-weather endured? What border-agents eluded? And all that the message be delivered intact.... This quality is easily appreciated by children and by their co-conspirators, the poets. Many of us can remember receiving a letter as children and being rapt with the feeling of touching an object whose origins seemed rooted in some far-off fairy country.

While the more rebellious among us may still send each other letters, in any case, many young people today have never received or sent a letter, and nowadays, whether young or old, the mysterious fallen star encountered on one's doorstep is more often than not yet another parcel from Amazon. There's hardly a need to remind us that the internet, and more specifically social media, presently hold the mercurial realms of communication and information in a fatal choke-hold. This is to say that reality itself is held in a fatal choke-hold: for is not Logos, and the numeric and alphabetic garments in which it tends to dress, an animating principle of the universe itself?

This book is about reality. It has as its axis the ecotone between language and the land. It employs the epistle form as a means of sabotaging the suffocating ontological artifice erected by the internet and social media. It has been written for the witchcraft being reborn all around us, under the clandestine auspices of Hermes Chthonios.

The Epistolary Form

While we all know that letters have been a prominent medium of communication for thousands of years, it is less known that the epistle has also enjoyed pride of place as a preferred (if not *the* preferred) literary form for the expression and propagation of complex philosophical, scientific, mystical, or political ideas.

The epistle as a literary genre was cultivated in Ancient Egypt and Greece, and subsequently developed further by the Romans. Epistles were written in these civilizations not only for communication or didactic purposes, but were also addressed to the Dead and the Gods. An aspect of letter-writing all but lost in our age, yet one that the present collection, in its own way, seeks to rekindle.

Many of us may have first encountered the term epistle in the context of the New Testament, which is made up in part of the Pauline Epistles and the General Epistles. Here we have an example of the epistolary form not only expressing theological and ethical concepts, but forming a part of a tradition's religious canon. A similar example would be the *Rasā'il al-Ḥikma* [Letters of Wisdom], a collection of texts held sacred by the Druze faith. We find parallels to this in several branches of contemporary paganism and witchcraft, in which letters by prominent personages are treasured by their initiates, lineages, and other practitioners who they might have inspired.

The epistolary form was so highly regarded during parts of the medieval period that rhetoric was taught in some universities as a subcategory of letter-writing, and not the other way around. Here, the term epistle refers to a literary form somewhere between a message and a treatise.

For example, we see the term epistle used in this way in the *Rasā'il Ikhwān aṣ-Ṣafā'* [Epistles of the Brethren of Purity]. This notorious epistolary, written and compiled by the Brethren of Purity (a secret society from tenth century Basra, Iraq, the identity of whose members remains a mystery), covers subjects as diverse as natural sciences, mathematics, music, religion, astronomy, ethics, politics, and magic. *The Golden Epistle* by William of St. Thierry or Ibn 'Arabī's *Risālat al-Anwār* [Epistle of Lights] are but two more famous medieval examples of the epistle form employed in a mystical context.

In addition to their composition for communication, mystical illumination, or the propagation of ideas, epistles also functioned at times as the chief medium through which religious and philosophical polemics raged. One need only think of the polemical letters that were shot back and forth during the second phase of the Maimonidean Controversy (the Hebrew equivalent of the *risāla* is the *iggeret*).

The epistles in this collection pay homage to this past, and remind the reader of a time when a simple handwritten letter could mystify, illuminate, or spark a revolution. The form is employed here as an alternative, or even a challenge, to the more cursory blog post or the essay whose structure is shackled by Aristotelian logic and its derivatives. Poetic inference is applied alongside logical inference, and story and discourse are manipulated in a way in which ideas are rarely developed in the logical sequence of premise-premise-conclusion. The epistle opens the doors to direct, polemical writing, without losing scientific rigour, and permits an interdisciplinary approach that should not be exclusively seen as "cutting edge" or "post-modern," but traditional, standing on the shoulders of the ancestors.

Anti-Fascist Philology

The nine epistles that comprise this collection are broad in scope, and treat subjects proper to a number of disciplines and traditions, including philosophy, literature, history, mysticism, and politics. One element that brings them all together is their focus on language as a way in which the soul of Nature expresses itself through the prism of the human body. Another binding element is its subtle and recurring treatment of three taboo themes in leftist thought: time, tradition, and identity.

With each passing year, the world is ever more polluted, people grow ever more desperate, and politicians ever more openly and unabashedly rancid. Climate change threatens all life on earth, and fascist tendencies are on the rise. This hostile atmosphere of lethargy and despair presents us with many challenges. Fortunately, brilliant writers, thinkers, and doers have come out of the shadows to meet them, and discuss how we can batten down the hatches and survive in a low-energy future, or combat the menace of fascism and its ugly cousins. Theories are developed, pacts are forged, and different initiatives are carried out to overcome the machinations of the enemy. However, there are pitfalls all around, and the left seems ever plagued by in-fighting, blind spots, and other debilities. The present contribution does not focus on exposing the enemy, or exclusively seek to ring alarm bells for the lugubrious state of the political or natural climates. There have been lucid and inspiring works dealing with these that have come out in recent years, some of which are included in the Bibliography herein. Rather, it proposes a reappraisal of and a different way of relating to time, tradition and identity, in hopes of fortifying our rhetoric and that of our allies, and overcoming the pitfalls—perhaps some of the greatest pitfalls that we currently face—that these three volatile subjects have given rise to. Besides the crane-skin bag of the poet, the tools employed towards this end are those of the student of Arabic, Hebrew, and Romance philology.

What is philology? Philology is the crossroads between language, history, linguistics, and literature. It is etymologically derived from *philos* [to put it simply, *love*] and *lógos* [to put it simply, *word*]. So philology is the love of words. It is alternatively translated as the love of learning. It is the study of texts, yet it also encompasses the study of languages in oral historical sources. While texts tend to turn up at the heart of philology as a discipline, one cannot unlock a text without complementing their foray with knowledge of the literature of the language in question, its linguistics, and the history and culture of the people who speak that language.

Yet, in some Western universities, the term philology has been excised. For example, instead of Romance philology, one might encounter Romance Studies. This is due in part to the efforts of some Western powers to distance themselves from the term given its association with German nationalism in both world wars. Philology has been used to uncover, exalt, and canonize national literatures, upon which are constructed national narratives and identities. Like tradition, it has had to bear the weight of a lamentable and at times mistaken association with fascism and far-right politics.

It is a goal of the present collection to use philology to explode the myths of nationalism, not to canonize them. Sometimes, when dealing with the more toxic of these, it seeks to finish them once and for all. In other cases, the goal is more of an unmasking, or temporary stripping down, which in some cases can serve to invigorate the identity in question. It's about fertilization, cross-fertilization, and forging pacts. This is an ongoing process.

While some have been a long time coming, in the twenty-first century at least, the aforementioned pitfalls in leftist thought and organizing are often the ugly spawn of the internet. If the internet unscrewed the locks from the doors, it opened them to an illusory labyrinth full of minotaurs, pregnant with mirage, where your steps are not only watched or tracked, but are forcefully flown along pre-programmed paths. Meaning is up for grabs. Who controls the liminal herm, wins the war. This is a particularly problematic issue for Paganism, in which symbols, myths, culture, tradition, identity, and so on have at times been seized and perverted by the fascist enemy towards their own despicable ends. This is like a gang of cutthroats robbing a museum, appropriating the artefacts, and re-writing history to their own morbid tune. A thing not unlike colonialism.

With its focus on language and the land, it is only natural for the present work to fall under the auspices of Hermes Chthonios. It is this cunning god of language and shapeshifting, of boundaries and their transgression, that can help us break through the rigid compartmentalization of identity, knowledge—and indeed, of reality itself—brought about by modernity, capitalism, and the internet. As underworld deity and guide of the dead, He can help revive dead or dying languages, and thereby put us back in touch with our ancestors. In this way, we are provoked to approach time and tradition with new eyes. This is philological necromancy. By the tricks of the god, and the cunning of the poet, the bones of texts are enfleshed once more and shocked into speech.

The Poet as Go-Between

> Poet, be God's spy, if God exists.[1]
> Lawrence Ferlinghetti

Intellectuals from all sides of the political spectrum often base their rhetoric on history. The most frequent readings of history employed tend to be those more reduced, black-and-white, kings-and-conquests type narratives. While the events that make historical headlines are in no way to be ignored, nor these types of narratives to be downplayed, there are many seemingly smaller events and lesser-known figures that are almost never discussed. However, these figures often end up having an enormous role in shaping the flow of subsequent events, for good or ill. One such figure is the go-between. Examples of go-betweens, to borrow Metcalf's terms and definitions, include *1) physical/biological go-betweens (those who create material links between worlds; carriers of plants animals and disease; bearers of children of mixed-race), 2) transactional go-betweens (those who facilitate social interaction between worlds; translators, cultural brokers, negotiators), or 3) representational (those who write, draw maps, and represent the "other" culture through texts, words, or images).*[2] Other types of go-betweens include spies and undercover agents, witches and other "shaman-like" figures who mediate relations between humans, spirits, and the natural world.

We see the importance of go-betweens and of dominance in the mercurial realms of communication, travel, and information highlighted in the *Art of War* by Sun Tzu which insists that the adept deployment of spies is imperative if the enemy is to be defeated:

1 See Ferlinghetti, *Poetry as Insurgent Art*, 12.

2 See Metcalf, *Go-Betweens and the Colonization of Brazil: 1500–1600*, 12.

> Thus, what enables the wise sovereign and the good general to strike and conquer, and achieve things beyond the reach of ordinary men, is foreknowledge. Hence the use of spies, of whom there are five classes: (1) Local spies; (2) inward spies; (3) converted spies; (4) doomed spies; (5) surviving spies. When these five kinds of spy are all at work, none can discover the secret system. This is called "divine manipulation of the threads." It is the sovereign's most precious faculty.[3]

In addition to spies, it is common to see bridges and post offices being considered critical objectives for control. Postal workers can be considered go-betweens, and travel also falls under the domain of Hermes. In Spanish, one sometimes hears the verb *comunicar* used in relation to roads, borders, and so on. The idea is that one road connecting to another is a form of communication. If a road or bridge is damaged, that communication is broken.

Perhaps it is due to their dominance in the mercurial arts that poets have a proclivity for espionage and that "divine manipulation of the threads" alluded to by Sun Tzu. While at times involved in the politics of their day, the secret agency of the poet reveals itself more broadly in their acting as lyre and mouth-piece to some furtive yet omnipresent voice or voices. Mark David Kaufman writes:

> Historically, writers have made excellent spies. It seems a life of letters provides the perfect cover for a life of plotting, of coding and decoding, of crossing borders and blurring identities. The list of English writers who may (or may not) have been involved in clandestine operations is long and distinguished: Geoffrey Chaucer, Christopher Marlowe, Aphra Behn, Daniel Defoe, Somerset Maugham, and Graham Greene, to name only a few...[4]

It this association of poet as go-between and mercurial saboteur that is invoked throughout this collection.

---

3 From section XII of *The Art of War*.

4 See Kaufman, "The Hermeneutics of Recruitment: The Case of Wordsworth."

The Opening

> Ahora todo se ha roto en el mundo. Todo. Hasta las herramientas del filósofo. Y el salmo ha enloquecido: se ha hecho llanto, grito, aullido, blasfemia... y se ha arrojado de cabeza en el infierno. Aquí están ahora los poetas. Aquí estoy yo por lo menos.
>
> Now everything on earth has broken. Everything. Even the tools of philosophy. And the psalm has gone mad: it's been crying, shouting, howling, blaspheming... and thrown headfirst into hell. The poets are here now. Well, I am here at least. [5]

The word *risāla* [letter] comes from the root 'r s l' [ر س ل] whose many derivative verb forms cover a semantic range that includes various actions such as "to correspond," "to send," or "to exchange letters."[6] The noun *rasūl* [messenger; prophet] is also derived from this root. In addition to acknowledging the flowering of *rasā'il* [s. *risāla*] during the Islamic Golden Age (what Western historiography calls the "medieval period" or the "dark ages"), the term *risāla* is used to refer to the epistles in this collection as an allusion to the spiritual connotation in the receiving, recording, and relaying of a message. *Rasūl* differentiates itself from *nabī*, an alternate term translated as prophet, in that the message is not received merely in visions or dreams but via contact with an angel. This is not to insinuate that this work is a prophecy or its redactor a prophet, but to establish the epistle as a two-way channel of communication between humans, the dead, and the gods upon a horizontal plane.

---

5 See León Felipe, "El poeta y el filósofo." English translation by Lucy Fuggle.

6 *Risāla* [رسالة] is primarily translated throughout the present collection as either "letter," "epistle," or "message," depending on context. With regard to transliteration, I have omitted the final (frequently) silent *ta marbūṭa* [ة] in most cases, to facilitate pronunciation by non-Arabic speakers. The exception is in possessive constructs in which the *ta marbūṭa* is included, also to facilitate pronunciation. Which is to say, transliterating the word *risāla* would be omitting the *ta marbūṭa*, and transliterating it *risālat* would be including it. Likewise, in cases where there is a *waṣla* in Arabic phrases, I omit the *alif* [ا], and in cases of sun letters (as opposed to moon letters) I omit the *lām* [ل] and double up the first consonant of the word being modified by the definite article. Again, to facilitate pronunciation.

And so a petition is aimed at Hermes Chthonios, that cattle-rustling thief at the gates who sends dreams or lifts sleep with but a flick of his wanton wand. Of the epistles herein he is declared the remitter.

And so a petition is aimed at you, friend, to tranquilly and critically consider the message relayed. You are declared *destinataire*, at once recipient and destination, delicately determined by the dealings of destiny. Merry meet. Grace and peace upon you.

And the poet Slippery Elm is declared amanuensis and courier. If, after receiving these messages, a return address is sought, the *destinataire* may resort to the verses by León Felipe cited above, which locate the poet in the underworld that we all know and love, the rose-gardens of Hell or the quartz caves of Fairy.

Thus having opened with the traditional declaration of remitter, courier, and *destinataire,* we may begin. However, since the communication at play in this work is forked, open-ended and travels there and back, another *destinataire* is hereby acknowledged and invoked as guide.

To Nebiros

Hell-hound, border dweller, chthonic angel
Howler, curser, doer and doer
Sagely miner, herbal healer
Jackal who haunts Death's wasted deserts,
Hades' watchdog, Hekate's pup,
Who speeds with Hermes down and up
Whose howls rouse the sleepers under roots
And by whose glorious hand the Moon's bright children
Walk unseen, fly to the stars,
Or plumb the dark Earth's crystal depths—
O fearsome guard dog, snake-tailed and wingèd,
By the fallen Sun, the golden fleece
Of St. John's Wort bursting 'neath a Midsummer sky
I bid thee come! Amen.

1

Risāla fī sh-sharq wa l-gharb

[Risāla on the East and West]

☿

The poet is a master of time. A petrified magician with proleptic eyes and analeptic feet who stands so still and moves so slowly they can appear inanimate, yet hip to that secret by which the clay pots of Story and Discourse are filled with breath and made to spin. Story: the series of events in the order in which they really unfold. Discourse: the order in which those events are narrated. A story has a beginning, middle, and end. Discourse can make the end the middle and the beginning the end as it sees fit.

The poet has an intimate relationship with time; by metonymy, therefore, she or he is also a witch, or in other words, a Minister of Fate. Truly in poems and tales there is a sign, and in them one sees expressed in the diminutive the same notes and time signatures to which dance the stars and all things. What better way to learn about concepts like Zeno's 7th Paradox, the Laws of Relative Motion, Entropy, or Gravity, than by contemplating the structure of a poem or tale? Edgar Allen Poe celebrated Metaphor and Simile, because, as he asserted, they are the very laws of the universe. Indeed, the laws of the universe are naught but poetry. Listen close. I mean that in the best sense of the words.

Thanks to Einstein and his Theory of Relativity, science has found a way to express a shade of what our witches and magicians have always known. Time slithers, folds in on itself, bites its tail, and can give light to fractals and spirals of ineffable complexity. The understanding that there is more to time than meets the clock has become quite commonplace. What is less common is the realization that like her sister time, space is also relative. This might be difficult for some people to grasp, as space arguably appears more tangible than time, but truly, space might prove to be the more relative of the two.

Let us consider cosmogony, and that erotic ecstatic moment that astronomers came to term the Big Bang. This is somewhat of a misnomer; a more accurate term might be the Big Expansion. Astronomers who work in the field of cosmogony believe that rather than a big explosion giving birth to the universe, all the fabric of what would come to be the universe as we know it was condensed into a small and incomprehensibly compact point. This point—or seed, as some might choose to view it—did not explode. Rather, it unravelled and continues to unravel even now.

Think of what happens when a leaf of paper crumpled into a dense ball is subsequently unravelled. This makes us ponder: if everything that exists was condensed in that seed, what could it expand into? Would there not be a something, or maybe a nothing, outside of that seed? The truth is, it would not have expanded into a something, or even a nothing. In the time of that seed, the idea of an outside did not exist.

Consider the North pole. When one is standing on the North pole, the idea of "North" ceases to exist, as any which way one may step, any which way the wind may blow, leads to the South.

And so the Rose of Winds sheds its petals. There is no North, East, South, or West without a subject. We see this in the Sun that rises in Japan as it sets in Samoa. Or in the way the Incas traced their constellations; not stars upon a depth of black but black shapes upon a depth of stars. Or in pop culture drawings that contain optical illusions and allusions to Freud. Or in the word for China in Mandarin, *Zhonggou:* not Eastern Kingdom, but Middle Kingdom. Or in the profoundest of oceans where up can be down and down up. Or in the underworld where, per D.H. Lawrence, darkness is awake upon the dark.[7] And in the underworld, that, per *The Vision of Er*, projects its deepest asphodel meadows upon the starry sky, where souls descend into earthly grottoes only to emerge refreshed or fatigued from craters on the moon, where the stars of heaven strike the lowliest plants and whisper to them: "grow." [8]

The ancients knew this; the geography of their myths witnessing more than one Mt. Olympus pick up its skirts, pull up its roots, and travel for leagues across land and sea.[9]

Let us remember that the same spatial subjectivity applies when we speak of the cardinal directions in terms of political entities. East and West do

7 Cf. "Bavarian Gentians" by D. H. Lawrence.

8 See the version and subsequent commentary included by Jake Stratton-Kent in his *Geosophia*, vol. 1, 368–98.

9 See the section "Mythic Geography" in *Geosophia*, vol. 1, 149–51.

not refer to fixed territories with fixed characteristics. This is demonstrated by the way in which Native Americans and First Nations were until fairly recently commonly referred to as Indians, or in how Australia is considered part of the West.

When one writes about the supposed clash of civilizations, one is writing about an Orient and an Occident of the mind. Edward Said famously wrote, "everyone who writes about the Orient must locate himself vis à vis the Orient."[10] Frequently, the Orient is taken to be the world of Islam and the Occident is Europe and her offshoot, the USA. It is important to make this distinction between the world of Islam and the so-called Far East, which "Western" culture tends to perceive as less of a threat to and less of a direct antithesis of itself, due to its distance and due to the fact that Far Eastern civilizations are not so much derived from Abrahamic religions. In contrast, Islam is Christianity's first cousin. Familiar, but seemingly unassimilable, similar but not exactly the same, where the West sees its own face reflected in a mirror of alterity. Let's not forget that in the lands that would become Europe, Islam was not initially viewed as a separate religion, but as a Christian heresy.[11]

The terms East and West have always been evocative of a dichotomy, of a history defined by wars and the inevitable clash of two opposing opposites. Of course, this is not the truth. What is considered Occidental today is in grand proportion made up of "Oriental DNA" and vice versa. These mental territories have always been heterogenous, subjective, and permeable; the borders thought to define them, both mental and physical, have never been able to keep much of anything or anyone out or in. We see this in al-Andalus during different periods, in Frederick II's Sicily, in Saladin's Egypt and Syria, among many other places, where by a trick of the light and an anachronistic multiculturalism that was by no means utopian, the medieval becomes the post-modern.

There are innumerable ways in which the "West" is indebted to the "East," and the other way around. Simply put, Europe would be without many of its most positive contributions and best-loved hallmarks were it not for Classical Islamic civilization, which in turn found the kindling for its own growth and innovation thanks to the cultural legacy left behind by

10 See Said, *Orientalism*, 20.

11 On this point see Menocal, *The Arabic Role in Medieval Literary History: A Forgotten Heritage*. 27–71.

the Greeks, who in turn were profoundly influenced by the cultures that surrounded them and with whom they interpenetrated.[12]

For example, the luminaries of Classical Islamic civilization made numerous breakthroughs and advances in science, literature, medicine, and agriculture. These breakthroughs were later absorbed and imitated by medieval Europe which profoundly effected the development of "Western" civilization.

Words like alchemy or algebra are both arabisms [*al-khīmiyā'* and *al-jabr* respectively]. To put this in perspective, the word "chemistry" is derived from the word "alchemy," and algebra is one of the cornerstones of mathematics, which is itself the cornerstone of practically all modern technology. Both alchemy and algebra have roots in pre-Islamic cultures, but Muslim luminaries made important advances and theoretical developments that gave them the form that we know today. In the case of alchemy we can cite Jābir ibn Ḥayyān, and in that of algebra we can cite al-Khwārizmī, author of *Al-Jabr* and first to treat algebra as a discipline in itself, or ʿOmar Khayyām (yes, *that* ʿOmar Khayyām!) who is thought to have been the first to identify the foundations of algebraic geometry.[13]

In virtually all the sciences, from astronomy (some Muslim astronomers like Ibn Bājja, of whom more anon, have craters on the moon named after them), to botany, to physics, Muslim luminaries made significant contributions as well as in the visual, social, and literary arts. Ibn Khaldūn is considered by some to be the founder of sociology. Arabic script influenced European calligraphy as scholars sought to imitate the elegant contours of its letters, while architects did the same with those of "Islamic style" buildings (cf. Mudéjar architecture). In the literary arena, we can cite the great debt that troubadour poetry (which some consider to be the very essence of European civilization) owes to the poetry of al-Andalus.[14] None of these advances would have been possible without a highly advanced and healthy agricultural tradition.[15]

---

12 See for example, *The Legacy of Muslim Spain* edited by Salma Khadra Jayyusi and Manuela Marín.

13 On the question of "ethnicity" among the luminaries of the Islamic world see *Risāla of the Inner and the Outer*, (page 49—52).

14 This point is treated in detail in *Risāla of the Arrow in the Heart* and *Risāla of the Closed Garden*.

15 This point is treated in detail in *Risālat al-Filāḥa*.

Most people would agree that aside from the Bible, the textual nerve at the foundation of "Western" civilization is made up of the works of Plato, Aristotle, Galen, and other luminaries of the Classical Greek and Roman worlds. Less people are aware, however, that an overwhelming amount of these texts (and indeed luminaries) have come down to the "West" through an Islamic filter. Indeed, if it was not for the preservation, translation, and further development of these texts and their textual tradition by luminaries of the Classical Islamic world Europe would never have had its "Renaissance," nor would Europe be able to claim descent from those who it counts today as among its most venerated ancestors.

This last point in turn highlights the debt that the Islamic "East" owes Greek and Roman civilization. Yet, Islamic luminaries did not just follow what they received from the Greeks by rote; rather, they experimented, put things to the test, and discarded that which was disproven or proved to be useless. Furthermore, much of the advances of Greek and Roman civilization were based upon those of the Egyptians, Babylonians, or Indians (not to mention those of other African cultures that scholarship is just starting to give credit to), so were they really ever "Western" to begin with?

It is largely irrelevant and nearly impossible to claim this or that breakthrough as wholly "Western" or "Eastern." What is relevant, however, is that this very impossibility is what makes terms like "East" or "West" become void of meaning, and therefore void of power when despots use them in attempts to demonize "the other," or oppress and control "their own" people.

The terms "East" and "West" only serve to make thinking less complex, more black and white, more economical, and to serve as justification for colonialism, the seizing of wealth and resources abroad, for the control and oppression of populations at home; in short, for religious and political leaders who go cheap for power. In this sense, in one way or another, all of us are "victims of a map."[16]

The borders that delimit the "East" and "West" and the territories that each of these compose are also subjective from "Islamic" perspectives. Less so than cardinal directions, these tend to be thought of as the *dār al-islām*—or, the house (territory) of Islam—and the *dār al-kufr*, or the house (territory) of disbelief. The *dār al-kufr* is also sometimes known as *dār al-ḥarb*, or house of war. An important concept that serves as the mercury

16 Cf. *Victims of a Map: A Bilingual Anthology of Arabic Poetry* translated by Abdullah al-Udhari.

or mediating agent between these two entities is *hijra*, or emigration as a religious duty.

The meaning of each of these terms, as well as the borders between them, have been redefined and redrawn throughout history in a process that continues today. This has been and is usually done in accordance with the specific religious and political needs and agendas of different religious jurists and politicians arising in response to shifting political climates.

To recognize the meanings of these terms as subjective, malleable, and shaped by those who control the liminal herm at any given time, is to recognize that they can also be seized and redefined by artists, activists and revolutionaries who seek to employ them toward healing, regenerative, and emancipatory purposes. Therefore, what follows is a survey of how "Islamic" spatial conceptions have shifted over time, with a particular emphasis in changing interpretations of the word *hijra.*[17]

In its earliest context, *dār al-islām* refers to the city Medina, where, we are told, Muhammed and his companions were given shelter from their persecutors. Here, *dār al-kufr* refers to Mecca, where the idolaters are still in control, and *hijra* to the emigration that the Muslims in Mecca are obliged to make to join their companions in Medina. In this context, we also see the relation between the term *hijra* and the term *jihād,* in that Muslim men were expected to emigrate in order to join the "holy" struggle against the disbelievers who threatened them.

As Islam spread throughout the Arabian peninsula and the Muslims conquered new territories, the borders between the *dār al-islām* and the *dār al-kufr* were continuously renegotiated. These borders become blurred, and the meanings of the terms become mutable and fluid, as we see *hijra* also being used to denote a Muslim who lives surrounded by disbelievers, but cuts off all connections with them without actually uprooting themselves and emigrating; to a Bedouin who leaves behind their nomadic life and adopts the sedentary life of an urban centre; or to some members of the nascent Muslim community who emigrated voluntarily to Abyssinia.

Posteriorly, the verses of the Qur'ān used in discussions of whether or not the *hijra* is obligatory are often Sūra VIII (*al-Anfāl*) verse 72 and Sūra IV (*an-Nisā'*) verses 97–100. Some consider these verses to have proceeded from

17 For more on the following discussion of the concept of *hijra* and spatiality see María Isabel Fierro "La emigración en el islam: conceptos antiguos, nuevos problemas."

the same period discussed above, when the Muslims were a minority community surrounded by hostilities. Whatever the case, throughout the centuries and to this day, different traditions of Islam and different schools of Islamic jurisprudence (*fiqh*) have given these terms their own interpretations. For the *khawārij* (s. *khārijī*) the term *dār al-kufr* encompassed territories controlled and inhabited by Muslims, but specifically *non-khārijī* Muslims.

In *ṣūfī* thought, *hijra* can imply an emigration from evil to good, from ignorance to light, or from forbidden practices to the path of God. In this case, to emigrate does not necessarily imply a physical journey. From a *shāfiʿī* perspective, as long as there is one Muslim in a territory denominated *dār al-kufr*, this territory becomes *dār al-islām*, allowing this Muslim to remain living there without obligations to emigrate. The *shāfiʿī* school of jurisprudence also identifies another sphere, called the *dār aṣ-ṣulḥ*, in which disbelievers have signed a treaty with the Muslims, and are therefore permitted to retain their properties in exchange for paying a special tax. But from a *ḥanafī* perspective, this type of sphere would still be termed *dār al-islām* due to it being governed by Muslims.

As we can see, the borders between the different types of territory are grey, something which has given rise to several questions for the jurists to solve when treating specific cases, for example, that of the *moriscos* in the Iberian Peninsula. What happens when a Muslim is living in a land previously denominated *dār al-islām* but has been conquered by disbelievers? Must they abandon their former home and emigrate?

Some jurists assert yes, in these cases, emigration is the only option. Others would argue that they are permitted to stay if, in spite of not being able to profess Islam publicly, they lived their religion in their hearts and intentions (another example of the *dār al-islām* being interpreted as an interior space). It's worth mentioning that in some moments throughout the history of Islam the old, weak, women, and children have been exempted from the obligation to make *hijra* when caught on the wrong side of the fence.

In addition to all these interpretations, for many practitioners of *sunnī* Islam, the *dār al-islām* is a territory governed by a Muslim, or a territory which, although Muslims are not in charge, they are permitted to freely practice their religion. Other jurists, such as al-Wansharīsī, have asserted that Muslims are obliged to emigrate at all costs from a land denominated *dār al-kufr* to one denominated *dār al-islām* even if the first is a just society and the second is not. The fear of these jurists is that Muslim women would marry non-Muslim men, or that Muslims would adopt foreign languages and customs such as foreign styles of dress, and that these would inevitably lead them into apostasy. This is a fascinating concept: that identity must be preserved at all costs, even if this means forfeiting justice for injustice.

The concept of *hijra* has also been subject to shifting interpretations in the context of European colonialism. One thing that almost all the cases have in common from Nigeria to India is the role that the concept of *hijra* has played in the rhetoric of the Muslim leaders fighting against the Europeans on the one hand, and in that of the Europeans themselves after having made conquests.

In the first case, the concept of *hijra* was used by Muslim leaders to compel their coreligionists who lived in areas recently conquered by the Europeans, to emigrate to the *dār al-islām* (here defined as the territories that they themselves controlled) in order to fortify their troops and bases. In the second case, we see how the European colonialists requested that a *muftī* from Mecca issue new *fatāwā* (s. *fatwā*) regarding the concept of *hijra* under non-Muslim governors if these permitted them to continue freely practising their religion. Such was the tactic used by the French in Algeria whose colonial agenda was disrupted by the Algerian population emigrating en masse to other countries such as Morocco or Syria.

In India the concepts of *hijra* and *jihād* became complicated when some Muslims were not obliged to fight against the English or emigrate from territories the English had conquered, as they were seen as a salvation for the Muslims in their struggle against the Hindus!

To complicate things further, in contemporary times the term *dār al-kufr* has been applied to some Muslim governments by certain fundamentalist groups in order to legitimize their struggle against these, as has been the case in Egypt, Indonesia, or Pakistan.

The term *hijra* has also been interpreted in contemporary times by authors such as Ibn aṣ-Ṣiddiq as the emigration a Muslim might make to Europe or the USA for economic reasons. According to Ibn aṣ-Ṣiddiq, Muslims would be permitted to remain in the *dār al-kufr* as long as they had intentions to work or study there.

The liminal herm that marks the grey boundary between terms such as East or West, or *dār al-islām* and *dār al-kufr*, can also be seized by artists, activists, and revolutionaries who see the so-called "extremist" proponents of each of these "poles" not as the defenders of their respective civilizations or religions locked in an inevitable and holy struggle, but as a single party of despicable greedy and violent villains who have sold this world at the cost of the world to come. The world to come not in the Qur'ānic sense of an eschatological paradise, nor in the "Western" sense of a Las Vegas (Jerusalem) in the Sky, but as the world that will be inherited by future generations, among which, ironically, the children of these same villains will be counted.

The ways towards this are manifold. One extremely powerful starting point for people who find themselves on the "Western" side of the divide is to make an earnest effort to learn Arabic. There are truly so many practical benefits in doing this, not least of which is that learning new languages re-wires your brain. In this sense the false divide between the mental territories of East and West—a divide which serves only to justify the machinations of tyrannical religious and political leaders—can be decimated, and thus make it much harder for us to be manipulated and controlled.[18]

Our exploration of spatial relativity also applies to concepts such as the hinterland, the global *sertão*, to urban human habitats and wild nature. Borders and limits writhe and fork like snakes and lightning and can be reinterpreted to good effect in all manner of rewilding or regenerative permacultural initiatives.[19]

The German word *hinterland* literally means "the land behind." It is commonly taken to mean the rural inland territory surrounding a port, though it can also refer to the rural territory surrounding a town. Implicit in the term's literal meaning is that the port (as locus of commerce, which is therefore also often taken to mean locus of "progress") takes pride of place. The hinterland is subject to the port, by which it is exploited, and to which it is obliged to provide food and raw materials for trade. In the context of European colonialism in Africa, the term hinterland was used to

18 This point is treated in detail in *Risāla of the Dead Hermes*.

19 One of David Holmgren's permaculture principles is *Use edges and value the marginal: The interface between things is where the most interesting events take place. These are often the most valuable, diverse and productive elements in the system*. The ecotone as locus of biological diversity and therefore resiliency will be further explored in *Risāla of the Dead Hermes* and *Risālat al-Filāḥa*.

refer to the outlying areas around a colony, those areas not totally colonized, but still falling under the colony's sphere of influence.

The closest equivalent of the word *sertão* in English might be "back country." In a colonial context, the "global" *sertão* refers to a spatial concept used by Portuguese colonialists to denote the vast inland wilderness areas they encountered in Africa, Asia, and South America that were not under their control or that were yet to be conquered and colonized. In the travelogues of early Portuguese colonialists, as well as in Portuguese cartography, the term *sertão* is used in a near symbolic manner to represent the unknown. It came to refer to an amorphous unmappable region, whose borders were never really fixed. The fact that the *sertão* initially referred more so to an abstract concept or symbol for Otherness is precisely what made mapping it as physical territory an impossibility. Just as the terms *dār al-islām* or *hijra* have been reinterpreted by different jurists, the same can be done with terms like hinterland or with a concept similar (but different) to the meaning of "global" *sertão*. From the Portuguese perspective, the *sertão* was more than just terra incognita, but associated with the "savage" or "uncivilized" other:

> In effect, the sertão signifies what Janaína Amado designates "aqueles espaços desconhecidos, inacessíveis, isolados, perigosos, dominados pela natureza bruta, e habitados por bárbaros, hereges, infiéis, onde não haviam chegado as benesses da religião, da civilização e da cultura" [those unknown spaces, inaccessible, isolated, dangerous, dominated by raw nature, and inhabited by barbarians, heretics, infidels, where the benefits of religion, civilization, and culture had not yet arrived].[20]

The way the *sertão* is represented in early Portuguese cartography clearly demonstrates the way in which maps have been used as hegemonic devices. Through the creation of maps, the unconquered unknown is transformed into the known and land becomes territory. Nielson writes:

> Maps provide navigational assistance, yet they rarely represent space in an innocent manner. As symbolic representations of the world, maps frequently bear the signs of calculated political and economic desire. As Linda Hutcheon, Djelal Kadir, and Mario

20 Nielson, "The Unmappable Sertão," 9.

> J. Valdés note, "Societies produce space as 'territory,' as a manifestation of culture. In seeking to map such territory, [we must] be aware of the less than innocent nature of cartography and, indeed, of geography. Mapping has always been a way to make something exist for imperial eyes." Thus, more than merely satisfying "the desire for symbolic mastery of the world', maps serve important administrative functions: 'ruling over a province, a nation, a kingdom, an empire, protecting or conquering a territory, imposing upon it the rationality of an administrative grid, a political project of reform or of development." Accordingly, maps operate as important tools for power... The sertão symbolizes a concept that resists the epistemological power and effect of maps. As a Portuguese symbol for the unknown, for that which stood outside of European knowledge, the sertão maintained an elusive presence in early modern maps. In a sense, the sertão paradoxically represented a space that could not be mapped. To map, that is, to locate the sertão within the rationality of the epistemological grid of European knowledge would be to endow the sertão with qualities that contradict its very definition as a sign for the unknown. As such, the sertão emerges as an uneasy, unstable, and even fluid sign within early modern Portuguese cartography. The sertão shifts locations from one map to another and moves easily, always resting just beyond the grasp of cartographic knowledge. This fact should not be interpreted as evidence of a failing or inconsistency of cartographic skill, but rather as a result of the sertão's conceptual essence. How could it be otherwise? The sertão is a sign that resists the symbolic order.[21]

Early modern Portuguese maps often included pictorial representations of the territories they attempted to chart. In this way, the European fantasy of the *sertão* as an inland terra incognita inhabited by fabulous beasts, uncivilized savages, and brimming with brazilwood, gold, or emeralds was projected onto the maps through drawings. For example, Lopo Homem's map from 1519 depicts the Brazilian interior as "filled with thick and red woods, exotic, multi-coloured birds and animals (even dragons!), and indigenous figures."[22]

21 Ibid, 10–11.

22 Ibid, 13.

In a similar vein, Diogo Homem's map from 1558 shows "graphic images of natives shooting bows and arrows and holding other weapons, and also cooking human body parts, including legs and arms, and hanging them on the branches of trees." It is clear that these images attempted to entice potential colonialists to set sail in search of wealth in exotic, rich lands, while the depiction of those lands' occupants as "savage" served to justify their violent, greedy, forays into the "godless" unknown.[23]

For the artistically inclined, the creation of a map (or maps) is a powerful way to not only take steps toward reclaiming or liberating subjected territory, but to claim power on an ontological level, by sabotaging the attempts made by Empires and States to control reality through visual depictions of space.

Personal maps drawn by witches and similar can flip traditional cartographic orientation, draw rhumb lines according to different (and more healthy) ways of viewing the world, change the language(s) of some (or all) toponyms, and use art and image in sundry cunning ways. In addition to more solid or physical regions, great benefit can be reaped from the drafting and adorning of maps of the Underworld, of Fairy, or of the starry firmament.[24]

Just as the terms dār al-islām or *hijra* have been reinterpreted by different jurists, the same can be done with terms like hinterland or with a concept similar (but not identical) to the meaning of "global" *sertão*.

With regard to hinterland, the focus should be shifted: the hinterland should be acknowledged as superior to the port or marketplace, as it is the very territory upon which the other two spaces depend. As urbanized humans, we tend to take places like Paris, New York, or Beijing as "the centre of it all." or in a religious sense places like Rome or Jerusalem, instead of reorienting our sense of spatiality and belongingness to the wilderness that bore us and continues to give us life. The inversion of the relationship from the coast to inland reaches also serves the purpose of disrupting colonial cartography, which, before the invention of airplanes, saw oceans and waterways as the foreground and continental expanses as the background.[25]

---

23 Ibid, 13.

24 More on map-making in a permacultural context will be explored in *Risālat al-Filāḥa*.

25 This inversion need not take place for island countries or among cultures who

To an increasing extent, the internet is taking the place of the port and offline reality is being cast as a hinterland, a backward space, a less important space. This insidious casting must be dispelled and reversed with conviction, cunning, and urgency.

With regard to *sertão*, I am not advocating that this particular term be reinterpreted and repurposed, as it has a specific history that is explicitly linked to Portuguese colonialism and the struggle of Africans and Black and indigenous Brazilians. Wherever the term *sertão* is mentioned in its "abstract" colonial context this should be duly acknowledged. By "abstract" I mean *sertão* as concept, and not necessarily the subregion in the North-East of contemporary Brazil (though the *sertão* as concept certainly plays a part in why that region is known as the Sertão today).

Rather, to think in terms of a similar yet culturally and historically un-specific concept—the concept of an amorphous, global wilderness space, whose borders are never quite fixed, and where the State holds no (or less) power—is a concept that can be useful in a more universal context. Like the dār al-islām, this can be understood at times to refer to an interior space as much as an exterior space, to the wilderness we carry within us and travel to for the purpose of communion, healing and emancipation.

It is becoming increasingly imperative that our understanding of "urban space" undergo a profound transformation. To acknowledge that space is relative is to acknowledge that this is not only possible, but perhaps a task not as insurmountable as we might imagine it to be. If cities are to survive into the future, the (illusory) border between human and nature need not only become more permeable, but disappear. This is not a call to "savagery"; truly, it is precisely the opposite. For is there anything more savage than carrying out, engaging in, defending, or tacitly consenting to colonialism, industrial civilization, or capitalism—forces which continue to destroy, poison, and threaten all life? The "away" in "throw it away" does not exist. Away lies before your very feet. Away is right here. The voice of the lyric poet has avowed to steal away from the agoras and online forums, and work for, and as, a *vox clamantis in deserto*.

With this sort of manipulation and redefinition of space, both one's own spatiality and that of one's surrounding environments, we leave the realm of the poet and enter the realm of the dancer. The poet is a master of time,

primarily depend on the ocean for their sustenance, or whose cultures and myths are primarily oriented toward the same.

the dancer a master of space. This is why the marriage of poet and dancer signifies an end for time and space.

2
Risālat al-ʿandalīb
[Risāla of the Violet Smile]

☿

The calcined stones come back.
The fallen temples come back,
The bursted whore houses, the green courtyards
Where the smile of Priapus
Keeps warm the memory of fountains.

My love, let us go along the vanished streets,
Across the bright geometry which still points
To mysterious love and hidden
Pleasures, still so sweet in the night.

Here is the house of the goddess. In the blue
Sanctuary, you can still smell the perfume.
Of sea foam and jasmine and
Carnations salty with her flesh.

The phallic symbol, jolly as ever
Riots in the thick foliage—stretched out
On the happy pan of the balance
Which offers it to love. It is heavier
Than all the fruits of the earth.
Aphrodite smiles in the shadows
As she feels the sea throb in her buttocks.

O ancient brightness! O far off light!
Naked light, love, shine on us always
And when the day comes when we are no more than stones,
After we too, my love, are only ruins,

> Let us lie like these stones singing in the sun,
> Leading others to love along our vanished ways.
> —Rafael Alberti[26]

Some say the lyric was born in exile. This is only partly true, as the lyric was born when language itself was born. Born from humans mimicking the cries of birds and beasts, of the sound of the rain in the branches. Of thunder, waves against the shore, and the reverberations that all of these made in the bodies of our earliest ancestors. Those bodies were humanity's first instruments.

But the lyric does thrive in exile, and like a recalcitrant dandelion or wild rose breaking through layers of outworn concrete, it has always been reborn with renewed vigour at moments in history coloured by the fracturing of Empire and State. Moments where, through song, we are connected to our most primal beginnings.

The ancestor of vocalized human language is bird language. Therefore, birds have pride of place among the ancestors of poets, and there is no bird more emblematic of this relationship than the Nightingale.

María Rosa Menocal puts it thus:

> In the beginning, the bird is all things: Zen object of contemplation, singer like the poet himself, solitary like the soul—or is it God?—mourning witness to the lover's blight, innocent, joyful beauty itself—or is that the Lover? They are clan brothers (some say it is a cabal) these poets and birds, survivors from forever, from the age of dinosaurs, but they are still, stark on the horizon. They keep us guessing: is he our soul? is she my lover? is she the singer? Does he clarify? Does he mystify? Will he fly away, just as I thought I finally had him in sight? [27]

There is indeed a cabal between poets and nightingales. Between poets and things that fly and sing in the night, that animate the trees' branches where sounds and sweet airs tryst and disappear. In turn, this highlights the connection the poet has with that other daughter of nocturnal birds: the witch.

26 Translation by Kenneth Rexroth. See Rexroth, *Thirty Spanish Poems of Love and Exile*, 9–10.

27 See Menocal, *Shards of Love*, 57.

Empire and State are inimical to lyric poetry, and instead have tended to favour the epic and the panegyric. Hence the lyric thrives when these fall apart, or when it is banished and forced to re-inhabit the wilderness that bore it. This is the lyric nightingale that Mahmoud Darwish referred to in his "Diary of a Palestinian Wound":

> And we came to know what makes the voice of the nightingale
> A dagger that shines in the face of invaders.[28]

A singing totem he inherited from Lorca, who inherited it from Don Luis de Góngora y Argote, who inherited it from the ghosts of troubadours and the Moorish ghosts that still haunt the streets and flower covered patios of his native Córdoba.

The truest poet is the lyric poet, whether her voice be accompanied by the lyre, the harp, the guitar and hand claps of flamenco, the *berimbau*, or the kick-kick-snare of an adept beat-boxer.

Yet, by the standards of the contemporary literary establishment, and even by those of some small journals that fall on or just outside the margins of the mainstream, lyric poetry is derided and labelled mere "confessional poetry." Nature is something to ignore, deny, or collect specimens of in small flasks to be later displayed in chic exhibitions. The lyrical celebrations of the *joi* of youth, the ecstasy and abandon of love, wine, and song, are considered immature and juvenile indulgences. Poetry, having lost its music and its *duende* reads more like the most sober of prose, despite the fact it is at times written out in stanzas, which is to say, despite it at times being dressed in the typographical garb of poetry. But even stanzas are on the wane as more and more poets abandon them in favour of the "prose poem," under pressure to constantly seek out new visual forms and to adopt a posture "more-avant-garde-than-thou." Otherwise, they get scarce or no attention from many mainstream editors and judges who care little for music, magic, or strength of poetic vision, yet care much for what they consider to be the most topically trendy and formally "cutting edge."

Gone is Enheduanna. Gone are Sappho and Catullus. Gone the scops. (The griots would be gone were it not for the emcees true to the elements, though the work of these is hardly ever considered literature). Gone wild Majnūn driven mad by his lost Laīla. Oisín and others like him have disap-

28 From his poem "Diary of a Palestinian Wound" [Yawmīyāt jurh filasṭīni].

peared in Fairy never to return. The descendants of William of Aquitaine have forgotten how to trobar. The wish of Novalis was granted; his soul was erased by the love the night brings. Baudelaire's spleen exploded. The lyric tree that Lorca sought to prune to make it flower again all the more exuberant and beautiful, that lonely wind-blasted fairy thorn, that Golden Spruce of Haida Gwaii, that wide-leafed poison-milk witch's fig, has been given to the axe and sold for pulp.

Modern "Western" civilization banished the Nightingale long ago, and instead claims as its ancestor the Empires of the Classical world. In simple terms, the modern "Western" telling of history goes as follows: our civilization was born with Classical Greek civilization, and was further developed by the Romans until their empire fell apart. Then the lights went out for about a thousand years until the advent of the modern period and beginnings of the Nation-State in 1492.

This is the *grand récit* or master narrative that has been told and re-told over the centuries and is still the dominant model employed by the textbooks of today. What seldom appears even in our contemporary textbooks is the detail that this narrative was written by Renaissance scholars who tended to re-write history to the tune of their own ideologies and political agendas, or to those of the politicians to whom they rendered service.[29]

Thanks to these scholars and their intellectual descendants, to this day, the medieval period is often thought to be a synonym for "the dark ages," for what is archaic and outworn, a wrinkle in the fabric of progress, of the smooth linear telling of "Western" history.

But nightingales sing in the dark, and the fracturing of the Roman Empire brought about a whole cacophony of "vulgar" Romance vernaculars, vernaculars that co-existed and co-mingled with various Berber languages as well as a great number of Hebrew and Arabic dialects and hybrids with Romance. And of course, the poems that were composed and sung in all of these.

It is important to recall that what were "the dark ages" for Europe was the "Classical" or "Golden Age" for Islamic civilization. However, the fact

29 For more on this point, see the aforementioned *Shards of Love*, where this and other ideas relevant to this risāla are running themes throughout.

the lyric favours political splintering is still reflected, to give one example, in the explosion of poetry in the *badīʿ* style, a literary heresy closely associated with religious heresy, that was cultivated in al-Andalus during the *taifa* period after the disintegration of the Umayyad-derived caliphate there.[30]

The Nation-State has no room for the lyrical riot of voices, languages, and cultures living together in the intimate conditions (an intimacy that bore dazzling cultural fruits, alongside some violent conflicts) that characterized what came to be known as the medieval period. It makes perfect sense that the historians of the Renaissance re-wrote history to smooth over the expulsions, ethnic cleansings, witch-hunts, wars against women, and linguistic discriminations that had to happen in order for the Nation-State to come into being. The dominant aesthetic of the Renaissance is derived from the smooth symmetries of Classical taste in art, of well defined categories and identities, and in some instances, of the mute and minimal. This is the aesthetic of the cool, smooth, and well-polished pearl, and not the cacophony or spectacular lyric excesses of much medieval art and literature, or their younger cousin the Baroque, a word thought to come from the Spanish *barrueco*, which literally means a rough or imperfect pearl.

Just as modern civilization claims its roots in Classical civilization, so too does modern literature and art in many ways drink from the fountains of Classical aesthetics. This perfect pearl and the polished and learned cherub voices that sing its praises are a far cry from *la perle en brute*, raw and natural, robust and godly as the kiss of Pan.

The Romantics challenged this view and sought inspiration in the often politically fractured yet culturally fertile medieval period, while they simultaneously fought against the societal changes brought about by the Industrial Revolution. However, the engines of modernity proved too powerful to bind with lyric enchantments. This is reflected in the tastes of the contemporary literary establishment referred to above, and in the meanings the term "romantic" has come to be associated with.

Nowadays, "romantic" is often used as a synonym for "escapism," "whimsical nostalgia," or "hollow fantasy," and has been mostly emptied of

30 Robinson defines *badīʿ* as "unprecedented, marvelous, unique; poetics coined in Baghdad in the late ninth century A.D. involving ostentatious use of metaphor and ornamental devices." It is linguistically related to *bidaʿ* [innovation; heresy], the same word that shows up in the phrase *ahl al-bidaʿ* [lit. people of innovation; heretics]; see *In Praise of Song*, ix; see also Suzanne Stekevych's article "Toward a Redefinition of badīʿ Poetry."

its political connotations. Far from an attempt to escape reality, Romanticism is really a passionate and fearless plunge into the very marrow of the same. The edict of the English Romantics was to call for love, wine, and snuff until you cry out, "hold, enough!," yet at the same time be tempered by the tranquility and ferocity of Nature, to get out walking in the rain and mud. To dive in and Live. In its truest sense, it does not project some hollow fantasy onto a cold, stark, inert reality. Rather, it asserts that reality in and of itself is inherently magical. All of it. The whole spectrum of existence and experience, from joy to suffering, youth to old age, is innately imbued with spirit and wonder. This only ceases to be the case when one changes the syntax with which they communicate with reality, a change that is often associated with the loss of childhood innocence.

Surely, to focus obsessively on one's self does no service to poetry. And yet, the age old axiom stands: as above so below; as within, so without. The lyric poet is not given to self-indulgence, but to feeling the world so deeply, seeing it so profoundly, that their own soul is erased in the soul of the world. Think of the anonymous lyrics of popular or folkloric poetry; in these, the "lyrical I" belongs to no one but the Wind. How wise the youth, who knows the insights and feelings they have are unique and ephemeral, knows there is oh so much more to learn, and takes advantage of all of their *joi* in employing death as copy editor. How wise the elder who defeats death by kindling the black flame of their innocent heart.

Romanticism, the age old lyric traditions that it in some way preserves, as well as the traditions it inspired that in some senses parted ways from it, are bearers of the violet smile. The violet smile of true poetry, a smile beyond the fictitious divides of literary currents, languages, and time periods imposed by the most learned poetry critics and their anthologists. That smile at once innocent, wise, and mischievous that seems to say "I know a secret that you don't know. But I can show it to you if you but come with me and take my hand."

It is a sad thing that today "romantic" is used as a derision. If a poet is inspired by the Romantic current, she or he usually feels a pressure to apologize for it.

Furthermore, the notion that Romanticism is not political is utterly false. We see this in Wordsworth's alleged activity as undercover agent around the time of the French Revolution, in the radical activities of Shelley with his infamous *Masque of Anarchy*, and those of Blake with his *Proverbs of Hell*, to give a few examples.[31]

There is a reason that the incendiary book that sparked the Romantic revolution in English was titled *Lyrical Ballads*. Surely, lyric poetry has a long history of political commitment. Think of Dante in exile, champion of the vernacular poets, of the troubadours, of the sweet new style. Think of the troubadours themselves, often considered heretics by their opponents. Their connections to Catharism is noteworthy, but it's not the whole story, nor is it analogous to the "heresy" expressed by many troubadours and Trobairitz. This is due to the Cathars' denial of sex and the body, whereas the heresy of the troubadours was more often a *fin'amour* whose physical consummation (when consummation was to be had) was celebrated before or as dawn broke, as demonstrated by the *alba* genre.[32] This heresy was decidedly a religion of love, or, *dīn al-hawā* to use the equivalent Arabic term.

We can go back further and think of the aforementioned poets of *taifa* period al-Andalus, whose poetic model with all its lyrical, anarchic, and debauched mystical components was absorbed by their neighbours north of the border of the *taifa* of Zaragoza (in Arabic, Saraqusṭa). Let's not forget that William of Aquitaine was for a time companion of arms to some members of the Banū Hūd of Zaragoza. It is clear the Occitan verb *trobar*, from which the troubadours take their name, is connected with ṭaraba, if not the Arabic verb itself adopted into the Occitan language. The meaning of the verb root ṭ-r-b [ط ر ب] and its derived forms is as follows:

> **Arabic Verb Form I**: to be moved (with joy or grief); to be delighted, be overjoyed, to be transported with joy;
> **Arabic Verb Form II**: to delight, enrapture, gratify; to sing, vocalize, chant;
> **Arabic Verb Form IV**: to delight, fill with delight; enrapture, gratify, to make music; to sing, vocalize, chant; to play music (with object pronoun, "for someone"), to sing (with object pronoun "for someone").

This has been more than demonstrated by many scholars over the years, and in recent years we can highlight the work of Cynthia Robinson that I

31 There have been several investigations into Wordsworth's clandestine operations, whether as revolutionary or counter-revolutionary. For one, see *The Hidden Wordsworth: Poet, Lover, Rebel, Spy* by Kenneth R. Johnston.

32 For more on this point see Paz, *La llama doble: amor y erotismo*, 73–106.

have drawn upon here.[33] And yet, sadly, due to ideological reasons, this is something many Romance philologists and medievalists continue to deny at all costs.

The legacy left behind by the notorious Abū Nuwās, and others like him who used homoerotic lyrics to subvert the religious and political authorities of ʿAbbasid Baghdad, was carried on by the *taifa* sovereigns and their poet-courtiers, who took things to a whole new level in being themselves kings who subverted the very notions of kingship. With their poems of love and praise to the charming, coquettish, and somewhat androgynous cupbearer (androgynous and gender-blurring whether this cupbearer was a boyish young woman, or, more often, an effeminate young man, and very frequently an eroticization of the Christian other) completely pulled the rug out from under the rigid commonplace hierarchies...[34]

Let it be known that whether sung to as *rosinhols* in Occitan, or *ʿandalīb* in Arabic, the undeniable totem of both of these groups of poets was our lyric Nightingale.[35]

Returning to Romanticism. It should be specified that Romanticism itself is far from homogenous, and when we use that term we are referring to a wide range of thinkers and artists across a wide range of languages and political landscapes, and across a time-frame whose start and end dates are rarely the subject of agreement. Furthermore, I am in no way advocating any sort of "neo-romanticism" (whatever that means) and understand there are also aspects of Romanticism worthy of critique.

In any case, much of this has been forgotten or denied. After Shelley "suffered a sea change," so to speak, in what can almost be seen as a strange poet's offering to the gods of the ocean, his washed up dead body was thrown into a bonfire on a beach at Viareggio.[36] The story goes that this

33 For a definition of *ṭaraba* and related verbal forms see Robinson, *In Praise of Song*, xxiii. Robinson later discusses this verb and its relation to trobar throughout 342–53.

34 On the *sāqī* as Christian other and the subversion of hierarchies, again, see Robsinon, *In Praise of Song*, 371–97. This point will be touched upon again in the present collection, in the epistle entitled *Risāla of the Closed Garden*.

35 Nightingale literally means night-singer, as *gale* is an archaic English word for wind, breeze, but also "to sing." This meaning is preserved in many other Nordic and Germanic languages. Cf. Dutch, *nachtegaal*; German, *nachtigall*; Danish, *nattergal*; Swedish, *näktergal*; or Icelandic, *næturgali*.

36 Shelley drowned at sea in the Gulf of Spezia and was alleged to have been

was done by, or at least done in the presence of, his friends Lord Byron, Edward Trelawney, and Leigh Hunt. His heart was alleged to have been salvaged and kept as a keepsake by his widow and fellow writer Mary Shelley in a silver case. Yet for many, that charred-black heart, its silver coffer, and the Memory behind it were cast back into the sea.

In the succeeding years, after the Victorian poets entered stage right, we arrive at the advent of literary modernism, and with it a strange paradox comes into play. While ideologically very different from the Romantics, much of Victorian era poetry can still be described as lyrical. This might have less to do with the poets themselves and more to do with their environment. In the nineteenth century, magic and a magical worldview was on the wane but still had a considerable foothold, especially in rural areas. "Western" civilization was becoming industrialized at an ever more alarming rate but wild nature was not yet so suffocated by concrete and smog.

In contrast, while modern poetry flung open the doors for experimentation, it closed them on the lyric. modern poetry can hardly be called lyrical, and some would argue that it should not even be called poetry. There are of course exceptions. Whitman is hailed as a father of modern poetry for flinging open the doors in his espousal of free verse, but his were songs primarily to the open road, not to the city street choked by pollution. Also, the fact his poems were meant to be ecstatically chanted, combined with their intensely personal nature, makes them, in a way, lyrical.

Or ee cummings with his nod to the medieval lyrics in "All in green went my love riding." With cummings we have a formally and orthographically experimental poet when one first sees his poems upon the page, but all his experimentation is done in the service of music and lyrical themes, as it must be. In many cases, it's less the modernists themselves who are responsible for the prevailing derision of the lyric in contemporary poetry. The guilty party is more the critics who posthumously enshrined the modernists, as well as the many poets of later decades taken to avant-garde posturing.

---

subsequently burned on the beach at Viareggio. His remains were later buried in the Protestant cemetery in Rome. His epitaph reads: "Nothing of him that doth fade,/But doth suffer a sea-change,/into something rich and strange," a reference to Shakespeare's *The Tempest*, Act I, Scene 2.

It is notable how two of the most famous poets in their respective languages, poets who often get lumped in with the modernists by the critics and editors, are at times conspicuously absent from anthologies of modern poetry alleged to be "definitive." These are Federico García Lorca and William Butler Yeats, poets that in large part can only be considered modernists if you deem them guilty by association.

It matters little if each of these poets pruned the lyric tree of his respective tradition, but in the connections they maintained with the land beneath their feet, with its folklore and the spirits that imbue even rocks with life, they represent something quite different. Lorca's entire *oeuvre*—even the plays!—have been sung and absorbed by flamenco lyric tradition. Yeats' poems have also been sung, and there are few poets in English who have such an exquisite sense for the musicality of language as he does.

Both these poets lived during the modernist era in literature and were associated with some of modernism's biggest names, yet while others were looking forward they were looking backward. Each in his own way and toward different ends carried out a mobilization of folklore, to borrow a phrase from Peter Grey and Alkistis Dimech.

These poets defy rigid classification into any particular literary current. This is to be expected from any poet whose output is based upon trafficking with fairies and *duendes*. It is worth mentioning that *modernismo* in Spanish literature is different from modernism in English, and, as exemplified by the bacchic and pagan Ruben Darío, in some ways is much closer to Romanticism.

Also, different languages got their modernisms at different times. Modernism or the term "modernist" should never be used as a mere synonym for what is revolutionary, iconoclastic, or innovative. What differentiates modernists proper from their innovative counterparts of all time periods are the specific connections those innovations have with modernity, with industrial civilization.

In Yeats' case, Yeats the magician is incompatible with Yeats the modernist, hence the omission or enormous understatement of this facet by subsequent anthologists, a facet which is more than a bit important to arrive at a nuanced understanding of both the man and his work.

Of course, there are also magical aspects to the work of T.S. Eliot, but these are expressed in a completely different way. In his short essay "Modern Poetry is Prose," Lawrence Ferlinghetti makes the following commentary:

> Modern poetry is prose because it sounds as subdued as any city man or woman whose life force is submerged in urban life… Like modern sculpture, it minimized emotion in favor of understated irony and implied intensity. As such it is the perfect poetry for technocratic man… and the nightingales may still be singing… but we can hardly hear them in the city waste lands of T.S. Eliot, nor in his Four Quartets (which can't be played on any instrument and yet is the most beautiful prose of our time). Nor in the prose wastes of Ezra Pound's Cantos which aren't canti because they couldn't possibly be sung. Nor in the pangolin prose of Marianne Moore (who called her writing poetry for lack of anything better to call it)… nor in the outer city speech of William Carlos Williams, in the flat-out speech of his Paterson. All of which is applauded by poetry professors and poetry reviewers in all the best places, none of whom will commit the original sin of saying some poet's poetry is prose in the typography of poetry—just as the poet's friends will never say it—the dumbest conspiracy of silence in the history of letters… Most modern poetry is poetic prose but it is saying plenty, by its own example, about what death of the spirit our technocratic civilization may be dealing us, enmeshed in machines and macho nationalisms, while some continue longing for some nightingale among the pines of Resphigi. It is the bird singing that makes us happy.[37]

It is in such a mesh of macho nationalisms that we are all increasingly finding ourselves. I recall not long after the events of October 1, 2017 in Catalunya walking the streets of Granada and seeing the city become gripped

37 See Ferlinghetti, *Poetry as Insurgent Art*, 85–90.

in a fit of flag fetishism. The gazpacho-red and paella-yellow banner of Spain being unfurled over numerous balconies throughout the city centre, and anti-Catalan sentiments (with a healthy dose of renewed hate speech toward *Rojos* and environmental activists, yet with no specificity as to who or what exactly these are) began to boil over.

Only individuals as despicable as Mariano Rajoy and his government could make the perhaps equally ill-reputable Carles Puigdemont look like the victim, or worse, a hero, from the perspective of governments and media sources outside of Spain. Yet within the Spanish mainstream, Rajoy, the National Police and the Civil Guard were seen as the heroes for giving the Catalans a *paliza* or beating of which they are considered to be the well deserved recipients.

Is it any small wonder the heraldry of the Civil Guard, the heraldry painted on all of their vehicles to this day, is a sword crossed with a fasces?

Rajoy was the head of a party (Partido Popular) founded on the same "España, una, grande, y libre" ideology of Franco, Primo Ribera, and The Catholic Monarchs Isabel and Fernando before them. A party founded on Christianist principles, or in other words, principles of "political Christianity" (cf. Islamism or "political Islam"). The PP thrives off of insurgent Basque and Catalan activity and more recently Islamic terrorism because it needs them as external demons in order to make every one feel more united and together under a flag that stands for stolen gold and spilt blood. We all know that Catalunya is Spain's economic and industrial powerhouse and therefore the Spanish government cannot afford to let them separate; but ironically, the PP also benefited from what happened due to the widespread awakening of Spanish nationalist sentiment that it aroused, swelling in power like a blood-fattened tick.[38] Likewise, the independence movement in Catalunya also benefits from acts of brutality committed on behalf of the authorities in Madrid, as well as the anti-Catalan sentiments propagated by these authorities. It's worth pausing and asking another question. Is it any small wonder the tragic attacks of August 2017 happened in Barcelona

38 While arguably less sympathetic towards Franco's legacy and its mythos, the PSOE (Partido Socialista Obrero Español) also benefits from external enemies in the same way the PP does. Since writing this epistle, the neo-fascist Vox party has emerged onto the Spanish political scene. They actually employ the word reconquista in advocating a reconquest of Spain from the hands of immigrants, who, according to them, are responsible for the decay and decline of all that is "good" and "Spanish."

just a month and a half before Catalunya's referendum?

All of this is directly related to our discussion of Empire, State, and the lyric. In order to understand why, let us return to our commentary on mainstream historiography and consider the year 1492 in a bit more detail. We all know it as the year that Columbus and his crew "discovered" the New World, and some people also know it as the year the Catholic Monarchs finally took control of the Nasrid Kingdom of Granada—an event that meant the end of what remained of al-Andalus and the birth of Spain. Others know it as the year the Sephardic Jews were expelled from the peninsula, but few know that in addition to all this, on August 18 of that same year—just a few weeks after Columbus set sail—1492 saw the first publication of the first Castilian grammar, codifying that language and establishing its hegemony in the Iberian Peninsula, a linguistic hegemony that it still enjoys.

Spanish, when referring to the language, is a misnomer. The language is more correctly referred to in Spain as *castellano*, in the same way it is also referred to in much of Latin America. Spanish, like the Spain it refers to, in reality does not exist. Both were founded, like most nations, and many other modern languages, on ideological fictions. It was this cacophonic cultural pluralism of Galician, Catalan, Euskara (Basque), Aragonese, Hebrew, Arabic, Berber, Caló—and all the hybrids between them and different dialects of the same—that had to be smoothed over to create modern Spain, highlighted by historians as a prime example of the beginnings of the Nation-State. This is one of the dead horses of the medieval period that was thrown overboard in the calm seas of the Horse Latitudes (between 30 and 38 degrees North and South), as Menocal insightfully showed us, sacrificed in order for the winds of progress and modernity to blow, in order for Columbus' ships to be able to continue sailing onwards toward a brave new world.[39]

Keep in mind that Castilian (especially in its Andalusian and Valencian varieties) is ripe with words derived from Arabic (arabisms); indeed, Catalan too has arabisms. It should not be forgotten that once upon a time the area that would come to be known as Catalunya was also part of al-Andalus.[40]

---

39 For a historical discussion of "the horse latitudes," see *Menocal, Shards of Love*, 1–55.

40 Toponyms and other proper nouns not withstanding, there are perhaps less arabisms in Castilian than some studies have previously asserted, but this does not detract from the point being made. However, more are being discovered,

The *Reconquista*, the Spanish nation's most beloved myth, is exactly that, a myth. Spain did not exist at the time of the so called *Reconquista* and numerous scholars have challenged the degree to which the different Christian Crowns considered themselves to be engaging in a *re-conquista* as they went about making land grabs to the South and in the Balearic Islands, not to mention fighting amongst themselves. Berbers have always been crossing the Strait of Gibraltar, have always lived in and done business with the peoples of the Iberian Peninsula, and before they were converted to Islam, many were Christian and some even Jewish (cf. al-Kāhina). If Morocco belonged to Christians and was later conquered by Muslims, by the same twisted rhetoric of the *Reconquista*, that would give Christians the right to "reconquer" Northern Africa, something that only the most despicable members of Spanish society would advocate (cf. Alfonso XIII and his role in the Rif War). Many of the Spanish flag wearers and '¡Arriba España!' chanters would find this barbarous. Furthermore, Monroe and Pettigrew assert that the word *reconquista*

> ... is a neologism; it was not recorded by the Real Academia de la Lengua Española until the nineteenth century, and does not appear in any known medieval texts. The verb reconquistar was first used in the late eighteenth century by Leandro Fernandez de Moratín (1760–1828) and Gaspar Melchor de Jovellanos (1744-1811), but was not recorded by the Real Academia until 1843. It designates (retroactively) the period between AD 722 (battle of Covadonga) and 1492 (fall of Granada), as if the 770 intervening years constituted one single, long, uninterrupted war, which it never was.[41]

Also, scholars like the controversial Emilio González Ferrín deny that there was a Muslim conquest in Spain, hence the ceaseless efforts of right-wing oriented scholars to silence him and punch holes in his research: for naturally, if there were no conquest, there cannot be any reconquest. González Ferrín insists that what happened in the Iberian Peninsula was

---

documented and recorded every year. See Federico Corriente's *Diccionario de arabismos y voces afines en iberroromance.*

41 They then advise the interested investigator to consult Joan Corominas and José A. Pascual, *Diccionario crítico etimológico castellano e hispánico* (Madrid: Gredos, 1981), vol. 4: 719a, for more information on this point.

not a conquest, but a revolution, or a gradual process that slowly assimilated Islam and Islamic culture over time.

He makes the following points: all the sources that describe the conquest were redacted much much later than the events they describe. The population in the South was largely Arian Christian rather than Catholic; Arians deny the trinity so their beliefs are actually very similar, or at least compatible with, those of Islam. How could it have been possible for some 300 ragtag soldiers (the oft cited 10,000 from the sources is likely highly exaggerated) to conquer just about the entire Iberian Peninsula in a few short years—taking into account the very difficult topography—when it took the Romans almost 200 years to do the same? These are all mysteries that the appearance of a coin from the eighth century whereupon it is written Muhammed is the prophet of God fall very short of answering.[42] Whatever the case, there is fortunately a growing new generation of Arabists, Hebraists, and Romance philologists who are committed to using their disciplines to destroy the toxic myths of Nations and Nationalism, and not the other way around, as has been the case for much of the previous century and earlier. Indeed, philology has been used on equal-footing as that other most powerful way for the greedy and power hungry to prove their nations: war. And in the ostensible absence of war, international sports (the World Cup, the Olympics). No Spaniard feels so Spanish as when they see *la selección nacional* take to the pitch, nor when Spain wins the World Cup.[43] It arouses pride in those who don't even like football, and in pretty much all Spanish citizens, be these *catalans, gallegos, valencianos, euskaldunak* (*vascos*), *aragoneses, castellanos, calés* (*gitanos*), or *andaluces*.

Mastering philology is one of our keys to mastering reality, to unravelling the *grand récit* and making room for all those other voices that don't make the canons of national literature, for the lyric poets singing in the streets

42 See González Ferrín, *Historia general de al-Ándalus*; See García Sanjuán, *La conquista islámica de la Península Ibérica y la tergiversación del pasado*.

43 See, for example, *A Sea of Languages: Rethinking the Arabic Role in Medieval Literary History* edited by Suzanne Conklin Akbari and Karla Mallette. While this isn't to say that the scholars who contributed to *A Sea of Languages* have a radical agenda, whether they like it or not they are contributing to a philological upheaval and all that that entails (i.e.; concurrent epistemological and ontological upheavals). I am more so referring to an even younger generation who are presently educating themselves by any means necessary and have yet to hit the scene.

and leafy bowers. To speak with Bob Kaufman, "*for all those ships that never sailed, the ones left scuttled in their stalls with their seacocks open.*" Ships that could have sailed toward a very different future than the one brought about by Columbus' voyage and the events surrounding it. "Today we bring them back Huge and intransitory. And let them sail forever."[44]

All reality is quantity and quality. Numbers give the quantity, words give the quality. Hence operative Kabbalah or other (almost all?) magical systems that employ numbers and words—the true roots of all things—to make change in the world. Languages come from the elements, from roots (cf. Empedocles). We see this so clearly in Hebrew and Arabic in that all words are derived from verbs of three (and some two and four) letter roots. Verbs are superior to nouns, because they represent the animating principles that substantiate nouns, that make them move. Therefore, we can flip the adage of the concrete and very "modern" William Carlos Williams: No ideas but in movement.[45] As Empires and States continue to crumble, now's to declare our intent in all our myriad babel tongues, in all our lyric and varied *voces magicae*: the homecoming of love (and wild nature) among illustrious ruins.

---

44 From his poem [All Those Ships That Never Sailed]. See Kaufman, The Ancient Rain: Poems 1956-1978, 55–56.

45 Empedocles did not use the word *stoicheion* [στοιχεῖον] to refer to earth, air, fire, and water. Rather, he referred to them as *rhizōmata* [ῥιζώματα], literally, *roots*. On verbs and nouns cf. Antonio Machado's famous verses in which the poet asserts that nouns and adjectives are naught but the "accidents" of verbs: El adjetivo y el nombre,/remansos del agua limpia,/son accidentes del verbo/en la gramática lírica,/del Hoy que será Mañana,/y el Ayer que es Todavía. From his notebook Los Complementarios. The original is: "No ideas but in things." From Book 1 of William Carlos William's Paterson.

3

Risāla fī l-bāṭin wa ẓ-ẓāhir

[Risāla on the Inner and the Outer]

☿

> When the young prince arrived perched atop his thoroughbred steed, with his mouth of ambergris and his teeth a string of pearls curled into a smile, and began to unbutton his fine linen sūsīya shirt just so, and to expose the moon-coloured upper reaches of his shank, just above where it was bronzed by sunbeams or henna—the poet Ibn Quzmān had fallen in love. Oh, if it wasn't for fear of the lad's father, the powerful noble, Abū Bakr!

The images with which I open this piece are drawn directly from a poem by the notorious andalusī poet Ibn Quzmān (d. 1160). It is a curious poem, this. Formally a *zajal*, yet with some features that make it closer to a *muwashshaḥ*, it is a mock panegyric which becomes a mock satire which becomes a mock panegyric and on and on, allowing the poet to satirize his "patron" and subvert his authority right under his nose, yet still end up getting paid for it.

Ibn Quzmān is famous for his expertise at composing poems in the *zajal* form, a type of sung strophic poem written in a popular or colloquial vernacular of Arabic that often included loan words from Romance, and whose content frequently dealt with the taboo themes of wine, love, and sex. He is also famous for seeming to take delight in subverting the authorities of his day at every chance he could get, for his intense love of wine and for gleefully boasting of his sexual adventures with all manner of women and men, regardless of their class, ethnic, or religious background. Exactly how he was able to go about his drunken weaving way through the streets of Córdoba and Sevilla singing his wine-soaked songs on corners and in the marketplace during the reign of the Almoravids without getting his head lopped off continues to amaze us.

As many contributors to Gods&Radicals are poets not only dedicated to the multiplication of beauty in the world, but to employing the satirical register to curse our enemies—the high priests of capitalism and their pseudo-religious puppets—we can learn a lot from Ibn Quzmān, a true master of the subtleties of satire.[46] In an age where all our movements and words are tracked, and in which internet call-out culture and aggressive trolls make it difficult for any would-be dissident to express viewpoints that fall outside of party lines, it seems timely to be reminded of the poetry of al-Andalus and in particular that of arguably its most saucey knave.

In addition to a discussion of some of Ibn Quzmān's poetry, this epistle is intended to be a work of banishing, to dispel some of the misconceptions that have been sold to us about al-Andalus in particular and Classical Islamic civilization in general. A further intention will be revealed toward the end of this inanna-dance of rent illusions, as the misconceptions finish their fall to the ground around us garment by garment.[47]

Ibn Quzmān has been referred to by some researchers as "a prince of disorder." He often boasted in his poems of his great appetites for love and wine, his masterful poetic prowess, his blond hair and dashing good looks. His literary idol was that other great saucey knave of Arabic literature, a poet both simultaneously hated and loved—Abū Nuwās. It would certainly be reasonable to award Ibn Quzmān the title of "Abū Nuwās of the West."[48]

Citing a few verses from the poem which the anthologists title "Zajal no. 90" would be a fitting way to introduce this colourful character.

---

46 See www.abeautifulresistance.org

47 For more on this point, see González Alcantud, *El mito de Al-Andalus: Orígenes y actualidad de un ideal cultural.*

48 See Monroe, "Why was Ibn Quzmān Not Awarded the Title of "Abū Nuwās of the West?" ('Zajal 96', the Poet, and His Critics)." While it is quite clear that there is no poet more deserving of the title in the medieval western Arab world, the critics of Ibn Quzmān's day instead awarded him the title of "the Mutanabbī of the zajal." As to the reason why, Monroe comments: "Incorporating and applying these concepts, the Maghrebi critics concluded that, as Al-Mutanabbī had done before Ibn Quzmān in the East, and for the classical qaṣīda, the latter had placed greater emphasis on the internal meaning (maʿn) than he had on the external wording (lafẓ) of his colloquial zajal poetry, as a result of which he was honored with the dubious compliment of being 'the Mutanabbī of the zajal' as if we were to say, in contemporary terms 'the Shakespeare of rap songs.' These same scholars, however, never comment upon, or discuss, the internal meaning of Ibn Quzmān's poetry." (298).

For me to repent would indeed be absurd,
And my survival without a wee drink would be a mistake.
Wine! Wine! Ignore what others say.
In my view, it would be folly to give up depravity!

Hey, let us clink glasses together in a toast!
Drunkenness! Drunkenness! What is soberness to us?
And, whenever you wish to take a morning drink,
Wake me up at dawn's early light.

Take my cash, and spend it on wine,
And my clothes, and divide them up among whores,
And assure me that my approach is correct;
I have never gone wrong in doing this!

And when I die, my style of burial
Will be to lie neath a vine in the vineyard,
While you gather grape-leaves over me as a shroud,
And on my head let there be a turban of tendrils.

Let the Evil One summon all my dear friends there.
Commend me to Him at all moments,
And whoever eats a bunch of grapes,
Let him plant the stem on my grave!

I'll pour Your [i.e. the Evil One's] great gift of joy from
the krater itself:
Take Your glass, raise it high, and empty it.
How good is that gift of joy with which You favoured us!
Whatever You command, will be done by me![49]

After the request is made to his companions to perform this rather devilish, bacchic ritual on the poet's grave after he dies, he then goes on to describe a night of rollicking sex he had with a Berber lass, and the food fight and brawl with her husband and family that ensues the morning after. Here I will

49 See Monroe and Pettigrew, "The Decline of Courtly Patronage," 140–42.

spare the reader the graphic descriptions the poet gives of their genitals when aroused, or the precise "honey-sweet" manner in which he claims they fucked. Interested readers can look for this poem themselves in Arabic or in Spanish (trans. by F. Corriente) or the English version I've drawn upon here, translated by Monroe. Any pursuer of Ibn Quzmān's *dīwān* however will discover that he wrote plenty more poems similar to this one.

At first glance, this seems a tasteless macho boast about his night of love. Yet, if we scratch below the surface—with the help of Monroe's detailed analysis of all the poem's contradictions and ins and outs—we see that there is much more to this poem than the alleged confessions of a drunken fool. While ostensibly trying to poke fun at the Berbers, the aims of the poet are actually to subtly criticize the anti-Berber sentiments and prejudices commonplace among his andalusī contemporaries. The poem is a ruse, and though it might have been based on some real events, in this case the poet's misadventure likely never took place, at least in the way he relates it. It was crafted with a political purpose in mind.

Written in an age when the Christian crowns to the North were becoming increasingly aggressive, our poet is making a plea to the diverse ethnicities and followers of different religions that made up andalusī society to put aside their differences and unite against the advances of what at this point in the history of al-Andalus was mostly a common enemy.[50] It's true the Almoravids in some ways did not do good service to the cultural achievements and religious tolerance of the Umayyad and *taifa* sovereigns that reigned in al-Andalus before them (i.e.; by burning books, destroying ornate palaces, and massacring groups of people who weren't like them), but in painting a more nuanced picture of these veiled invaders (the Almoravid men were famous for covering their faces with veils), the poet is actually way ahead of his time. Arabic philology is still to some extent plagued by the prejudices of last century and earlier: that Arab culture is the high and the exquisite, and that andalusī arabized culture especially is tolerant and more "Western" compared to the "barbaric" ways of the African Berbers. Naturally there is much more complexity to this and as the new generation of philologists starts to come into its own I predict there will be more studies that come out challenging this overly simplified dialectic.

While for those who are dedicated to studying these things it's become normal, our daily bread and olive oil per se, some readers are likely sur-

50 See, again, Monroe and Pettigrew, "The Decline of Courtly Patronage."

prised to hear about so much wine and illicit sex (illicit from a hardline religious perspective) in a primarily Muslim society, or to hear that this society had a very diverse ethnic make up.

Our enemies have sold us an imaginary line in the sand with "light-skinned" Christians to the North and "dark" Muslims to the South, as if both of these societies were totally homogenous. Nothing could be farther from the truth. In al-Andalus, though culturally and politically dominant, ethnic Arabs who had come from the East were a minority (and even within this minority alone there were tribal differences and different regions of origin and so on). The majority of the population were the same old mix of Iberian peoples (with all the influences from all the various peoples and civilizations that had come through the Iberian peninsula and left their mark, Iberian, Ibero-Celtic, Phoenician, Jewish, Roman, Visigoth, Byzantine, Berber, Arab, etc.) who had at this point in history become arabized in culture, customs, and language. Some were *muwalladūn* (s. *muwallad*), arabized Iberians (often Goths or Hispano-Romans) who had converted to Islam. Others were what has come to be called mozarabs, arabized Christians. Others were arabized Jews or arabized Berbers (or non-arabized Berbers in the case of the Almoravids). Others still were sub-saharan Africans or arabized Nordic or Slavic peoples.

These last three groups mainly came to be in al-Andalus due to the slave trade (the English word "slave" comes from Slav). Many were kept as eunuchs, but the arabized Slavs did come to power for a time in the *taifa* of Almería (in Arabic, al-Marīya). It has even been postulated that Ibn Quzmān's name is an arabization of the germanic surname Guttman (which might explain his alleged blond hair, although I'm not entirely convinced by this theory).

Even in the Christian crowns to the North, various kings and popes at different times tried to enforce members of each religion to wear special clothing to distinguish them from one another (people didn't always go along with this). The idea was that rather than there being clear dividing lines between light and dark, everyone pretty much looked, dressed, and acted the same, hence the need for other items of clothing to enable the political and religious authorities to detect those differences between people and in so doing, profit from them.

Some apologist researchers today (usually with right-wing orientations or orthodox religious affiliations) claim that all of the erotic poetry and especially the homoerotic poetry that was written in al-Andalus, and indeed the wider Islamic world, was all just make believe, or just jokes, or that the male pronouns are masks for lovers who were actually female. It is true in some cases that male pronouns were used to disguise a female beloved, but in other cases this argument becomes futile when descriptions of the beloveds are made that include explicitly male attributes like beards or phalluses, or when the beloveds are compared to well known male cultural figures like Moses or David.[51]

It is true that we should be cautious about taking every poem as autobiographical reality (as we noted in the case above), but the existence of wine parties, homoerotic relationships, and other types of taboo sex in al-Andalus (and Classical Islamic civilization in general) are thoroughly documented in a wealth of sources besides the poetry, such as in anecdotes and works by the historians of the day, among others. I do not mean to insinuate that al-Andalus was a drunken fuck fest, but to dispel the common misconception about Classical Islamic societies being strictly puritanical and/or "homophobic."

When islamophobic (and often right-wing oriented) historians draw on the widespread homoerotic motifs in Arabic literature as a way to degrade Islamic civilization, they ought to take a closer look at the Greeks and Romans whom they idolize, with their famous love for ephebes and ganymedes.

The same goes for when islamophobes and anti-arab writers insist that all of the cultural and scientific advances of Classical Islamic civilization were made by thinkers who weren't "ethnically Arab" (for example, Persians). It is true that many "non-ethnic" Arabs produced great works of science and philosophy, but just because they were born outside of the Arabian peninsula or were of a different ethnicity is irrelevant.[52] For better or for worse they were arabized, Arabic speaking, and belonged to the same cultural

51 See Scheindlin, *Women, Wine, Death: Medieval Hebrew Poems on the Good Life.*

52 One thing that is indisputable is the Arab contribution to literature, especially poetry. This was something that almost all Hebrew and Arabic luminaries were in agreement on during the medieval period; in this regard, the opinion of andalusī Hebrew poet Moshe ibn Ezra is but one example of many. Another thing that should be kept in mind is that when the Arabs received knowledge from the Greeks, Persians, or Indians, they did not just apply it by rote, they put everything they received to the test. One example of this would be the high sophistication that was reached in agriculture and animal husbandry. In hindsight we might dub this a truly scientific approach. This point will be touched upon again later on in the present collection, in the epistle entitled *Risālat al-filāḥa.*

milieu. How many luminaries of Greek or Roman civilization were actually from Anatolia, Syria, or Northern Africa? Plenty! Or even, as in the case of Seneca, from places as far afield as Córdoba? The same place, strangely, where Ibn Quzmān would be born centuries later.... No one who fetishizes "Western" civilization would ever question the "Romanness" of their idols. And for good reason, while from disparate places, they were all Romanized, and part of the greater Roman world.

Some left-oriented writers could also benefit from getting over a few too-often touted exaggerations of their own. For example, that al-Andalus was a cultural and ethnic utopia and a place where women were "liberated" more so than they were in the East. This is simply untrue. We are talking about a period of about eight hundred years. Different regimes came and went. Under some, different ethnic groups got along better; under others, less so. [53]

Similar to other Mediterranean societies of the time, at least "officially," the society of al-Andalus was undoubtably a "man's world" in which sexual hierarchies rotated around an axis of a "politics of penetration." However, there are of course many nuances to this, plenty of exceptions, and a noteworthy number of women (many of them poets) who defied these norms. It might be untrue to say that women were better off in al-Andalus compared to the eastern regions of the Islamic world at the time (not to mention we'd have to define what "better off" means in the first place), but the relatively high number of woman poets and women in positions of power in al-Andalus compared to other Islamic societies contemporary to it should at least give us reason for pause.[54]

Does it make our arguments any less strong if we are realistic, say, about the number of books in al-Ḥakam II's library? (The previously oft-cited 60,000 is probably closer to 600). Doing the best we can to get our history right can only make our arguments stronger. Even if it was only 600 books, it still likely would have been one of the biggest (if not the biggest) and most important libraries on the European continent at that time.

Another misconception is that, although there might have been ethnic

53 See Nirenberg, *Communities of Violence: Persecution of Minorities in the Middle Ages.*

54 See Wright, "Masculine Allusion and the Structure of Satire in Early 'Abbāsid Poetry." For more on this point see Viguera, "Aṣluḥu li 'l ma'ālī: On the Social Status of Andalusī Women."

diversity in al-Andalus, the different ethnicities did not mix or interact with one another. This is utter nonsense. How many right-wing or orthodox Jews and Christians, for example, continue to paint the illustrious andalusī Hebrew poet Yehuda ha-Levi as some sort of "proto-zionist" and yet totally ignore, censure, or deny the great wealth of wine and love poetry (in which figure both male and female beloveds) that he sang before his fellow Muslim courtly courtiers at court? Does this make him any less of a Jew? Does this mean he loved Zion less?[55]

Some deny these things at all costs because they would in many ways nullify their political rhetoric and rattle their religious and ethnic identities. Even Isabel the Catholic, who, with Ferdinand, is famous for finally taking control of the last remaining corner of al-Andalus—The Nasrid Kingdom of Granada—and for eventually expelling the Jews from the Iberian peninsula, had a Jewish gynaecologist in her personal employ.

Furthermore, the numerous normative texts left behind by the religious and political authorities from each of the three Abrahamic religions are proof that romantic relations across ethnic and religious divides were a widespread and significant problem (in their eyes, of course), such that they were kept busy writing laws and making decrees to try and keep it under control. Strangely, these same authorities were fine with their male coreligionists keeping concubines belonging to one of the other two religions (from which many an "illegitimate" child was born), while attempting to guard their female coreligionists from contact with men of the other two religions at all costs.[56]

Having now been acquainted with Ibn Quzmān and (hopefully) having dispelled a few misconceptions regarding al-Andalus, let us return to the striptease with which we began.

55 On medieval Jewish poets writing panegyrics and performing love lyrics at Muslim courts see Brener, *Isaac ibn Khalfun* or Scheindlin, *Wine, Women, Death* to cite just two of the innumerable studies that deal with this subject.

56 See Park, "Medicine and Natural Philosophy: Naturalistic Traditions"; or Mazo Karras, *Sexuality in Medieval Europe*; or Rivera Garretas, "La construcción de lo femenino entre musulmanes, judíos y cristianos (Al-Andalus y reinos cristianos, siglos XI–XIII)."

In premodern Islamic civilization there was no word for "homosexual," hence my choice to use homoerotic here. Although it was religiously proscribed and could be punishable by death, desire from a man toward another man was not considered psychopathic (as in Christianity) but natural, derivative of, or comparable to the same desire a man might feel toward a woman. However, the permissibility (or not) of sexual relations rotated around an axis of a politics of penetration. This is to say that in male-male sex, the penetratee would have been more severely punished than the penetrator. Likewise in female-female sex, the penetrator (if any) would have been punished more than the penetratee for upsetting gender norms. Furthermore, men of higher class could usually get away with penetrating younger men or men of lower classes without it being frowned upon.[57]

In saying that Abū Bakr's son is a flirt and a dandy with whom he wants to romance (not to mention one of a higher class), Ibn Quzmān is indirectly satirizing his father. Yet he is also turning the politics of penetration on its head by offering himself as sex object to the whims of this younger man.

In his excellent essay "The Striptease That Was Blamed on Abū Bakr's Naughty Son: Was Father Being Shamed or Was the Poet Having Fun?" Monroe gives the following commentary:

> By couching his rebellion in the form of a pseudo-panegyric that is, in reality, a satire against a member of the ruling class, the voice speaking in Ibn Quzmān's poem carries its rebellion one step closer to total anarchy, attempting through subversion of the genre to disrupt the entire social order. However, the speaker's program is presented from the very outset as unsuccessful. He is doomed to failure in his attempt to win the boy's favours because of his prudent, pusillanimous, and decidedly unheroic fear of Abū Bakr, if for no other reason. Thus it may be concluded that the speaker's anarchic program is being presented ironically, as one of which the implied author heartily disapproves. In this sense, Ibn Quzmān's Zajal No. 133 seems to validate the eternal truth contained in the Qur'ān, to be far less licentious than a preliminary reading might suggest. Paradoxically, licentiousness, insofar as it is presented as

57 See Oberhelmen, "Hierarchies of Gender, Ideology, and Power in Medieval Greek and Arabic Dream Literature."

> being unsuccessful, may in certain cases have the ritual function of reaffirming the very values it seems to flout.[58]

And yet, this is all part of the plan. Monroe continues:

> A mock panegyric, such as Zajal No. 133, has the potential to become a satire... but if, as in this case, the satire is also undercut, what does it become?—a mock satire with the potential to become a true panegyric? Since that panegyric is also undercut, the poem becomes a satire that is a panegyric that is a satire that is a panegyric that is a satire that is a panegyric, with no amen. Thus the poet has found a unique way to circumscribe his patron with a vicious circle from which he cannot escape and within which he is rendered utterly neutral and helpless. The poem is therefore an instrument for patronly entrapment: having been roundly insulted, the patron must now graciously pay the poet for his efforts while secretly remaining thankful that matters have gone no further. In this sense, the poem illustrates the poet's superiority over the patron, based upon the poet's unique mastery of words. But when a superior poet praises an inferior patron, the genre of panegyric has been totally inverted.[59]

Ibn Quzmān has cast a binding spell. And like any good magician, he has also used his wits and a dash of trickery to neutralize his adversary. By the time Abū Bakr realizes what's going on, it's too late. Our poet has effectively snared his patron in a lyric brocade and has him at his mercy.

In proposing we can learn from Ibn Quzmān, I don't mean to imply we have to go out and peddle our poetry to this patron or that, although studying his work would of course be helpful to any recalcitrant poet who ekes out a living with her craft yet at the same time will never compromise her poetic principles.

More so, what I want to draw our attention to are some of the techniques he uses. Ring composition, unsaying away his satire and his panegyric *ad infinitum*, and the potent mix of inversion, wine, and taboo sex to undermine authority. This is beginning to sound a lot like witchcraft.

Wine, poetry, and "illegitimate" sex are all proscribed in the Qur'ān. Not

58 Monroe, 125.

59 Ibid, 125–26.

least of the reasons why being that they are strongly associated with the pagan rituals of the *jāhilīya* (lit. ignorance: Age of Ignorance; pre-Islamic Arabia). Many of the poetic forms most typical of Arabic poetry—like the *qaṣīda* for example—actually arose out of whole ritual frameworks and poetics of gesture and movement. Anyone who's read the *sūra* known as *ash-Shu'arā'* [The Poets] knows that the Qur'ān makes poets out to be liars and cheats.[60] The common pre-Islamic image of the poet in the Arabian peninsula was that of a wandering sage or magician, sputtering out poems and prophecies, whose powers of eloquence and strength of vision were said to have been bestowed upon him or her due to undergoing possession by *jinn*.[61]

Which brings me to the interesting moment we are at now. It appears we're experiencing a turning point in magic (which of course, therefore, has potent political implications as well!) accentuated by several publications of magical texts and commentaries thereof, in which magical lore is shared and compared across the East-West divide.[62]

I imagine many "Western" readers who delve into these books will discover that something that has been made out to be so foreign is really much more familiar than we think. For truly, the *jinn* are all around us. Whether in the form of stray dogs, hot eddies of wind, or waiting in line right next to you to buy goods at a market stall. For I have heard say in the Maghreb that at every market two-thirds of the people that are there are actually *jinn* in disguise.

To illustrate this further I will make a somewhat piquant and picaresque confession: I have watched a significant portion of *The Fellowship of the Ring* in Arabic. It was fascinating to note that the word the translators used in this particular version to denote elves (i.e. Legolas) was *jinn*. The idea that the elves and fairies of the "West" are the same as, or are at least related to, the *jinn* is not some fantastical orientalist cut-and-paste job, but something affirmed by the very cultures to which the *jinn* belong. I am not saying that a *jinnī* is identical to a fairy. However, the parallels are too striking to overlook and are certainly worthy of prolonged reflection.

May the present *risāla* lend a wind toward the conjuration of the coming sandstorm. And may that storm erode the outworn bars that have kept us prisoner from each other for far too long, that have kept us from seeking

60 See Stetkevych, *The Mute Immortals Speak: Pre-Islamic Poetry and the Poetics of Ritual.*

61 See Stillman, *Jews of the Arab Lands: A History and Source Book*, 3–22.

62 One recent example is *Jinn Sorcery* by Rain al-Alim [sic].

intimacy and companionship instead of strife and distraction, while our enemies are free to profit off our fear and hate unopposed; the iron bars and barbed-wire walls that uphold the edifice of empire, greed, and burning disdain for all of life—both human and non-human.

Now that it is time to part, we will do so in the same way we have met. With a striptease.

In a famous anecdote about al-Mūʿtaman, one of the Hūdī kings of Zaragoza during the *taifa* period, the sovereign and his poet-courtiers are out wandering in the meadows looking for an ideal place to have a drinking party. His charming young cupbearer (who happens to be a Christian in this case) finds the perfect place and in exchange al-Mūʿtaman orders all of the revellers to obey him. The king declares himself the lad's slave, and is totally smitten with love for him (another topsy turvy subversion of the pecking order, typical in the literature that emerged from *taifa* court culture).[63]

For Ibn Quzmān the employment of taboo *topoi* in his poems was about political subversion, and yet at the same time about something more. However, for these *taifa* poet-courtiers, borderline-heretic devotees of the cult of pleasure and religion of love, these *topoi* were also about political subversion, and yet at the same time about something more. While the Qur'ān proscribes wine and beautiful virgins (both male and female) in this world, both wine and virgins are available in bountiful supply in the world to come, where wine flows in a river and ephebes dressed in emerald gowns are available to attend to the delights of the faithful who have made it in to Heaven. Therefore, the *taifa* drinking party also had a subversive mystical element: it was about invoking paradise in the here and now which, through the magic of poetry, is transformed into the nowhere and always.

On with the anecdote. The cupbearer, now revealed to be a bestower of immortality, begins to remove his armour and garments.

The authors of this anecdote use a curious string of religious symbolism when referring to him, not least of which using the word *ẓāhir* (exterior) to refer to his clothes, and *bāṭin* (interior) to refer to his body. You might recognize these words as also referring to two schools of Qur'ānic exegesis,

63 See Robinson, *In Praise of Song*, 381–86.

the *ẓāhirī* (or exoteric) which takes things at face value, and the *bāṭinī* (or esoteric) which searches for hidden meanings beyond the veil of the text.

This anecdote touches on something that witches will no doubt find familiar. Wine, that red spirit of sex and war captured in a goblet, effects the soul, not the body. Like those of sex, the pleasures of wine are primarily spiritual, not physical. For if wine were to solely effect the flesh and not the spirit, it would be contradicting its own *raison d'etre*.

The striptease in the sense of shedding exoteric religious identity in search of a deeper truth is something common to mystics the world over. Particularly in those who employ an apophatic discourse. In keeping with our andalusī theme, we will turn to Ibn ʿArabī, who seems to ask:

> When the fetters and trappings of religious identities and customs fall away, if only temporarily, *what's* left? What are the common jewels that shine there at the heart, often obscured by so many layers of cultural and political filigree?

May his immortal words ring out in the olive groves:

> Marvel, a garden among the flames.
> My heart has become receptive of every form.
> It is a meadow for gazelles, a monastery for monks,
> An abode of idols, the Kaʿba of the pilgrim
> The tables of the Torah, the book of the Qur'ān
> My religion is love. Wherever its camel mounts turn
> That is my belief, my faith.
> We have a model in Bishr, Hind, and her sister,
> In Qays [aka Majnūn] and Layla, Mayya and Ghaylan.[64]

---

64 Mystics often resort to apophatic discourse, or "unsaying," because the identities and entities their words attempt to describe are ineffable. Language will always fall short unless the poet is able to overcome its inherent duality (yes/no). See the section "Unsaying" in Michael Sells' *Mystical Languages of Unsaying*.

Both the words *jinn* [genies] and *majnūn* [crazy; possesed], as well as *janna* [garden; paradise], *janān* [heart; soul], *jannān* [gardener] and *junūn* [posession; obession; fury; ecstasy; rapture] are derived from the root 'j n n' [ج ن ن] which in verbal form I means to cover, hide, conceal, veil; to descend, fall, be or become dark (night); and in the passive voice of form I to be or to become possessed, insane, mad, crazy, to get madly excited, become frantic. To me, it seems the semantic connection between paradisaical gardens and the heart with the rest of the meanings is to be found in the sense of the "closed" or "sealed" garden, and

So let us be like wild eyed Majnūn (whose name is often translated as "crazy" but literally means be-jinned; bewitched), and ever be consumed by the spirit of love; oh cooling flood, oh black fistful of loam, oh fire that casts no smoke!

---

the heart as closed garden. See *A Dictionary of Modern Written Arabic*, 164.

4

Risāla fī l-hīrmīs aṣ-ṣāmat

[Risāla of the Dead Hermes]

☿

When Nature died, and a great voice erupted along the shores of the Mediterranean proclaiming *the Great God Pan is Dead!*, the winged sandals of Hermes were snagged upon cloud thistle, and he fell from the sky as Autumn leaves fall, for death to Nature means death to Hermes.[65]

To silence the bird calls, to disrupt the electric patchwork of mycelium, to gag glacial flows, is to sever human language from its source. Languages live and grow like plants. To suffocate the systems that give them life from the sun, soil, and water, will result in their death. The carnality of spoken human language, its origins in the contact of the human body with the more-than-human other, in spontaneous gesture as the *bodying-forth* of emotions, and in mimicking the soundscape of one's immediate environs will be familiar to readers of David Abram's *The Spell of the Sensuous*. Our first languages were rooted in place, and therefore moulded and given form by place. Language is not separate from the land any more than the mind is separate from the body. Language is the chance reflection glanced in a rain puddle; the audible and sensual looking-glass where Nature might marvel at her shining savage visage.

Biodiversity is directly linked to linguistic diversity. To illustrate this, it is useful to meditate on how approximately 60% of all Canada's First Nations languages are indigenous to the province known as British Columbia, which also happens to be the Canadian province home to the most biodiversity in the country. Indeed, and to some of the most biologically diverse

---

65 Cf. Plutarch's *De defectu oraculorum* [The Obsolescence of Oracles]: "Suddenly from the island of Paxi was heard the voice of someone loudly calling Thamus, so that all were amazed. Thamus was an Egyptian pilot, not known by name even to many on board. Twice he was called and made no reply, but the third time he answered; and the caller, raising his voice, said, 'When you come opposite to Palodes, announce that Great Pan is dead.'" [trans. F. C. Babbitt]. Many writers through the ages have cited this and interpreted it to their own ideological tunes. It also appears at the opening to Jules Michelet's *La Sorcière*.

regions on the North American continent. British Columbia is also very topographically diverse. Consequentially, although British Columbia's landmass is but approximately two times that of the Iberian Peninsula, there is more autochthonous linguistic diversity found there than in all of Europe.

Study any language map of British Columbia and wonder at the intense linguistic diversity found there. Compare with the Prairies and Eastern Canada which are less topographically diverse, and you will notice that the most prominent language family is Algonquian, and in particular two Algonquian languages, Cree and Anishinaabemowin (Ojibwe). In the Arctic, alongside the Algonquian family, languages from the Dene and Inuit families are spoken. In contrast, British Columbia is the traditional home to speakers of languages included in just about all of the above families (except maybe Inuit), plus Salishan, Tsimshian, Wakashan, Haida, and Kutenai.

To put this in perspective, keep in mind each one of these is a *language family*, not a *language*, meaning that each of these encompasses many other languages, in the same way the Indo-European language family encompasses many languages. In turn, each of the languages in each family outlined above has various dialects. For example, while Cree, a member of the Algonquian family, is considered a language in itself, there are at least eight different dialects of Cree.

Several hypotheses have been put forth to account for this. One asserts that British Columbia must be a linguistically old area from which speakers of different languages migrated to the south and east. This may be true, but at the same time it seems impossible to discount biological and topographic diversity as contributing factors to linguistic diversity.

Consider ecotones. An ecotone is the natural crossroads where one biome or ecosystem meets another. The forest's rim, river banks, the skirts of mountains, the alpine tree-line, or the beach are all ecotones. These liminal zones and edge spaces are much prized in permaculture designs as they often give rise to a great increase in biodiversity, and are among the most biologically diverse spaces in the natural world. Therefore, while we might affirm that British Columbia's linguistic biodiversity is wholly or in part the result of its diverse topography and species richness (due to the languages developing in isolation), we can equally affirm that it is the result of different bioregions *in communication* with one another. From the dry deserts of the Okanagan valley to the rainforests on the west coast of Vancouver

Island, these languages have emerged as expressions of the land, encountered one another, and given rise to a complexity of thought, culture, and tradition as beautiful as it is humbling.

The examples given were those of traditionally oral languages. However, while perhaps some degrees removed from their rooted, "indigenous" origins, written languages, and even the "high" languages of "major" world religions and their literatures, also emerge from the landscape and are interwoven throughout it.[66] We find this in the *Sefer Yetzirah*, in which the Hebrew alphabet is purported to be possessed of elemental powers and to have played a key role in the creation of the natural world. With this in mind, one could behold a garden as a physical vegetal manifestation of the elements, expressed through voice, body, and symbol.

Every language is an entire ecosystem unto itself, with the connections between words ever so beautifully and subtly mirroring the connections between species, climate, and minerals. This is especially appreciated in root-based languages like Hebrew or Arabic in which all verbs and nouns are derived from (mostly) three-letter roots. Meaning branches out from these roots in the manner of trees. Comparing words derived from a common root opens up vistas onto semantic fields whose contemplation draws us nearer to the hidden bonds and communications between all things, making it a truly Hermetic exercise.[67]

For example, take the Arabic three-letter root 'r s l' [ر س ل] In verb form I, its simplest form, *rasila* means "to be long and flowing (i.e. hair)." Form III (associative), *rāsila*, means "to correspond, carry on correspondence, exchange letters (with someone); to contact, get in touch."

In form IV (causative), *arsala*, to send out, dispatch, to send off, send away, to send, forward, ship, to send, transmit (radio), to release, let go, to set free, to discharge, to pour forth, vent, give vent, to utter; to shed (i.e.; tears), to let hang down (i.e.; hair), let it fall, to speak without restraint, to talk freely; to yield to ones natural impulse, do the natural thing, to (make)

---

66 Some islamophobic writers accuse Classical Arabic [*fuṣḥa*] of being naught but the invention of philologists. An ornate, inorganic, fabricated, faux-language, that is officially spoken nowhere. They forget that any language with a codified grammar and a dictionary can be accused of being "inorganic," and indeed, any such language is, in effect, the fabrication of philologists. Is there any country in which proper literary English is spoken at ground level? Is this the case with any modern language?

67 Cf. *The Corpus Hermeticum* or Agrippa, *Three Books of Occult Philosophy*.

someone feel at home; to feel at home, to follow one's own instinct or natural impulses; to radiate glowing heat; to give a short whistle; to talk long and broad, let oneself go.

In form V (reflexive form II, and usually intransitive) *tarassala*, to proceed leisurely, take one's time; to hang down, be long and flowing (hair). In form VI (reflexive form III) *tarāsala*, to keep up a correspondence, exchange letters; to send to one another, exchange (something); and in form X (considerative or resquestive of form I) *istarsala*, to ask to send, to have someone send something, to be relaxed, at ease, free from restraint; to be long and flowing (hair); to be friendly, affable, intimate, chummy; to act naturally, without affectation; to let something go; to give oneself free rein, to do without restrain or inhibition; to abandon, give up; to talk at great length, speak extensively, to surrender to one's thoughts, muse.[68]

A whole bouquet of nouns flower from these branches. We have already mentioned *risāla* (simply put: a message, letter or treatise) and *rasūl* (messenger or prophet), and can add *rasīl* (messenger, runner), *rasl* (easy, gentle, leisurely; loose, slack, relaxed; long and flowing i.e. hair), *mirsāl* (searchlight), *mursil* (sender: consignor; transmitter) to provide a few more examples.

There are a number of things about this exposition that catch our attention. For starters, speakers or students of Arabic will notice that 'r s l' [ر س ل] does not find expression in all ten verb forms. Not all roots do. Form IX, for example, deals exclusively with colour verbs. While there are some colour verbs in English, such as "to rouge," "to darken," "to azure," and so on, colours are rarely used as verbs. However, in Arabic, colour verbs are not only used, there is an entire verb form (the ninth), which is to say—an entire pattern upon which to conjugate the root consonants all the way from first person singular to third person plural—dedicated to colours. Colours in motion, colours in action, colours as verbs! The temptation provoked by such linguistic features to wax lyric makes the poet's heart thrill.

Another thing that stands out is the connection that becomes clear between letter writing or sending with an intuitive pouring forth, and the letting down of long flowing hair. Curiously this connection appears again when one considers that the word *sh'ir* [poetry] is almost identical to *sh'ar* [hair], and both derive from the same root, *'sh ' r'* [ش ع ر] In verb form I, this root means to learn or understand intuitively, to realize, notice, to per-

68 See *A Dictionary of Modern Written Arabic*, 391–92.

ceive, feel, sense, be conscious, be aware, to make or compose poetry, poetize, versify; and in form IV, to make feel, let notice, to notify, inform, to feel, sense, notice, perceive, realize, be conscious, be aware, to be filled with (a feeling). This semantic connection, which to English speakers might appear bizarre at first glance, appears to emerge from the connection between hair, the senses, and intuition. Hair is a sensory organ. The cat uses her whiskers to sense her whereabouts, and the recitation or singing of a powerful poem can make one's hair stand up on end.

As Nature dies, Language follows suit. With each passing year more and more species go extinct, the biosphere becomes ever less diverse, and therefore ever less resilient. While much protest is made over species loss and the destruction of the natural world, one hardly ever hears that the ethnosphere loses languages at a much faster rate. Wade Davis, the anthropologist who coined the term "ethnosphere," writes:

> And just as the biosphere, the biological matrix of life, is today being severely compromised, so too is the ethnosphere. Only if anything at a far greater rate of loss. No biologist, for example, would dare suggest that 50 percent of all species of plant and animal are moribund or on the brink of extinction. Yet this, the most apocalyptic projection in the realm of biological diversity, scarcely approaches what we know to be the most optimistic scenario in the realm of cultural diversity. The key indicator is language loss. There are at present some 6,000 languages. But of these fully half are not being taught to children. Which means that effectively, unless something changes, these languages are already dead...
>
> It's haunting to realize that half of the languages of the world are teetering on the brink of extinction. Just think about it. What could be more lonely than to be enveloped in silence, to be the last of your people to speak your native tongue, to have no way to pass on the wisdom of the elders, to anticipate the promise of the children. This tragic fate is indeed the plight of someone somewhere roughly every two weeks. For on average every fortnight a leader

> dies and carries with him or her into the grave the last syllables of an ancient tongue. *What this really means is that within a generation or two, we are witnessing the loss of fully half of humanity's legacy. This is the hidden backdrop of our age.* [Emphasis mine].[69]

Each one of these languages that is lost not only represents a cultural legacy, an identity, and a storehouse of wisdom, but *an entire reality*. Reality is inseparable from language, whether verbal or otherwise. We cannot escape it. Even Descartes formulated his affirmation of existence in language, for to do otherwise is impossible. The more languages we speak, the broader our reality. To speak but one language is to exist in a very limited sphere. Death to Hermes means death to the real.

Some might deem it nonsensical to say that reality could rot, rust, or be corroded. However, one cannot access the real without a mediating agent. Every age has a dominant ontological portal that acts as arbiter of what is real and what is not. In the most primordial sense, this portal is the body and especially the senses. Then came Language. Then religion. Then Capitalism, and now the internet, which is essentially capitalism turned digital shadow play.

If reality is composed of ideas, and the appearances which house these ideas become corroded, than so does reality. This is the premise of J. P. Kruses' philosophical treatise, *The Blue Spark*. As far as capitalism is concerned, things are only real insofar as they can yield a profit; that which is most profitable becomes the most real. And as for the internet, content is only real insofar as it generates likes, shares, and retweets. Which is to say, the content with the most likes is higher up on the ontological food chain.

Of course, when one makes a concentrated ontological investment in some ideas, it is done at the expense of others. With this in mind, it hardly bears pointing out that capitalism is likely the foremost cause of language loss. Some languages are profitable, others yield no profit, and may even get in the way, hence them becoming targets to be eliminated. Why would indigenous people, some might ask, teach their children their traditional languages when these languages will not lead to their children getting jobs,

---

69 It is not always easy to cite Wade Davis as he often restates his eloquent affirmations throughout his talks, class lectures, and books. This is from an interview he did with National Public Radio (NPR) that can be read at www.npr.org., but he also explores this in his *Light at the Edge of the World*, and indeed is a common theme throughout all his books.

becoming financially well-off, or "getting ahead" in society?

In the same way that monocropping in industrial agriculture can be a more efficient way of making a profit, and, in effect, of dominating a landscape, the elimination of languages, and indeed the elimination of words within languages, are well-known hegemonic devices. To provide a familiar example, think of the elimination of words like "peace" from the dictionary in George Orwell's *1984*. As species go extinct, their names are deleted from the dictionary. This becomes even more unsettling when one realizes that a dictionary functions, in a sense, as an ontological compass. Indeed, each year all kinds of words are deleted, regardless of them being related to species extinction or not, simply because they have ceased to become profitable, and thereby have fallen into disuse and ultimately, oblivion. Internet-speak is like a bioengineered capitalist monoculture, the mon in Monsanto. Old words and archaisms are the heirloom varieties of species that we all have a duty to seed-save; they are the mon of a monism that is star-struck and earth-fed by the divine in all things.

The continual and increasing exploitation and destruction of Nature mirrors that of the fast-food reduction of Language. One need only consider the depreciation of poetry and the increasingly marginalized, discarded, or even demonized role of the poet in most societies today compared to that of its illustrious past. The poets, those wild silversmiths of language, once fulfilled societal functions of a prestige comparable to a king or chief. They were remembrancers, diviners, magicians, healers, and sometimes occupied sapiential roles such as that of a judge. Poetry was intimately intertwined throughout all aspects of society, and was chanted to mark life's thresholds—births, marriages, deaths, and other types of initiation. This is true in traditional cultures all over the world, regardless of whether or not these are (or were) oral or literate cultures. In fact, it might be argued that it is even more true in the case of oral cultures.

And so the beasts of the wood and the birds of the air weep, and the trees and all rushing streams weep, weep for the monetization of language, for the de-eroticization of language. For hundreds if not thousands of years, monarchs and chiefs used poetry as a prime mode of communication. Epistles were composed in verse. Politics were conducted in verse, in the language of poetry. Even casual speech was once much more florid. Given the ongoing dalliance of Language with the real and the ideal, each increasing level of degradation that communication undergoes and has undergone can represent rungs on an ontological ladder. Is a spoken poem more real than a written poem, more real than a hand-written letter, more real than a telegram, more real than a phone-call, more real than an email, more real than a text, more real than chat apps, more real than a tweet? So the poets wail, and weep for dead Hermes, and curse the insidious advent of #poetry.

Language is one of our most potent tools in the struggle against the orchestrators of ecocide and the perpetrators of genocide. It is also one of our most potent tools to combat colonialism, or to be applied in the dismantling of capitalism and its subsequent necessary translation into a healthy way of conducting economics, of literally "managing the house."[70] In making this assertion it is important to remember that several self-proclaimed communist or socialist regimes, both contemporary and historical, have also taken a destructive toll on both the biosphere and the ethnosphere. It is a necessary first step to reject the aspects of some strains of leftist thought that deem anything even remotely traditional as counterrevolutionary or as an impediment to progress and the industrial machine.

Languages are masks. When one speaks a given language, one dons a persona [from Latin *persōna*, literally, a mask] proper to that language. Languages should not be mistaken for the real, they are shades and colours of the real. Likewise, your persona in one language does not represent the "real you," even if this language be your mother tongue. The more languages you know, the better your ability to shape-shift, walk unseen, or cover your trail. Additionally, observing your behaviour when speaking different languages may assist you in the acquisition of self knowledge, or in a word—power.

Languages can be useful in conflicts in both attack and defence. The highly militaristic Assyrian empire was famous for addressing the officials of besieged cities in their native tongue and in loud voices, so their threats and aggressions would be directly understood by the civilians sheltered behind the walls. This is an example of psychological warfare. Addressing a target in their native tongue aims to fill their heart with fear. A contemporary example would be the propaganda of some "Islamic" terrorist groups who produce videos in which the West is addressed and threatened by native speakers of English.

---

70 The word "economy" comes from the Ancient Greek *oikonomía* [οἰκονομία] which literally means "management of a household." This word can be broken down into *oîkos* [house] and *némō* [distribute, allocate].

With regards to defence, speaking an enemy's language may increase one's chances of survival if the going gets rough. In the same way some identify language (in the human sense) as a dividing line between humans and animals: when someone speaks your language you are less likely to view them as sub-human, uncivilized, or bestial. Humans are essentially good. Even the most vile, self-loathing, twisted, broken, and unbalanced people will have a tougher time executing an innocent if they do not view them as irreconcilably other. Unfortunately, this notion has been applied in reverse by many a scumbag throughout history. To other one's targets is to make it easier for one's cronies to do one's dirty work. Wade Davis explains:

> All cultures are ethnocentric, fiercely loyal to their own interpretation of reality. Indeed the names of many indigenous societies translate as "the people," the implication being that every other human is a non-person, a savage from beyond the realm of the civilized. The word barbarian in fact derives from the Greek barbarus, meaning one who babbles. In the ancient world if you did not speak Greek you were a barbarian. The Aztec had the same notion. Anyone who could not speak Nahuatl was a non-human.[71]

Languages can build and foment true solidarity. When one travels, it is imperative to make an effort to speak the local language, even if this is a simple "*I apologize for not being able to speak....* " This shows respect, humility, and sincerity. Would Trump have been able to cash in on Americans' fear of the Mexican other if more non-hispanic Americans spoke Spanish? What would the War on Terror have looked like if more Westerners spoke Arabic? Would activists be more effective if they could better organize across linguistic lines, and not simply expect (or force) their allies to all learn English or some other language of colonialism? What would contemporary identity politics look like? What happens to white privilege when the cops see pale-skinned people speaking indigenous languages, or demonized languages like Arabic?

Languages can provoke mystical ecstasy. Take Don Luis de Góngora y Argote for example. What the academic establishment thought useless, *rococo* in excess, or verbose, was really an invitation to a linguistic bacchanal,

71 Again, from the interview he did with NPR, though he has made this point on numerous other occasions.

for Góngora's poetry is truly a lyrical banquet. Just as poetry is an eroticization of communication, rituals, games, and other preliminaries in a sexual context are an eroticization of reproduction, or as poet Lenore Kandel so eloquently put it: *To Fuck with Love*. Like sex, language—and especially poetic language—should not always be engaged in exclusively as a means to an end, nor to fulfill their alleged function, but for their own sweet sake.

Learning languages re-wires your brain. To learn a language is to engage in an internal alchemical process; you will never be the same. If language is truly carnal then these changes and resonances will be felt viscerally. Your identity might change slightly, both in the way you view yourself, and, more importantly, in the way society views you. Your reality will expand.

If languages are vehicles for reality, and the present political climate is marked by the efforts of some to ruthlessly impose their reality upon everyone else, to eradicate any other way of being in the world, it should surprise us that those who oppose them overwhelmingly all speak the same language, and thereby inescapably inhabit the same reality as the enemy. This is a most complicated matter. How can one fight a harmful reality on its own terms? Especially when this reality relies on a hate-speech whose syntax forces one's mind to manoeuvre in the same ontological grammatical positions as one's opponents? Is it strategic to use racial language to oppose racist ideologies? To rely on a common language, or on the same or similar terms or buzzwords reveals one's trapped state—held under the enemy's thumb.

Perhaps one of the most profound ways to combat colonialism in the Americas is to learn one or more indigenous languages. For both indigenous and non-indigenous people alike, this truly comprises a decolonization of the mind. However, for non-indigenous people, it is of the utmost importance to remember that learning an indigenous language should only ever be done *on the terms of the indigenous community in question*. Not all communities will open their doors to outsiders, and if they do not this must be respected all the same. When they do open their doors, however, teaching the language should be orchestrated, overseen, or done directly by that community's elders. If an outsider wishes to use what they are learning outside of the community, they must seek permission from that community's elders or governing body. To neglect to do this is to engage in colonialism in the grossest sense of the word.

I am immensely fortunate to have spent two years learning a Salishan language. I can testify that several harmful thought forms that were imposed on me from without were decimated in the process. All of my classmates who were not members of the community (even if they were indigenous but from other communities) had to sign a contract stating they would not steal or otherwise appropriate the things we learned, and that if we wanted to use things we learned in class outside of the community, we had to make a formal request and have this request approved by the band council. It is for this reason that I will not name the language or the community in question, nor write any of its words here. Apart from having no right nor wish to *speak for* this community, a need for discretion makes asking permission in this instance impossible. Some members of the community in question are practicing Christians who do not share my politics and might be repulsed at the thought of being spoken of by someone who consorts with gods and radicals.

I will say, however, that this language is as rich as loam. Its linguistic complexity was mind-blowing, and made English or Spanish look feebly simple in comparison. I loved how there were two different definite articles that were used depending on whether or not the noun in question was seen by the speaker or not. Imagine the usefulness of this when hunting, or even more so, when story-telling. Switching back and forth between the articles modifying seen or unseen nouns is a way in which the storyteller can draw their audience into the story itself. A story-teller could be telling about some mythic events said to have taken place in the distant past and be using the article for nouns the speaker cannot see, yet in an instant, switch to the article for nouns the speaker *can* see, and all of a sudden, however remote in time or space the story might be, it begins to unfold before the audience's eyes.

Also, traditional ecological knowledge is embedded in the very language. For example, there is a suffix that is used in every word that refers to a species of salmon. English, on the other hand, calls steelhead trout a trout when it is really a salmon, and Atlantic salmon a salmon when it really belongs to an entirely different genus than the salmon of the Pacific.[72]

This language is consonant heavy, and always struck me as sounding very much like rain falling through a forest's canopy, a fitting comparison when one keeps in mind the people who this language belongs to made (and

72 Cf. Steelhead trout: a subspecies of *Oncorhynchus mykiss*; Sockeye Salmon: *Oncorhynchus nerka*; Pink Salmon: *Oncorhynchus gorbuscha*; and finally Atlantic Salmon: *Salmo salar*.

make) their traditional home in Pacific temperate rainforests.

One such consonant that stood out in this manner is what some linguists call the voiceless alveolar lateral fricative, or more colloquially, the "slurpy l." In IPA (International Phonetic Alphabet) it is represented with this symbol: ɬ. The best way to describe what this sounds like to those unfamiliar with IPA is as an "h" sound followed by an "l." Curiously, this sound is also prominent in Welsh, represented in that language as "ll."[73]

The class was held on the reserve and about half the students were band members, the other half outsiders. At the end of each term the teachers organized a potluck in which the students' families, friends, and any other member of the community could come, share food, and watch us perform little skits and dialogues that we'd been preparing throughout the term.[74]

It so happens that the same night that one of these potlucks was going to be held, a prominent pagan activist was in town and giving a talk. I felt somewhat torn, as I really wanted to see her speak, but at the same time, knew that the right thing to do was to go to the potluck, and in hindsight I am so glad I did. I will never forget something our teacher—a respected elder in the community who grew up speaking the language with his mother—said that night. He addressed the whole room (maybe between fifty and seventy people) and went on in his gentle yet powerful way to let us know how much it meant to him that we came to the community to help support the survival of his language, and to multiply the opportunities that speakers in the community have to speak it.

Two things he said gave me goosebumps. First, in very gentle terms he asserted that the Truth and Reconciliation Commission that was ongoing in Canada at that time, was, to put it bluntly, merely lip service, and that although we didn't know it, everyone in that room—sharing food, breaking bread, performing silly skits—*was the true reconciliation commission*. Second, he mentioned that even if we never spoke the language outside the community, or if we moved away, we would always carry the language with

---

73 Such as the sound at the beginning of the name of the Welsh town often abbreviated as Llanfair-PG, whose full beautiful name is Llanfairpwllgwyngyllgogerychwyrndrobwllllantysiliogogogoch, the third longest "official" toponym in the world.

74 Those of us who were not band members were from or were descendants of people from Europe, Africa, Asia, indigenous people from other bands, or a mix thereof.

us for having spent time learning it, and that was something that made him happy and proud.

It bears repeating, of course, that not all indigenous people or communities might feel the same way. In any case, what impacted me so much about his comments was the realization that, while arguably "less sexy" or exciting than blockading something or giving an impassioned speech at a protest, and arguably less thrilling than publishing blog posts on the internet, the work we were doing was not only political, but profoundly and enduringly powerful. It was face to face, on the ground, and yielded tangible results.

Other than those comments, things did not ever get as explicitly political as that night at the potluck save for one other night. In the city where this all took place, there was a parking lot slated for development that had great archaeological and ancestral significance for the community that I have been discussing. The lot was near one of their traditional village sites, and construction machines had uncovered archaeological remains and even skeletons (including those of infants). It turns out it was a burial ground and midden site. The community called for the construction to cease, which went unheeded by the developer. One day in class the teachers and those classmates who were band members informed the rest of us that the workers had resumed construction earlier that day, and that the community needed volunteers to oppose them immediately. They were particularly concerned about protecting the site and preventing any construction workers from accessing it throughout the night. I asked them to sign me up for whenever they thought best and was assigned the last shift of the night.

I remember making a thermos of broth before heading over. There were only two band members there at that point: one was a middle aged man and the other maybe in his twenties. They were standing at the gate of the lot and the younger man was holding the band's flag. It was a large flag complete with shoulder strap. I asked them how the night had gone so far. They said it had gone well, there were some initial confrontations with the workers but things had been quiet. In any case, they would not leave the lot unguarded, lest the workers return. I asked them what they wanted me to do. The younger guy handed me the flag and said, "here, take this. Stand here and don't let anyone through this gate."

They got in their car and left, and that's exactly what I did. I stood there alone for the next few hours, in the cold and dark, until more and more band members and their friends and allies started showing up after the sun rose and some people started to barbecue... In this, and a few other actions that followed shortly after, the band members were not just defending their ancestors in the figurative sense, but also in the literal sense by *preventing the destruction of the ancestors' very bones.*[75]

A decision was made to include this memory here to illustrate how learning a language can foment solidarity. None of my classmates who were outsiders came to talk politics, give speeches, or tell the indigenous community members how we thought they should organize. Most of the classmates had no experience with activism, or even an interest in it. I'm not even sure to what extent all of them were aware of the political implications of their learning an indigenous language. We came because each of us had personal reasons for wanting to take advantage of this wonderful opportunity the band was giving us by opening its doors. We got to know each other pretty well over the course of our time in class and surprisingly enough, instead of calling on some activist group from down the way who talked all the right talk or read and published all the right articles, we were among those called on to quickly mobilize and help out at a time when the band needed it.

Some might resonate with the ideas put forth in this letter, but be reluctant to actually go out and learn a language or three. I hear people say all the time, "but I'm not good at languages," "it's not my *fuerte,*" "it doesn't come naturally to me," and so on. It's true that some people might be naturally gifted at language, but that does not mean that they do not or did not have to put in work.

When learning a foreign alphabet for example, here's what you do. Take leaves of paper, one for each letter, and write that letter fifty times (in all its forms if it has more than one). Repeat this exercise every day or every few days as needed until the alphabet is second nature to you.

Music is also invaluable when learning a language. For the young at heart, cartoons and children's books might be useful resources. Don't give up, and don't be afraid to laugh or make jokes about yourself, especially when talking with native speakers. Although lessons might get increasingly more complex as you advance, like learning a dance or martial art, the hardest day is undoubtedly your first.

---

75 Development halted, a few actions followed this one to raise awareness and support, and the municipality entered into negotiations with the band. A few years later the land was returned to the band by the municipality.

There are of course other resources available to the magically inclined among us. Many spirits are said to be able to teach languages, grant eloquence of speech, and instruct in the correct drawing of symbols. There are several of these in Western grimoires, and there are many stories of congress between humans and fairies that result in the human being given the ability to compose spontaneous poems or the ability to sing like no other mortal. Parallels to these can be found in cultures all over the world.

These spirits are of enormous assistance when it comes to learning languages. They can be invoked before or during studies, and their sigils combined with different herbs, oils, waters, or powders dedicated to them, made under their auspices, or that otherwise resonate strongly with them, can be applied to the body and around the place of study. What will occur is that you will find yourself learning the language as if through some sort of uncanny osmosis. You will begin to dream in it—more often if you didn't already—and the learning process will be more akin to remembering something you always knew but forgot, rather than learning something totally foreign from scratch. These spirits will also help make you more comfortable and composed when trying to speak the language, especially when speaking with native speakers, as this can be a bit embarrassing when just getting started. You will find that in a more relaxed state you won't stutter or freeze up as much, and new vocabulary you've learned and stored away will flow out of you instead of remaining hidden in some cobwebbed corner of your mind.

In addition to learning languages, it is imperative for the dissident to cultivate modes of communication that cannot compute. Instead of relying on the internet or a large and likely untrustworthy postal service, groups of covens can develop communications networks in which the role of courier is filled by the initiates themselves, potentially in combination with trusted allies. These networks might consist of something as simple as a single courier carrying a letter from one neighbourhood to another (or from one farm to another if in a rural environment), or as complex as a chain of couriers that spans countries or even continents. Magical alphabets—and there are no shortage of these in the grimoires of various cultures—can be employed to confound border agents and others who might intercept the message. The important thing to remember is communication is power, and to have control over communication is to take back power.

Also, non-written modes of communication may be employed. These can include mimicry of bird calls, signal lights, or the dark speech of gesture. Messages can even be sent between coveners through astral travel or dreams, and one or more than one divination tool can be employed in these instances when further clarity is sought. While oneiric communication has its difficulties and potentially problematic aspects, this does not imply it should not be cultivated. Like any mode of divination, clarity and precision increase with practice and the refinement of one's technique. All of these modes can be used alone or in concert with one another, and arriving at the most practical combination will be specific to the group and to the place where they operate.

Hermes, as bearer of the helmet of invisibility, asserts that invisibility and clandestinity—especially online—are of the utmost importance in this work. This cannot be stressed enough. While some might have compromises that prevent them from deleting their online avatar once and for all—for example, a small-publisher whose readership is far-flung and whose work would not proceed were it void of an online presence—all would benefit greatly from deleting their personal profiles. The benefits come not only from making it harder for the authorities to track and watch you, but from smashing the shackles of the forms of harmful group-think, ego-fattening, conflict-mongering and time-wasting that the internet (and especially social media) brings about.

Albeit hollow and illusory, the internet comprises territory. The left cannot afford to cede online territory to the fascist and fascist-leaning enemy; therefore a degree of online presence is necessary. However, as the internet is a hard drug, it should be treated as such, and only used infrequently and in safe doses. It should be a country one visits from time to time, not a country one inhabits. And when one visits a potentially hostile country one would do well not to announce one's presence too loudly. In the same way unseen spirits make incursions into the visible, dissidents who publish on the internet must do so in the sense of making incursions into another world, only to vanish again not long after. When a witch or similar publishes online, she is, in effect, engaging in a haunting.

Apologists might moan about the uses of the internet to disseminate information, but this comes at too great a price. Remember, the advent of the printing press meant the advent (or at least a great intensification) of censorship... Or apologists might moan about the rapidity with which one might communicate. Remember, the artificial need for everything to move faster and faster, for transactions and initiatives to be carried out instantly, and to think in short spans of time—all things brought about by modernity—are a significant contributing factor to what's causing the great crises of our age. It is imperative to return to a longer, slower, experience of time, of mythic time, an experience that spirals and fractals, condenses, evaporates, and rains down, not unlike the water cycle.

> As the crickets' soft autumn hum
> Is to us
> So are we to the trees
> As are they
> To the rocks and the hills
> — Gary Snyder[76]

If we premise the internet to be harmful for our physical, mental, artistic and political health, and to the health of all Nature, then dietary measures must be taken immediately to curb that damage. Deleting one's online presence and limiting one's use of the internet has an equal if not greater positive impact than going vegan.

All of the suggestions made above are necromantic techniques capable of reviving dead Hermes. In most cases, dead languages are not actually dead, but sleeping, and they should be referred to as such out of respect to those who belong to a culture whose language is threatened or no longer spoken. Hermes Chthonios teaches us that no end is truly final and even the coldest dead are but sleepers sleeping the charmed drowse of apple trees.[77]

---

76 See Snyder, *Axe Handles*, 51.

77 Cf. Federico García Lorca's "Gacela de la muerte oscura," from his *Diván del Tamarit.*

5

Risālat as-sahm fī l-qalb

[Risāla of the Arrow in the Heart]

☿

Truly, the earth is a serpent's den of languages. Forests, deserts, mountains, swamps—all contribute to the emergence of vernaculars in accordance with their unique and myriad *genius loci*. Space moulds language, and thereby moulds reality. Yet, in harmony with the effects of space, languages may also be moulded by time. As the sun falls below the horizon, the permutations of syntax are subject to an ebb and flow in many ways irreconcilably foreign to those more bombast broadcastings declared by daylight. A syntax at times unintelligible to those who forget that night keeps a vernacular all of her own.

This nocturnal tongue, this owl call or bat chirrup, is at times a cold vernacular, at others a warm one, but is ever a moist vernacular. It is moss-agate-speech, lyre-speech, and heart-speech. Truly, it is a hermetic speech—sealed, inviolate—that passes from the shadow of *trobar clus* to the nacre-glow of *trobar ric* after the postures of wet black boughs and the moon's whereabouts at any given moment.

And tonight there is wind in the flutes' reed-hollows. There is a battery of hooves and the lone voice melodic of some far-off nightingale (or is it that of some long dead poet whose soul donned feathers?). Arrows of moonlight project a dappled calligraphy upon the forest floor, after piercing the heart-shaped leaves of the groves' canopy—leaves become shards of sea-glass wrapped in hushed and intangible sheaths of silver. Could this be theophany? Could this be Diana at her most immediate, her most intimate? Not so much a goddess of the moon but the moon poured out upon branches and glimpsed from below?

The love ravished poet fears no Fate. No slings and arrows of outrageous fortune. For to fall in Love is to rise above death, and to be unbound by death is truly the sweetest, the most precious, and outrageous of fortunes. Therefore, when asked of your condition, respond—whether hale or infirm—"*will of the Fates.*" Could this be a true meaning of *submission* in a religious or spiritual context, to submit to god as one would a lover? To be careless of where the next bright bolt may fall?

The heart pierced by an arrow has become a near ubiquitous cipher for love-sickness, which is, of course, in many regards indistinguishable from love-sweetness. In "Western" cultures, the heart-shape we know today perhaps has its origins in the shape of the seed of the aphrodisiac silphium plant, perhaps the leaves of water-lilies, perhaps in the *mons pubis*, or perhaps from all or none of these. The arrows, belonging to Cupid, need no explanation. In any case, this shapely cipher has also variously been employed to denote religious rapture, whether the five wounds of Christ, or the pagan poet cum stag cum god impaled upon a regal tree and bleeding roses of blood all the wistful while.

This emblem of blood and honey, bewitching in its enigmatic simplicity, is also evocative of cycles of courtly romance, of eerie love lyrics or medieval mystery plays. In the modern era, it is hardly possible to ponder this symbol without the mind alighting on that infamous and by now near universal romantic outlaw: Robin Hood.

Like the green tipped darts of the leafy Devil he serves, Robin's elf-shot may wound or ravish, and his personage can mean more than a mere plundering and redistribution of material wealth of the few, but a simultaneous plundering inflicted on the spheres of knowledge and the real. The good Robin that is being called upon here, a call made in the same breath as one to the troubadours (with whom he is often, and at times incorrectly, associated) is concerned with ambushing the arbiters of meaning and value.

These arbiters of reality and value have taken on different shapes throughout the course of history. Once upon a time they were the armies of Empires, or the Inquisition and other agents of religious monodoctrine, or the police-force of industrial Nation-States. More recently, they are the monopolies that control the latest portal opened to the ideal: the internet. This portal, apparently inoffensive, and while not entirely void of utility, perhaps represents the most crude and dangerous initiative yet carried out and co-opted by Capitalism to assert itself as an indisputable nonnegotiable law of Nature. Fortunately, as the troubadours show us, the gates between the real and the ideal erected and policed by the aforementioned arbiters can taste poetry's torch and be razed to the ground.

The Robin Hood most of us know is cast as a twelfth century contemporary of Richard the Lion Heart, a noble-man who, upon returning from the crusades, finds his lands seized by the Sheriff of Nottingham. This nobleman then turns political bandit in opposition to the Sheriff and the illegitimate Prince John, stealing from the rich and giving to the poor. While much of this comes from additions to the tale-cycle by post-medieval authors, there are several mentions of a "Robinhood" (or otherwise spelled "Robehod" or "Robbehod") in the thirteenth century up until the beginning of the fourteenth, leading some historians to assume it was a mask or alias that different ne'er-do-wells, outlaws, or bandits adopted as it suited them.

The earliest literary reference to Robin Hood is the ballad known as the "Pliers Plowman," which is thought to date from the late fourteenth century. This is followed by the "Robin Hood ballads" proper, thought to date from different times during the fifteenth century. In these ballads, Robin is not cast as a noble-born man, but as a yeoman; nor does he explicitly steal from the rich to give to the poor. However, many of the seeds that would grow into the image of the merry bandit we know today can be found there, such as his anticlericalism, his staunch Marianism and high regard for women, his skill as an archer and his partisanship on behalf of the lower rungs of feudal society.

While the medieval Robin Hood dates from a time when the troubadour phenomenon (at least in the case of the troubadours proper, which is to say, those who wrote in Occitan) was on the wane, there is much overlap not only historically but in the ethos and mystique of both. One such example is the *Jeu de Robin et Marion* written by Adam de la Halle, a French *trouvère*.[78] This piece is thought to date from around 1282. While it does not depict Robin or Marion the outlaws in their full Lincoln-green glory, it is a clear example of both characters' connections with the May Games, games of love and the Greenwood, an association that Robin the outlaw would assume in (likely) later additions to his mythic cycle.[79]

---

78 The ballad known as "A Gest of Robyn Hode" is another example of overlap between Robin Hood and the troubadours. The narrator of the ballad at times addresses the reader (audience), which has led historians to believe it was performed by minstrels before a public. Of this ballad, John Taylor has written: "The targets of Robin Hood's criticism are the justices of the forest and the common law, against whom grievances could have been felt by more than one section of the medieval community." Taylor, John. "Robin Hood." *Dictionary of the Middle Ages*. New York: Charles Scribner's Sons, 1988.

79 Trouvère is the French term for troubadour, and is roughly equivalent to the

Historians and philologists have perhaps been too quick to dismiss the *Jeu de Robin et Marion* as a possible early reference to the same folkloric character as the later Robin Hood, no doubt due in part to the long-mouldering shortcomings of philology in demarcating texts too rigidly along linguistic, national, and temporal lines. The *Jeu de Robin et Marion* at once illustrates the universality of different aspects of courtly romance, the lyric and the court as spheres of cultural interchange, and the interplay in troubadour and lyric poetry between the "courtly" and the popular. Clearly, this *pastourelle* can be seen as the written shadow of a longer oral tradition of Robin and Marion, one with undeniable pagan roots. In any case, historicity and its uptight arbiters need not overly concern us here. Truly, the personage of Robin Hood is a mask. A mask that undergoes changes in accordance with changes of culture, politics and the inspirations of new voices that contribute to his cycle of tales. In this regard, the poet Giles Watson's delightful depiction of Robin and the Men-in-Green as shape-shifting animists with Robin himself a sort of "crow-shaman," is both powerful and appropriate.

It might be true that much of the written Robin Hood cycle was composed in the modern period and not the medieval, but Robin Hood's fairy figure no doubt carries with it something of an *ubi sunt* for a half-forgotten world. It is certainly not puzzling to wonder why, against the backdrop of the Industrial Revolution and the advent of Capitalism, many Romantic writers would take up Robin's bow and quarterstaff and make our cunning outlaw into the hero of the people and the bane of the greedy ruling classes.

The troubadours, at times blatantly subversive, have more in common with Robin Hood than an association with courtly romance. This is true in many regards, not least of which is their employment of lyric poetry to subvert religious and political hierarchies, or their role as agents of satire or fabricators of value. In order to understand these roles it is necessary for the reader to find orientation in the world of the troubadours, the world that formed the backdrop of their songs, a devil's world of mystics, philosophers and apostates, of women and outcasts, of fractured and resurgent empires, of rapidly changing economic models and the ideological ebbs and flows that underpin these.

Let us establish a mark of time. According to the *grand récit,* the troubadour phenomenon begins with Guilhèm de Peitieus (1071–1127), who is

---

Occitan trobador that a Romance philologist might consider a "troubadour" proper.

more commonly known to English speakers as William IX Duke of Aquitaine, and lasts another few hundred years into the middle of the fourteenth century. Spatially, we are concerned primarily with the lands collectively known as Occitania (as, strictly speaking, a troubadour is a lyric poet who composed in Occitan) but also the Iberian Peninsula, the Italian Peninsula (especially in its northern reaches), and several Mediterranean islands. However, troubadour poetry and the culture of courtly love would spread further afield throughout the Mediterranean and the Northern reaches of what we now call Europe, prisming its song into a plethora of tongues.

When dealing with the troubadours, while it's necessary to establish a temporal and spatial frame (however rough) in order to display the socio-political context of their art with more precision, this frame reminds us that we are dealing with some 350 poets who lived and sang over a period that spans several hundred years. When openly painting with broad strokes, there is nothing problematic about asserting that troubadour poetry is subversive, or to make any other assertion about their poetry by general rule for that matter. However, at the same time we must keep in mind that there were troubadours who were markedly more complacent or pious than some of their contemporaries, and there are many instances of conflict and polemics of moral, political, or literary natures that occurred among the troubadours themselves. Furthermore, one can even detect seemingly contradictory opinions across different poems composed by a single troubadour. Indeed, this motley crew of poets included some bishops (for example, Folquet de Marselha) as well as other clergy members and even a pope (Gui Fouqueis, later pope Clement IV). However, many troubadours came to blows with the Church and some were outright anticlerical. The aforementioned Guilhèm de Peitieus, for example, somehow managed to earn himself the irreverent honour of being excommunicated not once, but twice!

The troubadours are often associated with courts. Some were directly linked to courts either by professional or political ties, and those who were not likely bear this association due to their espousal of the ethics and aesthetics of "courtly" love. However, courts should not be understood as homogeneous domains in which participants and guests were exclusively members of the nobility. Furthermore, troubadours came from many different class backgrounds. In addition to members of the clergy or the nobility (lords, and even a few kings) there were also merchants, tailors, tanners, craftsmen, peasants, and some were described as "poor knights."

There is also the distinction between *trobador* and *joglar*. The former was the composer of his songs, though did not always perform them. In contrast, the latter performed the compositions of the former and was often of more popular origins. We must not forget the *trobairises* [s. *trobairitz*], or women troubadours (e.g. Beatriz de Día or Tibors de Sarenom). Though not without exceptions (e.g. Lambarda), most of the few surviving examples were written by women of noble birth. This however does not occlude the existence of *joglaressas* and all other manner of singing and performing women from humble origins prominent throughout the medieval period.[80]

Furthermore, there seems to have been different kinds of *joglar*. A thirteenth century penitential written by Thomas of Cobham identifies three different types. It is noteworthy that the first type of *joglar* is made up of a confluence of dance, obscenity, nudity, magic, and masks, which all are things that have been associated with witches:

> Damnable ones who make unworthy use of their bodies in obscene gestures and dances, undress in a shameful way, meddle in magical practices, and wear masks; scurrae vagi, also damnable, wandering jongleurs who follow princely courts as professional flatterers and calumniators, and instrumentalists, either frequenting taverns or places of debauchery and singing foolish songs, or, finally good ones who sing saints' lives and chansons de geste.[81]

There were also many instances of upward or downward mobility along the social ladder. Many poets who would become troubadours in their own right started out as *joglars* (e.g. Pistoleta or Raimbaut de Vaqueiras). Some were lords who, after becoming dispossessed of their domains, were forced to gain a living by performing their compositions (e.g. Raimon de Miraval). Others were of humble origins and through their poetic grace and virtuosity carved out positions for themselves in powerful courts as official court poets (e.g. Peire Vidal, or Cerverí de Girona). Some had stable professions or privileged social standings and cultivated their poetry for aesthetic, spiritual, or political reasons; others were professional poets who made their livings in courtly courts, village taverns, or sometimes both (e.g. Marcabrú,

80 See Filios, *Performing Women in the Middle Ages: Sex, Gender, and the Medieval Iberian Lyric.*

81 Cited in Burgwinkle, *Love For Sale*, 25.

Bernart de Ventadorn, or Giraut de Bornelh). Martín de Riquer writes: "... against all that might imply a rigid compartmentalization of social classes in the Middle Ages, differences of social condition are not heeded when one troubadour relates to another." [82] Truly, in the medieval period, hierarchies were much more porous and dynamic than many believe. Some knights were utterly impoverished, while some merchants (technically belonging to a lower class than the knights) were materially quite rich. These comments are not to be considered an apology for feudal hierarchies, but to signal some nuances often overlooked, and to cite how the troubadours demonstrate that social class did not impede social interaction, whether that interaction be affectionate and good natured or hostile and deprecating.

The ethos and aesthetic of courtly love is also often excessively associated with courts and nobility. This also has its nuances. Often, court poets would emulate popular songs in their own compositions (songs which at times served as discrete host-bodies for pagan survivals). In turn, compositions by court poets were sung in taverns and would serve to further inspire song and courtly ideals of loving among lower classes (for better or for worse). With regard to culture, the court itself can be taken as a sort of nexus point in which the popular and the courtly coalesce.[83] De Riquer continues:

> If we accept the passionate thesis of Eric Köhler that situates the origins of troubadour poetry in the tension between low nobility and high feudality in their coexistence at court, which had created a common ideal that erases differences, conceived by the lower classes and accepted by the upper classes... this would imply that the lower class were the real winners of this battle, and achieved a personal equalization between high and low...[84]

Regardless of whether or not Köhler's thesis is correct, troubadour poetry and courtly love clearly have their subversive elements. First, the lyric poetry of the troubadours can be read as a seizure of the means of the production and consumption of emotion from the hands of the Church. Indeed, according to the *grand récit*, troubadour poetry marks the very

82 De Riquer, *Los trovadores*, 22.

83 This point will be further developed in *Risāla of the Closed Garden* and in *Risāla of the Anti-Court*.

84 De Riquer, *Los trovadores*, 25.

birth of secular lyric poetry written in vernacular in the "West." While we should be hard pressed to consider troubadour poetry a *creatio ex nihilo*, or as essentially Western (whatever that means), the explosion of troubadour poetry against the backdrop of Church monodoctrine, liturgical poetry, and the production and consumption of literature carried out exclusively in Latin is indeed a hair-raising phenomenon.

The rituals of the Church—with their employment of splendid precious artifacts and ritual paraphernalia, heady incenses and perfumes, torches and candles, and ominous chants and pronouncements—are designed to provoke emotion in their audience and thereby manipulate and control their audience per thaumaturgy. These rituals also served as a kind of release or emotional outlet, in which the emotions provoked could be vented under the controlled and "legitimate" auspices of the clergy. In contrast, the troubadours expressed emotion on their own terms, and produced pieces that provoked emotion that could be enjoyed and released without necessarily being subject to intervention or manipulation by the Church.[85] Thus the composition of poetry reclaimed emotion from the space of dogmatic religious egregore and in some ways put it firmly back into the hands of the lyrical *I*.

It should be restated that the lyrical *I* does not necessarily belong to the individual in the bourgeois sense, but to the wind, to the fourth person singular. The collective anonymous makes itself known in the poems of the individual and the individual, if their lyric efforts are successful, is dissolved back into the collective anonymous. Poems by named troubadours were not just sung by their authors, but by others, and (instances in which the author is explicitly named within the poem notwithstanding) who is to say they were always given credit? The *vidas* and *razos* which provide biographical details to the troubadours—details whose historicity must be called into question and viewed within the complex dynamics of power and prestige in their concurrent political contexts—were written a long time *ex post facto*. This highlights the biographies' dependence on the poems and not the other way around.

It is also important to keep in mind that to compose within the confines of courtly love—which is to say, courtly love taken at face value—might

85 Yet, we must not forget that troubadours were also at times subject to their patrons' demands and to other external political pressures, making the task of disentangling genuine emotional expression from political conceit an at times complicated enterprise.

seem to impose restrictions on emotional expression rather than a liberation of the same. According to the *grand récit,* the troubadours were champions of a spiritualized heterosexual love and the saviours of Western civilization from the homosexual "passion" of the Greeks.[86] Somewhat ironically, they are praised by many as "heroes" who "exalted" women and thereby "improved their condition" when much surviving troubadour poetry was produced by men and—despite the lyrics being read as addressing the poet's (allegedly) female beloved—were in many cases actually written with a largely male audience in mind.

There is certainly much to critique in the mainstream reading of the troubadour corpus, a reading that casts the Lady as fantastical object and makes too many problematic and unhealthy assumptions about women, sexuality, and gender in general. However, the truth is far from this clear cut. Courtly love is not the chaste spiritualization of heterosexual love that many commentators have made it out to be. Nor is it a monodoctrine; variations on the theories and practices of courtly love, as well as parodies and subversions of the same, differ from troubadour to troubadour (and also from trobairitz to trobairitz for that matter). Furthermore, as Burgwinkle has demonstrated, troubadour poetry is ripe with ambiguity regarding sexuality and gender, not to mention the fact the *cansos* [love lyrics] and *sirventeses* [simply put, moral or political lyrics] are often intimately intertwined, if not one and the same.[87] This point will be touched upon in more detail below, but let us first return to our discussion of the Church and its monopoly on emotion and religious expression

In his book *The Devil's World,* Andrew P. Roach seeks to showcase instances of the medieval person's "consumer choice" in terms of religion under the shadow of a monopolistic provider, the Church. Yet, his own examples seem to suggest the contrary. Medieval people would only have freedom of religious choice in a very superficial way—to go on *this* pilgrimage, to go to church on more days of the week than Sunday, the kind of offerings left at a local shrine, and so on. While these are all sundry ways of expressing devotion, any deviation from the monodoctrine was impermissible and elicited increasingly brutal reprisals.[88] Freedom of choice here does

86 Nietzsche is but one example of a canonized Western intellectual who held this opinion. See Burgwinkle, *Love for Sale*, 6–7.

87 See Burgwinkle,"Alternate Readings," *Love For Sale.*

88 In some medieval realms other religions were tolerated at different times but this

not imply a rupture in the monopoly, much the same way consumer choice under capitalism is as deep as the choice between brands such as Coca-Cola and Pepsi, McDonalds or Burger King, Windows or Apple, Google or Amazon, or indeed among political parties in Liberal Democracies, themselves but hollow products that are bought and sold on a daily basis.

Troubadour poetry is sometimes considered subversive in a religious sense due to their association with the Cathars. Yet, there are no troubadours who openly declared themselves Cathars in their poems. Furthermore, courtly love, with its sensual celebrations of the body, is inimical to Cathar doctrine that deems all matter impure. However, many troubadours wrote *sirventeses* [i.e. moral or political troubadour poetry; praise or satire] in which a sympathy to the Cathars and a hostility to Simon de Montfort and his forces can be detected. In the wake of the Albigensian crusade, there were troubadours who had to leave the Languedoc and flee to seek patronage elsewhere, such as in the Iberian or Italian Peninsulas.

The troubadours are far from constituting an organized heresy, but to express spiritual or amorous feelings outside the control of the Church does constitute a sort of heresy in the literal sense, which is to say, *choice*.[89]

In addition to reclaiming emotion, troubadour poetry and courtly love subverted religious and political hierarchies by appropriating religious language and the juridical language of feudalism in ways that undermined the hegemony of both.

For instance, when addressing Ladies, troubadours employed religious language including terms such as *pecat* [sin], *colpa* [guilt; fault], *obediensa* [obedience], *martir* [martyr], in ways that appear to subtly cast courtly love as a kind of religion unto its own. These terms are woven into the rituals of a *fin'amor* that was by no means an exclusively chaste love (contrary to what has often been proposed), but whose stages— intriguingly reminiscent of the Sufi *maqāmāt*—went from *fenhedor* [the shy one], to *pregador* [supplicant], to *entendedor* [knowing admirer], and finally to *drutz* [lover] before their love culminates in *fach* [the deed].[90]

came at a price. See *Risāla of the Anti-Court.*

89 From the Greek haïresis [αιρεσιζ], literally "choice," "thing chosen."

90 These stations are drawn from an anonymous text known as *Un salut d'amor* which is thought to date from sometime between 1246–1265. While relatively late when considering the troubadours proper, and while it should not be taken as an all-pervasive rigid codification, it does provide an interesting frame through

At the same time, they also used erotic or amorous language when addressing the Virgin. While many troubadours were anticlerical, this does not mean they were all necessarily irreligious. One example of this is Cerverí de Gerona's appropriation of the *alba* genre—a genre that Romance philologists have characterized as one of the most overtly carnal, given its depiction of the lovers at dawn [*alba*] after having spent the night together. In the case of Cerverí, the poet employs (and inverts) *topoi* from the *alba* genre in order to wax lyric in devotion to the Virgin as dawn breaks over the poet's footpaths.

Furthermore, the *joi* invoked in the troubadours' poetic-personas by their beloveds, green leaves, or bird song, is a feeling that goes beyond a trivial or cursory contentment. The *joi* of troubadour poetry affects the body, yet also critically affects the spirit (if indeed a distinction must be made between them), and is a state that can be compared to the *fanā'* [mystical annihilation; mystical "passing away"] of the Sufis. On the meaning of *joi*, Jean Frappier writes:

> Without a doubt, joi translates an interior exaltation, a state of spirit that elevates one above themselves, a joy so violent that one's whole being feels renewed. But in the texts joi does not appear totally separate from amorous desire or pleasure, the troubadours sometimes associate it with Nature in springtime or with the song of the birds, and other times with the memory or presence of the lady, and other times with greater precision, as much with her insignificant favours as with the total surrendering of her love. It sometimes occurs that joi personifies the lady or is a mere synonym of fin'amor. Despite the slightly esoteric connotation of the term (joi in the Provenzal sense should not be confused with a trivial joy or the simple joy of the May festivals), the idea of a carnal happiness is never totally erased.[91]

---

which to understand these terms as employed by the troubadours. For example, the use of the verb *s'entendre* [to understand each other] by troubadours with respect to their Ladies to denote a phase of the courtship characterized by the fact that the lovers know each admires the other, rather than an earlier phase of "undeclared admiration from afar" for example.

91 "... joi traduce sin duda una exaltación interior, un estado de espíritu que eleva al hombre por encima de sí mismo, una alegría tan violenta que todo el ser se siente renovado. Pero en los textos el joi no aparece totalmente separable

In a similar vein to the appropriation of religious language, the troubadours also employed the juridical language of feudalism when addressing their beloveds. They declared themselves the Ladies' vassals [s. *om*, in Occitan]. *Midons* [my lord] is an oft cited signal term [*senhal*] to mask the true *destinataire* of the poem, whether this be a poet's actual beloved or, more prosaically, their patron.

Many examples of the formulas and terminology of feudal juridical texts in Latin appear in the poems of the troubadours, albeit in Occitan, including *dreit e razo* [Latin: *directum y ratio*], "action of right"; *bona fe* [bona fides] "fidelity"; *servir* [*servire*] "fulfill vassalic services"; *ochaizo* [*occasio*] "pretext, alleged motive"; *fieu* [*feudum*] "fief"; *retener* [*retinere*] "retain, conserve" (i.e. that which a donator conserves in feudal contract); *blandir* [from *blandimentum*] "favour, approval, consent"; *bailia* [*baiulia*] "tutelage, protection, shelter, administration of assets"; *bauzia* [*bausia*] "treason"; among others.

In the poetry of the troubadours, *servir* [to serve; fulfill vassallic services] becomes a code term for *to love*. *Bona fe* becomes a fidelity to the beloved. The poets declare their hearts the *fieu* [fief] or property of their beloveds. *Blandir*—or, to seek favour, approval, or consent—becomes a code term for courtship. Cerverí de Girona titles one of his satirical poems "Acuyndamen," a term equivalent to the Latin *acuydamentum* which refers to the declaration of war by a vassal against his lord, an act which forcefully breaks the bonds of vassalage.

In some poems, even the meaning of the word *amor* is manipulated in subtle ways. In addition to amorous affection, *amor* in the feudal juridical context of texts that deal with vassalage refers to grace, favour, pact, or alliance. The commendation ceremony in which men made homage to their lords and swore oaths of fealty was also given an erotic re-interpretation by the troubadours, by referring to it in the context of commending themselves as vassals to their beloveds. In this way, the customary kneeling, clasp-

---

del deseo y del placer amorosos, y los trovadores unas veces lo asocian a la naturaleza en primavera y al canto de los pájaros, otras al recuerdo o a la presencia de la dama, y otras con mayor precision, tanto a sus insignificantes favores como a la entrega total de su amor. A veces sucede que joi personifica a la dama o es un mero sinónimo de fin'amor. A pesar del sentido un poco esotérico del término (el joi de la poesía provenzal no debe confundirse con una alegría trivial o la sencilla alegría de las fiestas de mayo), nunca se borra en él totalmente la idea de una felicidad carnal." Cited in De Riquer, *Los trovadores*, 90.

ing of hands [*immixtio manuum*] and kiss [*osculum*] on the mouth acquire a sensuality that results in a beatific illumination rather than a degradation of personal stature before a social "superior."

These are all examples in which Love is celebrated as the highest truth and good, and is something that cannot be bound by the chains of political tyranny or religious dogma. There is a constant interplay between domination and submission, of bindings and agency, and union and separation at work in the poems in which—by mystical paradox—the lover's chains become the very key to their freedom.

Yet, at the same time the language of courtly love possesses this subversive, amorous, or mystical component, it must also be read within the context of power dynamics between different feudal lords, as well as between the lords and their vassals. The Lady must be read as a place-holder, and not exclusively as a flesh-and-blood woman. In some cases, *midons* and similar signal terms in the masculine do not refer to the poet's beloved (whether female or male), but to his actual lord or patron. Or in other cases—if the poet be a lord himself—to rival or neighbouring lords.

With the increased fracturing of the husk of the Carolingian empire, power dynamics began to depend less on dynastic legitimacy, noble birth, lineage, or "traditional" vassalic ties between members of the aristocracy. Courtly love emerged to fill the void and provide a political adhesive in a fractured world, and it is here we encounter yet another of its subversive elements: according to the *ethos* of courtly love, one's social power is legitimized by their upholding of *cortezia* [courtesy], of courtly values like generosity, honesty, and good virtue. Within this model, nobility is not based on dynastic legitimacy, birth, marriage, or aristocratic lineage, but measured against the extent that one is noble with regard to their moral conduct. This model is an almost exact reflection of the courtly model of al-Andalus already in effect a century before the alleged *inventio* of Guilhèm de Peitieus, a point we will return to in the *Risāla of the Closed Garden*.

Therefore, it was in the interests of feudal lords to surround themselves with the most illustrious troubadours. Lacking any form of clear dynastic legitimacy, many feudal lords' claims to power were based on their alleged level of courtliness. They could embellish their own courtly image through poetry, and through depictions of and anecdotes about the lord in precious manuscript compilations of songs. If the lord was a troubadour himself, he could generate and propagate this courtly image through his own vainglorious compositions. More often than not, however, it would be the troubadours in his employ who would cast a courtly glamour about their lord through the praise poems disguised as love lyrics they wrote in his honour. Whichever lord had an allegedly higher level of courtliness could thereby acquire more social power in the face of his rivals. Likewise, love lyrics could be sent to neighbouring lords as a means of forming political alliances, alliances based upon ideals of noble friendship and courtly love rather than exclusively upon aristocratic lineage or traditional bonds of vassalage.

In this way, the troubadours are creators of cultural capital.[92] Their songs function as incorporated cultural capital, which also has the potential to become objective cultural capital when these are recorded or depicted in manuscripts, books, carved on ornate chests and boxes, and so on.

Therefore, depending on context, the Lady can be read as a mask for the poet's patron, for other feudal lords, and even for other troubadours. It should come as no surprise then that many signal terms employed by the troubadours are in the masculine. Yet, at the same time, blurring the lines of gender can give rise to other readings of the poems that in some cases suggest homoeroticism and male-male love.[93] Burgwinkle argues that there are too many studies that read troubadour poetry exclusively as *personal love missives*, instead of also reading them as *musings on language* in which aspects of *black mail, power, domination or sexual ambiguity* are interwoven throughout. Again, parallels with *taifa* period al-Andalus are clearly present, in which one sees the linguistic blurring of gender identities when referring to the beloved (the Lady) as strongly reminiscent of similar blurrings when referring to the andalusī beloved (the *sāqī*; the cupbearer).

With regard to the troubadours as creators of cultural capital, Burgwinkle makes this statement: "*Literature can produce reality. It can even be argued that that is its essential function.*"[94] It is here that the arrow fired toward the beginning of this *risāla* pierces its mark. Whether or not troubadour poetry reflects a prior courtly reality, or was actually responsible for inventing that very reality, is relatively unimportant. The poems—as well as the *vidas* and *razos* meant to provide context for them—are naught but a mirror. And truly, mirrors do not simply reflect reality; they affect it. This is a secret any

92 For more on the concept of cultural capital see Bourdieu, *The Forms of Capital*, 241–58.

93 See Burgwinkle, *Love For Sale*, 23–25.

94 Burgwinkle, *Love For Sale*, 14.

black-mirror gazing witch will know all too well.

Reality is made up of the realness that we *invest* in it, in accordance with the dominant portal to the ideal in any given age. When the Church controls the portal, things are more or less real insofar as they are deemed more holy, insofar as they are *invested* with holiness. When Capitalism controls the portal, things are more or less real insofar as they can generate a profit. When Capitalism takes on the garments of the internet, the investment of attention is made in online content, and realness is measured in likes and reposts.

At the core of each of these ways to measure reality are assumptions about *value.* In their role as creators of cultural capital, the troubadours conduct a re-imagination of *value*, which itself comprises a redefinition of *meaning*, which in turn comprises a reappraisal of *reality*. This does not only refer to reality in an abstract broad sense, but in the more intimate sense of social reality: the poetry composed and propagated by the troubadours was partly responsible for tying, breaking, and re-tying the webs of social power prevalent in their times.

There is a curious relationship that economics, culture, and politics have with literary forms. Often the former are the forces that give rise to and shape the latter. We see this in the emergence of the Arabic shadow play in Mameluke Egypt, and in the emergence of the *maqāma* (a tale written in rhymed prose in Arabic or Hebrew) in Baghdad once the ʿAbassids were reduced to puppets by their Bujid Persian overlords; in the Baghdad example, codes of courtliness no longer had meaning and were therefore redefined; this resulted in the courtly *qaṣīda* losing favour as a literary form for use at court, hence the emergence of the *maqāma* to fill the void it left behind.[95]

We have already noted that troubadour poetry emerged partly as a response to a fractured political landscape. We can equally note that the decline of troubadour poetry and courtly love are linked to re-emergent empires and changing economic models. For example, the Crown of Aragon who, attempting to style itself as the inheritor of the Holy Roman Empire, made increasing conquests followed by colonial enterprises that established it as the dominant power of the Western Mediterranean (although it also established colonies in the East as well, mainly for commercial purposes) during the thirteenth century. These conquests and colonial projects were made possible by a powerful new merchant class riding the wave of the change from a natural economy to a monetary economy. Goods were no

95 See Monroe and Pettigrew, "The Decline of Courtly Patronage."

longer produced to be consumed locally in self-sufficient fiefs, but to be sold in an international market. The value of goods ceased to be measured by their utility, and began to be measured in monetary terms, by their ability to generate profit.

By the end of the thirteenth century and even more so subsequently, we see courtly love playing less of a role politically, and the ties of love or noble friendship that bound different political entities or personages being replaced by trade deals, trade permissions, royal monopolies (for example, on salt or bread baking), that used coin and credit as the basic currencies for measuring social power, in place of the previous currency of noble lineage, or later—as we have discussed—of courtly virtue.

However, like all mathematical formulas, the formula of *economics + culture + politics = literature* can be inverted. Truly, literature is not merely a product of socio-political contexts, but can with equal facility be their cause. Poetry can shift culture, reappraise value, and change the way we relate to one another. It can create paradigms that guide the flow of material exchange, and reweave webs of social power. It can break the monopolies held by the arbiters of reality.

There are three steps to breaking any monopoly: 1) *Inspire an active interest in the product* (reality) *to ensure it is not taken for granted.* For example, do not believe the lie that argues Capitalism is a law of nature, or that to oppose it makes one by default an apologist for despicable totalitarians such as Stalin; 2) *Provoke a dissatisfaction with the current provider* (Capitalism); and 3) *Provide a viable alternative.* Step three is arguably the most difficult, but the efficacy of steps one and two are directly dependant on the extent to which it is developed.

These three points can guide the movements of revolutionaries in pretty much every action they perform.

John Michael Greer has argued that our present political, economic, and environmental crises have less to do with the "rational" realm in which one looks for a solution to a problem, and more to do with the "irrational" realm of predicaments that impede the application of those solutions.[96] In his book *The Wealth of Nature* he makes the following commentary on economist Ernst Friedrich Schumacher:

---

96 See Greer, *The Blood of the Earth: An Essay on Magic and Peak Oil.*

> *Schumacher* pointed out that the failures of contemporary economics could not be solved by improved mathematical models or more detailed statistics, because they were hard-wired into the assumptions underlying economics itself. Every way of thinking about the world rests ultimately on presuppositions that are, strictly speaking, metaphysical in Nature: that is, they deal with fundamental questions about what exists and what has value. Trying to ignore the metaphysical dimension does not make it go away, but rather simply ensures that those who make this attempt will be blindsided whenever the real world fails to behave according to their unexamined assumptions. Contemporary economics fails to predict the behavior of the economy because it fails to criticize its own underlying metaphysics. Thus, a hard look at those basic assumptions is an unavoidable part of getting out of the mess into which current economic ideas have helped land us.[97]

Thus, here is the mark after which me must take aim with our bows. Here is where the economic and environmental justice of a Robin Hood meets the capabilities for ontological sabotage inherent in the art of the troubadour. Presiding over this work we find the Lady, now revealed to be a mask for whomever is most beloved, regardless of gender. Whether cast in the feminine as *Domna*, in the masculine as *Midons*, or under even more ambiguous and enigmatic *senhals* such as *Bel Vezer* [Beautiful Vision], *Mos Aziman* [My Magnet] or *Na Dezirada* [Desired one], it is the icon of the beloved who presides over this insurgent art.

It is the eyes of the beloved—whose eyebrows are bows, whose irises shoot arrows—that with a dianic touch may, upon striking our hearts, enflame them with the cool silver of *fin'amor*.[98] A metal capable of undermining the hegemony of coin, reimagining value, and rupturing the circuits of currency currently touted as laws of Nature. For the *fin* [fine] in *fin'amor* is derived from the Latin *finus*, a term used to describe depurated silver and the coins minted from the same.

The *fin'amor* that is being referred to here, is not the type that clothes

97 Greer, *The Wealth of Nature*, 3.

98 The eyes of the beloved as wounding or shooting arrows is a common *topos* in troubadour poetry, as well as andalusī love poetry written in Arabic and Hebrew. See Scheindlin, *Wine, Women, Death*, 81.

verse hagiographies, nor imposes limitations on sexuality, gender, or Love itself. Rather, one that exposes the hollow hagiographies of the day for what they are, that puts ethics above religious dogma or political affiliation, and through the dark speech of enigma and emblem decimates the limits imposed on loving, limits that are indeed inimical to Love itself and its many ways. Furthermore, as *fin'amor* was originally perceived by some as a moral code of conduct, it should provoke the development of strong ethics with regard to sex and courtship, albeit these ethics be developed in the spirit of *fin'amor* rather than in its outdated letter.

And so now we will part by conjuring the shadow of a long dead troubadour, whose inverse flower seems to uncannily speak to our own times, with its allusion to radical weather events and the importance of *joi* in the face of misfortune or oppression.[99] The "inverse flower" is a fitting emblem for witchcraft. The eight words of power repeated in the poem form an eight-pointed star, that becomes further interlocked with each passing stanza as the concepts introduced are subject to ever deeper and more subtle levels of subversion:

Now glows the inverse flower

Now glows the inverse flower
Along jagged cliffs and hills.
What flower? Snow, ice, frost.
And it burns, stings, and cuts
And dead are the trills, cries, screams, and whistles
In the leaves, boughs, and branch-whips
But joy keeps me thrilling and green,
Though I behold the wicked ones withered.

In such a way, all is inverse
that meadows seem hills
that I keep flowers of frost
that cold by heat is cut
that thunder seems a song or whistle

99 This troubadour is Raimbaut d'Aurenga, brother of the trobairitz Tibors de Sarenam. The senhal he employs towards the poem's end—Joglar—is thought to be a mask for his friend (and possibly lover), Azalais de Porcairagues, also a trobairitz.

and into new leaf burst the branch-whips;
I'm so firmly bound by joy
nothing I see appears to me wicked.

A graceful fairy inverts them
as if they'd grown in hills
they wound me more than frost
and with their tongues they cut
in hushed tones and whistles
of no use are sticks or whips
or threats that would sooner bring them joy
when their deeds are such that men call them wicked.

For locked in kisses we become inverse
I cannot be kept by meadow nor hill
lady, nor ice nor frost,
lest my power yield and my heart be cut.
Lady, for whom I sing and whistle,
the glow of your eyes is a whip
that lashes my heart with joy
that within it may grow nothing wicked.

I've wandered as a creature inverted
long hours, among valleys and hills
weeping in the way of he who by frost
is tormented, broken, and cut,
for I've never been conquered by songs or whistles
more than the lying clergy conquer with whips.
Yet now, praise God, I'm sheltered by joy
in spite of the false and the wicked.

And so goes my verse, which I inverse
that it be not held back by valley nor hill
there, where none feel frost
and where cold has no power to cut
to midons, the song and the clear whistle

and may the whip enter the heart
of who knows to sing with joy,
which the wicked singer never will grasp.

Sweet lady, love and joy
Have bound us fast, despite the wicked.

Joglar, I have lost much joy
For the distance between us; my semblance grows wicked.

6

Risālat al-filāḥa

[Risāla on Agriculture]

☿

True wealth is born in the underworld. And truly, Pluto bears cornucopias overflowing with fruits, vegetables, nuts, spices, grains, dyes, fuels, jewels, and fibres.[100] Yet these are but the shadows of a greater wealth: the dark fertile conditions from which they all emerge, and indeed the balance and dynamic equilibrium of those conditions. True wealth, then, is measured by the health and proper balancing of matter—which we might choose to see as the interplay of earth, air, fire, and water—over time. *Over time* refers to the cyclical framework that makes it possible for the elements to reach and remain in dynamic equilibrium: life, death, and rebirth. Or alternatively read: growth, harvest, and regeneration. There can be no harvest without death, nor new life without regeneration. Therefore, true wealth arises not from unfettered growth, or from the ceaseless, senseless, and greedy accumulation of material goods, but from the halls of death. Below the ground, in the secret silent world of roots, insects, bones, and earth, crystals grow, precious metals take form, and sleeping seeds awaken...

And there is a word in Arabic that seems to carry the power of a seed within it. A teardrop jewel that is at once a thing's most primal beginnings as it is its fullest flowering and maturation. A tiny heart that beats against the green pulse of all the land as the infant's heart beats against its mother's before she opens a path for the babe to emerge, to know, to be greeted by the light:

Ḥayya 'ala l-falāḥ!

So sounds the call to prayer, and it rings out from the olive strewn mountains of the Rif to the rice paddies of Indonesia. And human worshipers are not the only ones who heed the call, or lay themselves low in remembrance of the divine, for the clouds might move slower, the streams run swifter,

---

100 Pluto (or *Ploutōn* in Greek) literally means "giver of wealth."

and all the green things of the land bow and draw nearer to the voice of the *mu'adhdhin*, just as they stretch and open to the sunlight that calls them to grow and fulfill their rich fates.

> Ḥayya ʿala l-falāḥ!
> Come to success,
> come to salvation!

This word is *falāḥ*. In the context of *ṣalāt*, daily prayer in Islam, the word *falāḥ* is often translated as "success" or "salvation," as in the case of the above quote. However, it is important to keep in mind that here salvation can carry a somewhat earthy connotation, given the fact that the word *falāḥ* is linguistically related to *fallāḥ* which is translated as "husbandman," "tiller of soil," or "farmer."

These words are both derived from the root f-l-ḥ [ف ل ح], which, in form I, literally means "to split, cleave; to plow, till, cultivate" but with particular regard to the cleaving, splitting, or tilling of soil. At the same time, in form IV and form X it means "to thrive, prosper, become happy; to have luck or success, be lucky, be successful."[101]

This verb gives us the noun *filāḥa* which literally means "cultivation, tillage" but is often translated as "agriculture" or more broadly as "husbandry." These semantic connections, considered alongside the appearance of the word *falāḥ* in the daily calls to prayer, reveal how Islamic culture traditionally attributes an eschatological dimension to agriculture, in which the nurturing of plants and animals is directly related to worship, and leads to success and well-being not only in the present world but in the world to come.

This attribution is made explicit by Ibn al-ʿAwwām, an andalusī master of agriculture and husbandry who lived in the twelfth century. In the prologue to his *Kitāb al-Filāḥa* [Book of Agriculture] he writes:

> In [agriculture] are one's needs [met], in [agriculture] one will attain [so much as] one wills. Consider [agriculture], [the way] by which the benefits [منافع] of this world [دنيا] and the well-being [مصالح] of the hereafter [اخرا] come upon you, by the blessing [توفيق] of God, the Most High... Who plants seedlings [غرسا] without [committing] injustice [ظلم] nor oppressing [anybody] will thereby

101 See *Dictionary of Modern Written Arabic*, 850.

have an ongoing reward from the Merciful Creator [by which they will] benefit...[102]

Perhaps this subtle association of plant and animal growth with the divine helped prepare the ground for premodern Islamic civilization to develop and practice some of the most interesting and effective agricultural traditions the world has ever seen. The early spread of Islam instigated what some scholars have described as a "green revolution." Recipients of the agricultural traditions of the civilizations that preceded them, Muslim luminaries synthesized and improved upon the most fruitful aspects of all of these, and discarded what they did not find to be useful. In so doing, they developed an idiosyncratic and highly successful agricultural tradition of their own, marking a change in the way farming was conducted by their predecessors.[103]

Eventually, this "new" agriculture gave rise to a literary genre known as the *Books of Filāḥa*. Part scientific treatise, part manual for practical husbandry, these invaluable tomes served as a repository for the wisdom of diverse agricultural traditions—such as those of the Chaldeans, Greeks, Carthaginians, Romans, Byzantines, among others—combined with the practical experimentation of their authors and the know-how of local farmers. However, these texts understand agriculture or husbandry not just in the context of field crops or livestock, but to overlap with horticulture, arboriculture, pharmacology, botany, apiculture, veterinary medicine, and domestic economy (bread-making, etc.).

Despite their immense value, these texts have garnered far less attention

102 Ibn al-ʿAwwām, *Kitāb al-Filāḥa*, 1. All translations of direct quotations from Ibn al-ʿAwwām that appear in this epistle are my own. Ibid, 3.

103 For more information on this point, see Fitzwilliam-Hall's dense and inspiring essay "An Introductory Survey of the Arabic Books of Filāḥa and Farming Almanacs" (Hereafter, Filāḥa) to which a portion of the research for this epistle is indebted: "Although the notion of a medieval Arab Agricultural Revolution, first proposed by Andrew Watson in 1974, of an Islamic Green Revolution as called by others, has been challenged by some scholars this is not the place to recapitulate the argument, which seems to revolve around matters of degree and detail rather than substance. What is clear is the marked change in the way farming was done, and its undoubted success. The new agriculture that followed in the wake of Islam and emerged across much of the Middle East and Mediterranean world appears to have been quite different from the Roman, Byzantine, Sassanian and Visigoth models that preceded it. It resulted from the synthesis of a number of new and old elements, skilfully worked into a productive and sustainable system, giving it a particular, characteristic stamp." Fitzwilliam-Hall, *Filāḥa*, www.filaha.org.

than they deserve, and in the "Western" world are very little known outside the circles of specialist scholars that translate and study them. Much scholarly discussion of these texts has focused on the philological issues of authorship, the teasing apart of the origins of different ideas, and the ways in which ideas and knowledge were cited and transmitted across civilizations and generations (the *Books of Filāḥa* are full of complete and incomplete citations and adaptations of earlier works). However, less has been dedicated to studying the potential implications and applications of these texts for agriculture in modern times, let alone in a post-industrial world.

Therefore, it is a goal of the present epistle to consider a drop of the wisdom and practical knowledge preserved in the *Books of Filāḥa* alongside those of another green revolution: permaculture. In this way, it attempts to act as a small link in the epistemic chains of transmission, and present the *Books of Filāḥa* in a manner that aims to place their theoretical wisdom and practical knowledge into the hands of the revolutionary.

Indeed, the *Books of Filāḥa* constitute a veritable treasure trove for revolutionaries today. In the context of our current political and environmental climates, husbandry more and more seems to not only imply salvation in the sense of success, prosperity, or abundance but in the bleaker sense of survival itself. No matter how good the year or full the granaries, industrial agriculture does not and cannot feed the world's population. It is not only unsustainable, but toxic to both humans and the natural environment. Due to pollution, resource depletion and climate as well as economic instability, it will increasingly fail those who have the privilege of currently benefiting from it.

In addition to basic survival, the *Books of Filāḥa* applied in concert with permaculture provide a number of tools that can be used to actively combat the toxic ideologies of capitalism, and enable one to wrestle a degree of autonomy from the hands of the State. The breaking of any political or economic monopoly ultimately involves providing viable alternatives. To take control of the food one eats, the air one breathes, the water one drinks, and the medicines one uses to treat disease or wounds is to wax in power.

While it might be incorrect to directly equate sedentary civilization with agriculture, agriculture is indisputably a core component of what comprises a civilization, or at least contributes to the rise of much of what are considered hallmarks of a civilization, including urban development, social stratification, a cultural elite who taxes the general population (the State), and the perceived separation from and domination over the natural environment.

If certain approaches to agriculture can give rise to these unhealthy types of societal organization, then seizing control of it and implementing other approaches can entail a complete unraveling and re-imagining of civilization itself. This work is made easier with the realization that industrial civilization is unraveling all on its own, and seizing control of agriculture begins and primarily occurs on your own farm, lawn, house, apartment, or in the empty lots and barren spaces of your own neighbourhood.

The word "husbandry" literally denotes "the care, cultivation, and breeding of crops or animals" as well as, critically, the careful "management and conservation of resources."[104] This concept is central to the traditional Islamic approach to agriculture, and indeed to the philosophy underpinning permaculture. Humans take an active role in natural systems as agents who care for them through proper remediation practices that ensure the health and flourishing of all the system's components. In this context, husbandry becomes a cipher for sustainability.

104 The word husbandry is derived from the Old Norse *hūsbōndi* which literally means a house [*hūs*] dweller [*bōndi*]. In the medieval and early modern periods, the word "husbandman" was originally used in English to denote a farmer or peasant, with the verb "to husband" meaning to till the soil. This is probably due to the assumption that a sedentary (as opposed to nomadic) house-dweller and member of the peasant class would practice agriculture. "Husband" later came to be defined as "master of the house" instead of simply house-dweller, and in this context eventually supplanted the word *wer* to refer to a married man. In some old works (even from the nineteenth and early twentieth centuries), it is still possible to encounter the word "husbandman" used to mean "farmer," though this usage has largely become obsolete. The word "husbandry," however, retains this connotation in its meanings of the "growing and nurturing of plants and animals" and/or "the careful management of resources." Through becoming familiar with the history of the word "husband," we can discard its connotation of master of the house and thereby redefine what it means to be a male-identified person in a marital context: not a master or owner, but someone who cares for, nurtures, and protects; one who tends to his family or partner with the same dedication and delicacy as he would a cherished garden. Of course, these are qualities that can (and should!) be cultivated in any person in a relationship, whether or not that person identify as male, female, or otherwise, and regardless of whether that relationship be marital.

The first part of this epistle is a brief survey of the *Books of Filāḥa* to introduce their content, context, and legacy, with comparisons to the theory and praxis of permaculture. The second part is an initial exploration of the books' practical applications, primarily through the creation of a calendar and a map. These fundamental spatial and temporal tools help to serve as decanters through which the wisdom and knowledge of *filāḥa* can be transmitted in a dense syncretic fashion.

Conveniently, the *Books of Filāḥa* place emphasis on "the preparation and levelling of new fields, the excavation of wells, and the reclamation of marginal lands."[105] Fitzwilliam-Hall is likely correct in assuming this suggests that the books' intended audience was made up primarily of "royal patrons, high officials, dignitaries and gentleman-farmers who were the educated and enthusiastic owners of new estates and gardens, keen to experiment with new crops and cultivars."[106] While this may be true, it suits our purposes wonderfully as the regeneration of abandoned, polluted, or marginal land become increasingly central agricultural and political concerns in our own times. Therefore the State may tremble with fear, for the same principles enjoyed by the cultural elite of al-Andalus can be employed by the landless, the urbanite, or the guerrilla gardener.

After the great agronomists of al-Andalus, my aim is to "synthesize the accumulated knowledge of the past with practical husbandry on the ground," and this *risāla* constitutes some first steps towards that end.[107] While my own journey into permaculture began about ten years ago, I remain a student with so much to learn. The voice of this epistle then should not be taken to be that of a master instructing an apprentice, but that of a friend eager to share and willing to collaborate. Regardless of your level of prior experience with farming, animal husbandry, or permaculture, I hope the ideas presented here will serve to invigorate and inspire fruitful experimentation in your own designs.

105 Ibid.

106 Ibid.

107 Ibid.

Filāḥa

Farming and husbandry have a long and rich history in the Arabian peninsula. It comes as no surprise how in a generally hot, dry environment, traditional agriculture in the Arabian peninsula would be centred on techniques for irrigating, or the harvesting, storage, and distribution of water. Thousands of years before the advent of Islam, watersheds on mountain slopes were terraced, wadis were cultivated by way of spate irrigation, and oasis agriculture involving subterranean *falāj* irrigation was developed.

As the Arabs moved into newly conquered territories, this expertise with regard to water transformed the agricultural landscape. Indeed, it is one of the main contributing factors behind the defining characteristics of the "new" agriculture that emerged alongside the spread of Islam. For example, in Mediterranean lands, summer—the dog-days of Sirius—were considered a dead period when the land grew barren. The Arab expertise with water helped enable farmers to claim the summer months as an additional growing season.

The extension of growing seasons led to another feature of this agriculture: crop rotation. Crop rotation was not practiced to the same extent in the agricultural traditions of the Romans or Visigoths, for example, in which farmers would typically only yield one crop per year, or sometimes one every two years. The Arabs supported their irrigation-intensive style of farming with an equally intense regime of soil remediation and manuring, enabling farmers to yield three or four crops a year from a single stretch of land without depleting the soil.

These practices contributed to the awe-inspiring biological diversity that premodern Islamic Agriculture would become known for.[108] Crop-rotation and multiple cropping led to an increase in the amount of cultivars grown, and advanced irrigation techniques coupled with the "soil first" approach of Arab agronomists led to the successful acclimatization and introduction of new cultivars or exotics from sundry corners of the growing *dār al-islām* into lands far from their origins. For example, the acclimatization and intro-

108 "The range of crops available to the medieval Andalusi [sic] farmer was extensive. Towards the end of the 11th century Ibn Baṣṣāl mentions more than 180 cultivated crops and plants, and at the end of the twelfth century Ibn al-'Awwām notes 585 different species and cultivars, though not all of these would have been cultivated." Ibid.

duction in al-Andalus of numerous tropical plants and trees originating in Central Africa, South-East Asia, or the Indian subcontinent.

As a discipline, *filāḥa* is said to have reached its apogee in al-Andalus, where indeed most of the *Books of Filāḥa* were written. Their authors were not just agronomists *in sensu stricto* but polymaths who were also accomplished mathematicians, astronomers, poets, courtiers, jurists, philosophers, physicians, botanists, surgeons, or pharmacologists. This holistic approach to knowledge no doubt made itself manifest physically in the agro-ecosystems of the andalusī landscape. Contrary to industrial agribusiness, rather than tending to focus exclusively on field crop or tree crop monocultures, the andalusī agro-ecosystem incorporated both of these with garden crops (flowers, herbs, vegetables), pasture lands and common spaces.[109]

Another major contributing factor that greatly facilitated the emergence of agro-ecosystems alongside other transformations of the agricultural landscape were changes in land tenure and taxation, which Fitzwilliam-Hall eloquently summarizes thus:

> The diffusion of new crops and cultivars, the adoption of new multiple-cropping and rotation regimes, the abundant use of manures, and the refinement and expansion of irrigation were supported, crucially, by changes in land tenure and taxation that accorded farmers more liberty and a greater incentive to improve their land, all underpinned by Islamic precepts and customary laws by which farming was conducted more fairly and more effectively. For the first time in many places, any individual—man or woman—had the right to own, buy, sell, mortgage, and inherit land, and most importantly, farm it as he or she liked. Relatively low rates of taxation, where they existed at all, were paid as a fixed proportion of output, freeing farmers from uncertain and capricious tax hikes, in contrast to the oppressive rural taxation prevailing in the late Roman, Sassanian, and Byzantine empires. Large estates, which had everywhere come to dominate and often monopolize agriculture, were often broken down into smaller ownerships, or at least had to compete with smaller farms and individual peasant small-

109 "The extraordinarily bio-diverse agro-ecosystem of Al-Andalus was composed of cultivated lands—a mosaic of tree crops, huerto or market-garden crops, and field crops, both irrigated and rain-fed—permanent meadows and pasture lands, and commons with rights of usage by local inhabitants." Ibid.

> holdings. The lands around cities were almost everywhere given over to small market gardens and orchards. Serfdom and slavery were virtually absent from the countryside in the early Islamic world—instead, "the legal and actual condition of the overwhelming majority of those who worked on the land was one of freedom."

This agriculture also brought with it a diversity of cultivars heretofore unparalleled. Diversity is of course highly valued in permaculture for its role in creating more resilient systems. This wide array of cultivars challenges the oft recited idea that in the medieval period people lived on a meagre diet of water and mouldy bread, or that it was a backward superstitious period pockmarked by scarcity and disease.

This diversity of cultivars can be glimpsed in Abū l-Khayr's *Kitāb al-Filāḥa*, whose contents include instructions for the planting, growing, and harvesting (alongside knowledge and lore on other matters pertinent to *filāḥa*) of many plants, trees, fruits, vegetables, and grains including: fig [تين], palm [نخل], olive [زيتون], holm-oak [بلوط], chestnut [الشاه بلوط], carob [خروب], golden shower [خيار شنبر], jujube [عناب], pine [صنوبر], nettle tree/hackberry [ميس], elm [نشم], walnut [جوز], bay laurel [شجر رند], myrtle [ريحان], cypress [سرو], tamarisk [طرفاء], Spanish juniper [ابهل], yew [طخش], strawberry tree [الاحمر حناء], ash [دردار], Mediterranean buckthorn [صفيراء], barberry [برباريس], moringa [بان], Judas tree [اوتاد الذاذي], Chinese palm [كاذي], mulberry [توت], almond [لوز], hazelnut [بندق], pistachio [فستق], rowan [غبيراء], pear [كمثرى], pomegranate [رمان], quince [سفرجل], apple [تفاح], citron [ترنج], lemon [ليمون], orange [نارنج], grape [عنب], rice [أرز], flax [كتان], cotton [قطن], madder [فوة], fenugreek [حلبة], cumin [كمون], black caraway [كرويا], white lupin [ترمس], butcher's broom [خيزران], acacia [برم], artichoke [خرشوف], tiger nut [فلفل السودان], mandrake [يبروح], ornamental rose [ورد الزينة], blue iris [الاسمانجوني سوسان], marshmallow [خطمي], henna [حناء], onion [بصل], saffron [زعفران], garlic [ثوم], Madonna lily [الابيض سوسان], white narcissus [بهار الابيض], narcissus [رنجس], banana [موز], colocasia [قرقاص], or sugar cane [قصب حلو].[110]

In *Kitāb al-Filāḥa*, each of the plants listed above is allocated its own "section." Abū l-Khayr also includes lore, instructions and information on many more plants, whether this be pertinent to their planting and cultivation, to companion and succession planting, or to their use as spices, medicines, gastronomic ingredients, fertilizers, or pesticides. A few of these

110 See Abū l-Khayr, *Kitāb al-Filāḥa*, 12–16.

include carrot [جزر], anise [انيسون], rue [فيجن], sandalwood [صندل], leek [كراث], thyme [زعتر], dandelion [طراخشقون], plum [انجاص], cherry [كراسيا], spinach [اسفناج], cabbage [كرنب], radish [فجل] loquat [مصع], jasmine [ياسمين], henbane [بنج], chickpeas [حمص], lentils [عدس], broad beans [فول], sumac [سماق], basil [حبق], sesame [سمسم], wheat [حنطة], spearmint [نعناع], and many more.[111]

There were many cultivars grown in al-Andalus as well as other parts of medieval Europe that over the centuries have fallen by the wayside of the capitalist measurement of value. Consequentially, they are grown no longer. This is not only true of the agricultural landscape but of biodiversity in general.[112] The Christian conquest of al-Andalus led to deforestation and re-purposing land previously characterized by more complex agro-ecosystems into cereal monocultures. Galicians, Asturians, Catalans, and other peoples from northern parts of the Iberian Peninsula were encouraged to repopulate areas of the South (such as in modern day Valencia, Murcia, or Andalucía) after the local *morisco* population had been expelled.[113]

As is to be expected, this had an impact on agriculture. These were colonists leaving one type of environment and arriving in one to whose climate, topography, and exigencies they were not yet accustomed. In the Alpujarra for example—whose dramatic landscape is very different to the homelands of much of its Galician or Asturian "re-populators"—irrigation on the high mountain slopes is based on a complex system of channels or *acequias.*[114] The Christian conquest and expulsion of the *moriscos* brought about the degradation or even loss of many *acequias* as they fell into disuse, as well

111 See Hernández Bermejo, J.E. and J. León (eds.). 1994. "Neglected Crops: 1492 from a Different Perspective." Plant Production and Protection Series No. 26. Rome: FAO, 303–32. Cited by Fitzwilliam Hall, *Filāḥa*, www.filaha.org.

112 "Examples include rocket, purslane, sorrel, dandelion, alexanders, scorzonera or black salsify, spotted golden thistle, milk thistle, comfrey, Spanish salsify, vetches, cow-peas, spelt, pearl millet, sorghum, lotus tree, service tree or sorb, azarole, and the hackberry or nettle tree." Fitzwilliam Hall, *Filāḥa*, www.filaha.org.

113 The term morisco refers to a Muslim convert to Christianity under Christian rule. Cf. mudéjar, a Muslim under Christian rule who is permitted to profess their religion.

114 The word *acequia* [*sāqiya*] is an arabism derived from the root s-q [س ق] which in Form I means "to give to drink," "make drink," "to water," "to irrigate," "to dip, scoop, or draw water," or "to temper steel." See *A Dictionary of Modern Written Arabic*, 468. The word *sāqī* [cupbearer] is also derived from this root. This is due to him "pouring the wine" and thereby "watering" or "irrigating" the drinking companions. See page 155 of the present volume.

as a cultural forgetting in all the intricate ways of how to work this highly efficient system of irrigation and water distribution.[115]

Botanical gardens served as important *loci* in the fomentation of diversity. They functioned as centres for the acclimatization of plants, the development of new cultivars, as well as places of learning where master agronomists (e.g. Ibn Wāfid) would transmit their knowledge to students (e.g. Ibn Baṣṣāl) in a practical environment. While some of these masters were connected to the royal courts, new cultivars prepared in the botanical gardens would, by emulation and word of mouth, be subsequently spread all over the agricultural landscape of al-Andalus. The practice of direct transmission is noteworthy and certainly is an approach with many valuable aspects. While books can make great teachers, there is really no parallel to having the opportunity to learn from an experienced teacher, outside, in a hands-on environment.

The andalusī masters of husbandry—the authors of the *Books of Filāḥa*—are a fascinating group.[116] In addition to being polymaths, many of them travelled widely collecting all manner of roots, buds, seeds, and specimens for study and introduction into the botanical gardens of al-Andalus, acquiring agricultural knowledge from the local population wherever they went. Abū l-Khayr, Ibn al-ʿAwwām, and Ibn Luyūn constitute three fine exemplars.

Abū l-Khayr, a luminary from Sevilla known as ash-Shajjār [the arboriculturist], was the author of a *Kitāb al-Filāḥa* and the likely author of the anonymous *ʿUmdat aṭ-ṭabīb fī maʿrifat an-nabāt li-kull labīb* [The Physician's reliance in the knowledge of plants for every man of understanding]. The *ʿUmdat* is a truly extraordinary work of botany and so much more. Abū l-Khāyr sought to document all the plants of the Iberian Peninsula. To this end he wandered all over the Iberian Pensinsula documenting its flora and plant lore. The *ʿUmdat* includes the biological, medicinal, culinary, cultural, and magical properties of plants and lists their distribution and their names in several languages including Classical Arabic, vernacular andalusī Arabic, Classical Greek, Byzantine Greek, Latin, Berber, Persian, Syriac, and several Romance vernaculars, in which one can distinguish Galician, French, etc. It is fascinating to note some of the Romance words

115 In spite of the great loss of knowledge, acequias are still in use in Andalucía today, especially in the Alpujarra.

116 This group includes: Az-Zahrāwī, Ibn Wāfid, Ibn Baṣṣāl, Ibn Ḥajjāj, Abū l-Khayr, aṭ-Ṭighnarī, Ibn al-ʿAwwām, Ibn ar-Raqqām, Ibn Luyūn, and anonymous Andalusī,

are among the first ever textual appearances of any Romance language. What does it imply for contemporary Romance identities, upon learning that one of the first instances in which their languages' ancestors appeared in text was in a work written by an Arabic-speaking Muslim? It is equally fascinating that Abū l-Khayr, in the eleventh century, was able to arrive at a criteria for plant classification that is today considered much more accurate than that of Linnaeus, who wrote several centuries later. Sadly, I have yet to meet one Western botanist who has heard of him.

Another author, Ibn al-ʿAwwām, was one of the few andalusī agronomists who seemed to dedicate himself exclusively to husbandry. He lived and worked in the Aljarafe district near Sevilla. Apart from being an eminently practical manual, his colossal *Kitāb al-Filāḥa* is comprised of thirty-four chapters that treat the following subjects: types of earth; types of manure; types of waters; establishing a garden; how to sow plants and trees; how to transplant; grafting; the size of trees; ploughing; how to manure; irrigation; pruning; artificial pollination; treatments for pests; innovative methods for improving the fragrance and flavour of several plants and fruits; conserving fruits, plants and cereals; how to prepare the earth; cereals and legumes that improve the earth; how to sow cereals; how to sow and grow rice, lentils and chickpeas, beans, hemp, cotton, saffron, root crops (eg. carrots) and other garden crops; how to establish a kitchen garden; how to grow aromatics, medicinals, spices, and many vegetables like artichoke or asparagus; how to harvest and store cereals; how to mill flour; talismans; nuts; how to press olives; how to distill rose water; how to make raisins; the weather; an agricultural calendar; the seasons; cattle raising; horses; medical treatment of cattle; chickens; peacocks, and other birds.[117]

A third author, Ibn Luyūn, was a poet, philosopher, jurist, and mathematician. His *Kitāb ibdā' al-malāḥa wa-inhā' ar-rajāḥa fī uṣūl ṣināʿat al-filāḥa* [Book on the principles of beauty and the purpose of learning, concerning the fundamentals of the art of agriculture] is an intriguing example of a "book of *filāḥa*" being composed entirely in verse. Aside from being a beautiful poem in and of itself, Ibn Luyūn states toward the beginning of the work that he wrote it in order to synthesize agricultural knowledge in a way that would make it easier for the material to be learned and committed to memory (rhyme and metre, of course, being mnemonic devices).

117 See Ibn al-ʿAwwām, Kitāb al-Filāḥa, 10–36, in which the author does a break down of the chapters of the book and summarizes their contents.

The intellectual ferment that bore the *Books of Filāḥa* was shaped by influences from figures belonging to a number of different time-periods and traditions likely including Aristotle, Bolos Democritos of Mendes (Egyptian), Mago (Carthaginian), Varro (Roman), Cassianus Bassus (Byzantine), and many others.

One monumental work that had an enormous influence was the text known as *al-Filāḥa an-Nabaṭīya* [Nabataean Agriculture], said to be a translation of Syriac manuscripts made by Ibn Waḥshīya (or Pseudo-Ibn Waḥshīya). Alongside it being a repository of agricultural knowledge (it cites earlier authors and works), it is full of myth and magic and preserves many of the beliefs and practices of the indigenous, rural, pagan population of pre-Islamic northern and central Iraq (i.e.; the Nabataeans).

While the *Books of Filāḥa* cover a wide range of subjects and were written over the course of a few hundred years by several different authors, there are certain traits common to all of them that seem to inform their underlying philosophy or approach to agriculture. It is useful to identify these traits in order to juxtapose them with the philosophies of permaculture on the one hand, and industrial agriculture on the other.

Some participants in today's biodynamic farming, organic farming, or permaculture movements curiously seem to perceive their work as innovative, new, or more advanced than the approaches of their forebears. A quick browse through the *Books of Filāḥa,* combined with a brief look at the history of premodern agriculture in general, exposes their hubris and demonstrates that linear progress is a myth. Time doubles back on itself, bites its tale, and spirals, urgently, from the future into the now. In a time plagued by pollution and green-washing, if you would like to style yourself as an organic farmer it would be a useful part of your learning process to get to know the *Books of Filāḥa* or another repository for premodern agricultural knowledge, as there is truly nothing more *organic* than the practices and philosophies documented therein.

Some noteworthy philosophical patterns that emerge from the *Books of Filāḥa* as a whole include: a strong emphasis on regeneration and the soil; effective waste management, composting, and manuring; crop-rotation, multiple cropping, and diversity; and viewing health as the result of balance and disease the result of imbalance.

As is to be expected, we find regeneration at the heart of *filāḥa*. Our andalusī agronomists were well aware that cultivation entails a cycle of growth, but also of death and regeneration. The ability to continue farming in perpetuity depends on the fertility of the soil. One cannot expect to be able to keep farming if the natural cycle is disrupted and the completion of its final key phase is neglected. Naturally, the emphasis placed on regeneration gave rise to complex systems for returning organic matter, plant nutrients, minerals and trace elements to the soil. Andalusī agricultural systems produced no waste; indeed, human, animal, and plant waste were all applied to great effect.

This approach has a number of parallels with permaculture. First, regeneration touches upon two of permaculture's core tenets: *Care for the earth*, and *Care for people*. If regeneration comprises an important stage in the natural cycle, then seeking to engage in or facilitate regeneration constitutes a way of *working with* natural forces rather than attempting to work against them.

It also encompasses several of the permaculture principles articulated by David Holmgren.[118] The principle *Catch and store energy* is present in organic matter—energy ultimately derived from the Sun (carbon cycle)—being composted, stored, and later returned to the land. This of course also comprises a practical example of the principle *Use and value renewable resources and services,* and of the principle *Produce no waste.* This approach is in stark contrast to that of industrial agriculture, which sees soil as inert and only useful insofar as it serves to administer industrially produced chemical fertilizers to plants, whose health becomes compromised and exploited in the name of short-term profit.

Crop-rotation and multiple cropping contribute to the system in a number of important ways. Of course, being able to grow more crops per season helps one to better *Obtain a yield*, but also helps prevent the build-up of pathogens and pests, as well as the depletion of soil nutrients that occurs when a piece of land is subject to continuous mono-cropping over a period of time.

Diversity, plant and animal guilds, and companion planting all contribute to more productive and resilient systems. Diversity provides a balanced diet to the human components of a system, as well as food security throughout the year, and resilience to disease, unseasonal weather, or pests. Andalusī farmers purposefully bred and adapted new cultivars to foment

118 See, Holmgren, *Permaculture: Pathways Beyond Sustainability.*

diversity. The mosaic-like multi-layer agro-ecosytems of al-Andalus are all examples-in-action of several permaculture principles: *Design from patterns to details*; *Integrate rather than segregate*; *Use and value diversity*; and *Use edges and value the marginal*. Companion planting, multi-storey cropping, and the wise integration of animals (both wild and domestic) into the system of course find their parallel permaculture principle in *Integrate rather than segregate*.

Again, these approaches contrast with those taken by industrial agriculture, which tends towards extreme specialization, monocultures, the use of artificially produced fertilizers, neglect of soil fertility, dis-integration of livestock with field crops or market vegetables, and which adheres to the illusory laws of capitalism instead of the ebbs and flows of the natural world.

Filāḥa considers health to be a state of balance. Pests or diseases, then, are the result of imbalances, of a plant receiving too much of one thing or too little of another thing (whether light, water, fertilizer, etc.). This approach finds its parallel in the organic farming movements of today that seek to get at the root cause of pests or diseases by making sure the plants are not ultimately suffering from incorrect growing conditions, rather than merely treating the symptoms. Interestingly—especially when considered in light of Hermetic thought and the laws of sympathy—our andalusī agronomists prescribe spraying diseased plants with decoctions made out of healthy plants of the same species. Alternatively, the healthy plants are burned and the diseased plants are dusted with their ashes. These ashes can be from dried leaves, pits, peels or even dried fruits. Ibn al-ʿAwwām asserts:

> And thus the ash from [each] tree is applied to benefit [اصلاح] those of its likeness [مثل]...it is foundational [اصل] that in the cultivation of every plant, whether tree or small plant, that something of the same is mixed in the manures that are used for each."[119]

We mentioned that the andalusī agronomists preserved much traditional knowledge as they based their treatises on numerous earlier sources such as Aristotle or the Nabatean Agriculture. However, a valuable aspect of their own contribution is that they did not follow their predecessors by rote but put everything they learned from the ancients to the test. In the prologue to his *Kitāb al-Filāḥa*, Ibn al-ʿAwwām confirms: "I do not vouch for [اثبت]

119 Ibn al-ʿAwwām, *Kitāb al-Filāḥa*, 103.

[in this work] any council [راي] without [having first] tested it [جربته] many times [مرارا]." Sometimes the results of their experiments led the andalusī agronomists to disagree with the ancient sources.[120]

This approach should be applauded as being truly scientific; and it is the approach we must take in applying the instructions in the *Books of Filāḥa* in a contemporary context. Magical operations should not be omitted but carried out with results, critique and notes made on how to improve for next time. Talismans and other seemingly strange practices for pest management and disease prevention should not be dismissed at face value. In one text, the author instructs us to bury a magnet in the ground in areas plagued by ants. While at first this seems to be a potentially useless or superstitious practice, we realize now that ants navigate underground in accordance with the earth's geomagnetic current. Placing a magnet underground amongst the ants slightly disrupts the current and confuses them, which ultimately makes them leave. A humble willingness to experiment as a means to arrive at understanding can help provoke a reappraisal of traditional knowledge in some leftist circles where atheism is the vogue, progress the god, and in which anything remotely "traditional" is perceived as hostile, counter-revolutionary—or worst of all—the purview of the fascist enemy.

Too many people, regardless of political leaning, look backwards in time and immediately dismiss the ways of the ancestors as primitive, naive, or barbaric. Of course, pre-modern traditional Islamic husbandry—*filāḥa*—while based on simple principles, is extraordinarily complex. The holistic, sustainable systems it produced could only have been made possible by prolonged engagement with the most important permaculture principle: *Observe and Interact*. Again, the great value placed on careful meticulous observation as imperative in designing a system that produces no waste, gives a yield, and functions harmoniously with its natural environment is ultimately a much more *scientific* approach than, for example, blundering around, bulldozing or clear-cutting trees with no careful observation or understanding of those trees in their greater context.

Just as it is grossly incorrect to call our andalusī agronomists primitive, Fitzwilliam-Hall opines that it would be equally incorrect to view them as the precursors of today's agro-scientists, whom he views as being situated

120 Cf. Abū l-Khayr's opinion of some of his predecessors' seemingly arbitrary attributions to different days of the month. Abū l-Khayr, *Kitāb al-Filāḥa*, 54–55.

on the total opposite end of the sustainability spectrum. How different is the approach of industrialized agribusiness bent on maximizing short-term profit, characterized by high chemical inputs, high carbon outputs, monocultures, and a great dependance on (often harmful) machinery. In remarkable contrast, premodern Islamic farmers were able to practice and create an incredibly successful sustainable form of agriculture without any of the tools and technology of modern industrial civilization.

Filāḥa and "Root Work"

In accord with the prevailing scientific theories of the day, the approach to agriculture that the *Books of Filāḥa* preserve was based on the humoural system.[121] The human body was perceived as a microcosm of Nature, so in *filāḥa* we see farmers taking philosophical approaches to their lands almost identical to those an andalusī physician might take toward the bodies of his or her patients. In his *Kitāb al-Filāḥa*, Abū l-Khayr states: "The greater part of vegetable sicknesses are due to the influence of the four elements: water, air, manure [fire], and earth, and it is beneficial for one element to agree with another or even a third."[122] We might be so bold as to define *filāḥa* as the art of balancing the four elements: earth, air, water, and fire.[123] The correct balance between these *roots* and the qualities and temperaments that blend and shift between them gives rise to healthy crops in healthy environments.[124] Indeed, the elements or humours in the humoural system do not operate in isolation from each other but are in a dynamic relationship. To make a change in one results in an effect on all the others. This is not the "more is always better" attitude prevalent in modern society. It is often necessary to have

121 These humours are blood (air), yellow bile (fire), black bile (earth) and pleghm (water).

122 Abū l-Khayr, *Kitāb al-Filāḥa*, 248. This English translation is based on Carabaza Bravo's translation of the original text into Spanish.

123 Cf. Starhawk's approach to permaculture in books like *The Earth Path* or in her incredible permaculture design course Earth Activist Training.

124 Cf. page (x) of the present collection for more on the classical elements as roots. It is also noteworthy in light of considering *filāḥa* as "root work" that much of the procedures for healing infirm or ailing trees involves doctoring their roots, whether this includes digging them up to directly apply an appropriate mixture of manure, making incisions in them, and/or inserting bits of gold, bone, or other minerals.

less of something in order for a person or plant to reach a state of healthy dynamic equilibrium. Let us now take a closer look at how the elements are conceived of and applied in the design systems of andalusī agronomists, alongside parallel ideas and techniques common to permaculture.

Earth

It is common in the *Books of Filāḥa* for an entire chapter (or more) to be dedicated to different types of soil and the proper preparation of land for cultivation. As these chapters are considered to be among the most important—if not *the* most important—they often appear toward the beginning.

Such is the case in Ibn al-ʿAwwām's *Kitāb al-Filāḥa*. He opens his chapter on soil with the following statement: "The first principle [مراتب] in the science [علم] of agriculture is knowledge [معرفة] of the earth, and knowing how to distinguish [ميز] the good [جيد] [earth] from the abject [دني]. Who does not know this is without merit and [in this matter] deserves to be called ignorant [جهل]."[125] He then proceeds to discuss the best kinds of soils for cultivation, classifying soils by colour and temperature, with black being the best (and hottest), followed by red, then yellow then white (the coldest). According to Ibn al-ʿAwwām, workable earth is formed through the breaking down of stones (and organic matter) caused by the heat of the sun and the moisture of the rain. Therefore, he explains that the soil near the surface (what is known as topsoil today) is the most fertile due to its proximity to the sun, and that earth brought up during the excavation of a well will not be brought to life until it becomes warmed by the sun. Heat in this context does not always refer to temperature, but to the level of fertility, to the quantity of organic matter.[126] The sun is the energetic force behind the carbon cycle after all. The energy in organic matter can be approached as a kind of heat or stored sunlight.[127]

In addition to colour and temperature, soil type was discerned through

---

125 Ibn al-ʿAwwām, *Kitāb al-Filāḥa*, 37.

126 For example, sandy soil is considered hot in the Summer and cold in the Winter. The inability of a sandy soil to hold water is likely what makes it "hot" in the Summer, yet lack of fertility/organic matter what makes it "cold" in the Winter. See Ibid, 44.

127 Ibid, 37–38

taste, smell, touch (texture), and by indicator plants.[128] Ibn al-ʿAwwām suggests a few different methods for discerning the type and quality of the soil one is working with including placing samples of earths in different bins, then covering and burying the bins for half a lunar cycle (fourteen days), and observing the changes in smell, humidity, temperature, that might have occurred in each soil sample, or whether or not insects have hatched in it (if so, the colour of the insects is to be noted).[129] Andalusī agronomists taught that there was an ideal soil for each plant and tree, knowledge of which enabled one to better plan where to sow different things, or how to correct the soil in accordance with the elemental, temperature, moisture, and textural needs of a given plant.

The attitude of andalusī agronomists toward soil was one of a physician to the body of a patient, attempting to correct the imbalances at the root of a disease in order to bring it into vitality. While loose black earth (what we call loam today) was the favoured type, they did not make such a rigid demarcation between so-called "arable land" and "marginal" or "non-arable" land. Instead, "inferior" soils were seen as bodies ailing from elemental imbalances that could be cured and brought to life. If a soil was swampy and had an imbalance from excess water, it could be drained. If the earth was too cold it could be warmed up with a particularly hot type of manure, dried plants or ashes. Valley land along rivers was prized, but this did not stop andalusī farmers from cultivating high and steep mountain slopes or along the coast.[130]

This directly resembles the attitude of permaculture. In addition to composting techniques, permaculture would advocate—after Paul Stamets—myco-remediation, myco-forestry, and myco-gardening.[131] Edge spaces are valued, and barren or unproductive areas are not discarded but seen as spaces that can be regenerated. The landscape is approached as a vernacular to be learned, the pattern of whose plants indicate soil type and reveal the distribution of heat, texture, and moisture.

---

128 Ibid, 47–49

129 Ibid, 57–58.

130 Ibid, 44–46.

131 See Stamets, *Mycelium Running: How Mushrooms Can Help Save the World.*

Fire

In the *Books of Filāḥa,* the element of fire does not usually refer to fire in a literal sense, but to manure.[132] Our agronomists believed that manure, when applied around a plant, functioned as an auxillary for the heat and light of Sun.[133] Even to this day I have heard some farmers in Andalucía warn not to apply too much chicken guano to the plants for fear that it might "burn" them.

Ibn al-ʿAwwām devotes an entire chapter to manures, in which he presents the manures in a hierarchical manner, with human and dove being the hottest and the strongest, and ox being the coolest. He gives detailed instructions for the proper curing and preparation of manures, a process which could take up to several years. Different mixtures of manures are used for different plants, depending on the plant's nature. For example, a colder or wetter plant will require a hotter and dryer manure. Decomposed plants (often of the same variety as the plant to which the manure will be applied), ashes, urine (human and camel), and other house waste are all added to the mix.

Ibn al-ʿAwwām advises against manuring during the waxing moon, and with regard to the solar year notes the time from Autumn to Spring is best.[134] However, he also refers to instances in which cooler, wetter types of manure are administered in Summer to revive plants burned by the Sun's heat.[135] Manures could be worked into the earth before sowing and planting, applied around a plant or to a tree's roots after uncovering them, or dissolved into the water that was used for irrigation.[136]

Contemporary science has shown that as substances decompose, heat is

---

132 In addition to manure, fire is often associated with the sun in *Books of Filāḥa.* Fire in a literal sense makes its way into *filāḥa* when used to burn pruning waste, reduce nutrient rich plants (like broad beans) to ashes, or even to provide literal heat to some plants that lack it in the winter. For example Abū l-Khayr asserts that some summer plants can be grown in winter by lighting little fires near them to provide them with heat. See his *Kitāb al-Filāḥa,* 235. Cf. The contemporary practice of lighting little paraffin or beeswax lamps in greenhouses.

133 See for example, Ibn al-ʿAwwām, *Kitāb al-Filāḥa,* 118–119.

134 Ibid, 132.

135 Ibid, 118.

136 Ibid, 124.

released, hence the half-decomposed interiors of hay bales being burning to the touch, and the common danger of barns catching on fire. Manure is a medium through which the energy of fire can be harnessed and added to the design in proper doses.

Applying manure to plants was compared to administering a medicine. According to Ibn al-ʿAwwām, "... these manures... rot until becoming like the medicines with which people are medicated [تتعالج]. By them, the tree, palm, vine and every class of plant is cured [يعالج] of all pests [افات] and damage [عاهات]."[137]

In permaculture, the parallels to this approach would be the employment of various compost regimes, compost tea and bio-brews, humanure, or even urinating around the base of fruit or nut trees in order to increase production.

Air

The appreciation of air is more straightforward in the *Books of Filāḥa*, and refers, as can be expected, to air itself, and to the wind. Just as our agronomists meticulously documented different kinds of soils, they did the same with winds. Hot winds, cold winds, moist winds, dry winds, dusty winds, and everything in between were all carefully observed, and their effect on different plants duly noted. Companion planting is advocated in order to deal with certain strong seasonal gales, or to facilitate the cultivation of plants at higher altitudes, such as the practice of planting delicate citrus trees under hardy olive trees to protect them from harsh climates or the falling of frost and moisture over night. The element of air is also treated when it comes to pruning to increase air flow, or uncovering roots to remedy puddling and waterlogged soil.[138]

Companion planting is of course a famous characteristic of permaculture. The element of air can also make its way into permaculture designs by way of flow diagrams and other site analyses showcasing the flow of movement, or of sectors and vectors.

137 Ibid, 106.

138 As Abū l-Khayr notes, cold damp conditions without sufficient airflow can create conditions in which plants are vulnerable to disease. See Abū l-Khayr, *Kitāb al-Filāḥa*, 248.

Water

Our agronomists also documented the many different kinds of waters according to their temperatures, mineral compositions, acidity, alkalinity, sediment and so on. In addition to the aforementioned *acequias*, they advocate the use of water-lifting machines, water-wheels, diversion dams, siphons, and storage reservoirs (called *albercas* in modern Spanish, another arabism).

The four main types of water that are catalogued are 1) rain water 2) river water 3) spring water, and 4) well water, with rain water being considered the best and most advantageous for plant health. Some authors (like Abū l-Khayr) add sweet water, salty water, and sea water to this list.[139]

Aṭ-Ṭighnarī, an agronomist from Granada, catalogues the four degrees of coldness found in well and spring water, noting their positive and negative effects on different plants and animals. He also recommends cutting two identical pieces of cloth, dipping them each in a different water, then hanging them both up in the shade and observing which one dries faster. The water that dried faster will be of a lighter constituency than the other.[140]

In some instances, different waters are indicated at different phases of a crop's growing cycle. For example Abū l-Khayr notes that onions planted in the fall are to be watered repeatedly (with river water, spring water, or sweet well water) until they germinate, then left to be nurtured by the rain and cold air until they mature. Onions planted in the spring will need more frequent watering (with the sweet waters listed above) as they flower and approach maturation. Once they reach a large size, Abū l-Khayr calls for them to receive no more irrigation and for their stalks to be cut, and claims thereby they will become enormous.[141]

One fascinating innovation involved the equitable distribution of water and water rights connected to a time of day or night. Originally, these times lined up with the Call to Prayer. Which is to say, different neighbourhoods or different farms had water rights at different times throughout the day, as different *acequias* were opened and closed. The descendant of this system is still in place in the Alpujarra today.

In permaculture, the element of water makes itself present in the digging

---

139 Carabaza Bravo, "El Agua en al-Andalus," 23.

140 Ibid, 24.

141 Abū l-Khayr, *Kitāb al-Filāḥa*, 332–33.

of swales (similar to *acequias*), water purification and filtration techniques, myco-filtration, the treating and harvesting of grey-water, drip and flood irrigation, or catching rain-water and rain-water runoff from roofs.

Sectors, Vectors, and Pest Control

In permaculture, a sector refers to the path of an energetic input that flows across your design. The most important of these are elemental forces: the path of sunlight, the flow of rain water, the course of the wind, or the patterns of different soil types.

The term vector refers to outside forces that flow across the design, but in distinction to sectors these usually have a negative connotation, and more often than not would refer to something like mildew, insect pests, destructive dogs or other animals, birds, diseases, and other forces that cause damage.

As we have mentioned above, the andalusī agronomists believed pests and diseases to be the result of an imbalance in the four elements. Mould, mildew, and harmful worms can afflict overly waterlogged plant roots where there is insufficient airflow, and where the soil is not properly prepared, or plants can whither from an excess of sunlight combined with a lack of water or manure of a cooling influence. This paradigm with regard to disease demonstrates how quickly a sector can become a vector, an observation made all the more poignant by the climate instability and increased frequency of extreme weather events that we are witnessing today. The rain brings life, and fire can have a regenerative effect, but both of these in extreme doses can spell the destruction of an otherwise healthy system.

Therefore, it is important for permaculture designers to not only think of sectors as potential vectors, but vectors as potential sectors in accordance with the design principle *The problem is the solution.* This will allow designers to create resilient systems capable of withstanding, or even thriving in, an unpredictable climate.

For example, in the landscape where I operate, wild boar are a vector of considerable difficulty, and tend to enter and destroy large swathes of garden with impunity. Some people put up electric fences but even these have failed to keep the boars out. I was able to keep them out of my gardens all year long without any fencing by frequenting these areas at twilight and after dark, and encouraging dogs and humans to urinate nearby. The boars were diverted to a hitherto uncultivated area on the edges of the design, which they dutifully rooted up. This area was chosen for cultivation the following year, as the "destructive" boars had done a great deal of work for me by ploughing that section and ridding it of aggressive plants and grasses. This area was then sheet-mulched with cardboard, over which was dumped several hundred kilos of straw and horse manure to provide nutrients but also to maintain a warm moist atmosphere underneath so the cardboard could break down faster in anticipation of the spring.

In addition to the boards, a second vector that was transformed into a sector during this process was the heavy rain that fell. Rain can be a vector when it induces flooding, or damages leaves, fruits, or flowers, or when it makes it difficult for work to be done outside effectively. However, I harnessed the rain's energy by leaving out the sheets of cardboard for sheet-mulching to be soaked by the rain, instead of having to laboriously soak them sheet by sheet with hoses or submersion in stream water (a big job when there is a lot of cardboard that needs soaking). I also coordinate tilling and weeding (if necessary) to be done the day after a rain fall, when the earth is soft and workable. If one primarily works with hand tools, this keeps energy inputs low as it reduces the need for physical energy to work the land, and allows one to eschew power tools and machinery, which are both types of tools that are very costly in gas, electricity, and money.

Every type of weather, even when extreme, can almost always contribute something beneficial to the system if approached the right way and with a little coordination. Blazing hot sun can effectively dry fruits and nuts for the winter, and wind storms can bring down old dry trees and dead branches facilitating the gathering and cutting of kindling and firewood. It might seem obvious, but all too often the attitude of many modern gardeners is to view these elemental forces as things to be contained, controlled, or repelled, instead of as potential allies.

For pest control, Abū l-<u>Kh</u>ayr recommends natural pesticides like a mix of ashes, strong vinegar and dry or fresh henbane, and calls for pruning equipment to be anointed with garlic and onions to repel wasps and other insects that can damage fruit.[142] Alternatively, sulphur is used as a repellent and plants like wormwood can be planted throughout gardens to discourage pests.[143] For further protection against unfavourable weather conditions,

142 Ibid, 245.

143 Ibid, 236.

he advocates hanging talismans in the branches of trees, burying pieces of different kinds of metals (such as lead or gold) near roots, or hanging holed stones on branches to prevent the premature falling of fruit.[144] Magically inclined permaculture designers can take similar measures. Spirits alleged to grant their supplicant the power to handle fire unharmed can be approached and petitioned during the confection of talismans for protection against wild fires, and those spirits that have influence over the rains and hail for talismans designed to protect against harsh weather. These spirits can also be consulted toward the end of an agricultural year to make weather predictions for the following one.

The Calendar and Map

Let us recall the first and most important permaculture principle: *Observe and interact*. As we have mentioned above, a prolonged period of observation in a place and interaction with its elemental characteristics is imperative to designing productive, sustainable systems that are not only passively inoffensive to the surrounding environment but actively *beneficial* to it. Before acting—especially when it comes to energetically costly actions such as digging a swale, clearing shrubs, or otherwise altering a system in a major way—one must have a grasp of varying temperatures, the onset and subsiding of winds and rains throughout the day and throughout the season, have contemplated the distribution of light and shadow, have a clear idea of possible vectors and how they flow across the system, know where the soil is most fertile and where it can be built up and healed: in short, understand the elemental composition of a place, as well as the dynamics by which that composition shifts in accordance with the passing of time.

The product of observing and interacting with this elemental interplay between time and space can take the form of a calendar and map. One is a tool for orientation in time, and the other in space. One is a reference for *when* to act, and the other for *where* to act. Annotated calendars are repositories for agricultural and permacultural wisdom and practices. In a comprehensive manner, they are the distillation of the entire year's round of agricultural activities. Both calendars and maps are the place where the designer records the observations they have made after spending prolonged

144 Ibid, 222–23.

time on the land. Therefore, they are extremely useful and practical tools.

Calendars are essentially divination tools. When one draws up a calendar, they are literally projecting themselves into the future. Indeed, they are peering into the future, as different paths, possibilities, and opportunities present themselves and disappear, and different doors open and close as things are erased or "penciled in."

Maps, on the other hand, function more like compasses, antenna, or dowsing rods, useful in locating different elemental components of a system, and detecting and following the paths along which they ebb and flow. Both calendars and maps offer the designer a chance to step back and get a big-picture perspective. Beginning a design by comprehending a year as a whole, and contemplating a piece of land as a whole, leads to a more integrated approach that can help us *Design from patterns to details.*

I will now offer practical instructions for the creation of a calendar and a map. Creating these tools are essential first steps for someone just getting into permaculture. Additionally, they might provide ideas that experienced permaculturalists can incorporate into their own calendars, maps, and designs. These instructions will be informed by the andalusī calendars and almanacs. Therefore, they will not only function as bare astrological, meteorological or spatial measuring sticks, but will encompass such things as medicine, gastronomy, poetry, art, and magic.

There is some confusion as to the origins of the word *almanac*. While there is no etymon for almanac in Classical Arabic, it has been proposed that *al-manākh* came into Western languages via the vernacular dialect of andalusī Arabic, in which it meant "the climate." However, the andalusī almanac encompassed so much more than just astrological or meteorological predictions. If we accept the Hermetic axiom *As above so below* it follows that humans, alongside other species, minerals, and natural forces are each a microcosm of Nature that contains the whole within it. Therefore, essentially every activity whether domestic, agricultural, medical, culinary, and so on has an appropriate time to be performed. These activities are all integrated parts of the system and are governed by the ebbs and flows of the stars and weather. Fitzwilliam-Hall includes the following commentary on almanacs in his survey of *filāḥa*:

> No survey of medieval Arabic agricultural literature would be complete without including the almanac, which if not specifically

devoted to agriculture often contains a wealth of information on weather, the seasons and the agricultural cycle, the sowing and harvesting times of crops, animal husbandry, and other matters of concern to the farmer (and to the agricultural historian). The almanac is essentially an annotated calendar, a month-by-month and day-by-day reckoning of changes in the natural world and a guide to the proper times for various agrarian operations and other human activities in accordance with these. Besides agricultural matters the almanac typically records a more or less diverse range of events and occurrences that can include day- and night-lengths, shadow-lengths for particular times of the day, entry of the sun into zodiacal constellations, star risings and settings, lunar phases and mansions, the first day of seasons, the onset and end of winds and rains, changes in temperature, the rise and fall of groundwater and floodwaters (especially of the Nile and the Euphrates), navigational periods, animal migrations and behaviour, the growth, flowering and fruiting of wild plants, historical events, as well as Islamic, Jewish, and Christian holy days. At the end of each month's listing there is usually a round up of relevant farming activities, including notifications of tax assessments on particular crops, and advice on appropriate dietary regimes, bodily hygiene, health and medical treatments...

...While the almanacs may have been inspired by pre-Islamic Arab folk astronomy and weather lore, and surely reflect the indigenous agricultural milieu of where each was compiled, they contain certain astronomical, calendrical and medical concepts that can be traced back to Assyro-Chaldean, Greek, Judaic, Hellenistic, Romano-Byzantine, Coptic, and even perhaps ancient Indian, Egyptian and Babylonian traditions. Underlying all, however, is the fundamental conception of correspondence between the regular movement of the stars, sun, moon, and other heavenly bodies, the unfolding of the seasons, the rains, the growth of plants, the round of farming and pastoral activities, the particular nature—wet or dry, hot or cold—of each food, the four bodily humours, and health. Not only agriculture, but all human affairs and activities, including diet, sexual activity, bathing, exercise, travel and medical

> treatment have their times and seasons in accordance with the natural cycle. As Ibn al-ʿAwwām remarks in the introduction to his farming calendar: "One of the most wonderful things in the ordering of time and the seasons is that each activity is ordained to be done at its proper time, such that when it is done at another the result is never as favourable." The Arabic almanacs present, in a nut-shell, a very ancient, perhaps universal, belief in the necessary order and harmony between the microcosm of man and the macrocosm of nature.[145]

A famous example is the *Kitāb al-anwā'*, also known as *The Calendar of Cordoba for the year 961*. True to the cultural heterodoxy that al-Andalus would become known for, the linguistic landscape behind the composition and copying of the calendar is a vignette of the co-existence and tensions between different languages and cultures. There is some mystery surrounding its authorship and the circumstances in which it was copied; scholars hypothesize it was written by ʿArīb ibn Saʿd—a Muslim polymath, physician, theologian, poet, man of letters, among other things—but probably based on the sanctoral calendar of Rabīʿ ibn Zaīd, a bishop from Granada. The calendar is composed in Judeo-Arabic (Arabic written with Hebrew characters) which makes it highly likely the copyist was a Jew. Alongside the Judeo-Arabic manuscript, there are a few other manuscripts of the same calendar, written in Latin. The calendar follows Christian months and also gives the names for the months in Syriac and Coptic.

Like other works pertaining to the *kitāb al-anwā'* [lit. book of seasons; book of epochs; simply put, almanac] genre, it includes astronomical, astrological, and meteorological information, as well as suggestions for when to carry out different agricultural chores, when to sow seeds or when to harvest, and suggestions for when to take medicines, alongside dietary considerations. It also includes dates for saints' days as well as other Christian, Muslim, and Jewish festivals celebrated in al-Andalus at that time. The calendar's preface, in which its purpose and contents are outlined, reads as follows:

> Abū l-Ḥasan ʿArīb ibn Saʿd the secretary—may God forgive him and ourselves—says: Here is a book that recounts the periods

145 Fitzwilliam-Hall, *Filāḥa*, www.filaha.org.

and seasons of the year, the number of months and the days they have, the sun's course through the zodiac and the mansions, the far points where it rises, the measure of its declination and its elevation, the variable length of the shadow it casts at the time of the meridian, the periodic return of the seasons, the succession of days with the increase and decrease of their lengths, the cold season and warm season and those, moderate and temperate, which separate them, fixing the date of the beginning of each season, the number of days it contains, after the doctrine of the astronomers who calculated the position and movement of the stars, and the ancient physicians who determined the seasons and their natures, for, in the division of the year there appeared among these scholars differences that will be mentioned and discussed in this book, God willing.

We will also set down those times that no one can do without concerning the times for sowing and planting, and for various agricultural operations, the first harvesting of fruit, the storage and preservation of foodstuffs, the onset of maturity of fruits that are eaten dried, the dates of parturition, as well as other details concerning the well-being and health of people, such as the most suitable times for the purification of the body through the absorption of medicines and phlebotomy, the gathering of herbs and medicinal seeds, and the preparation of drugs, syrups and preserves, when appropriate and possible.

We will also recount the knowledge regarding the changes of the winds and the theories of the Arabs concerning the anwāʾ and the rains, for they were particularly interested in these and the need to determine the dates of the rising and setting of the stars, to distinguish those that brought the rain from those that did not, in order to adjust their migrations in search of grazing and their transfer to water sources...[146]

146 Translated from ʿArīb ibn Saʿd (1961). *Le Calendrier de Cordoue publié par R. Dozy. Nouvelle Edition Accompagnée d'une Traduction Française Annotée*. Ed. C. Pellat. Leiden: Brill, 2-4. Cited by Fitzwilliam-Hall, *Filāḥa*, www.filaha.org.

The calendar offers an invaluable month-by-month look at the type of crops grown in Córdoba in the year 961, the chores and tasks carried out each month, as well as other cultural activities. The calendar categorizes months by the classical elements, qualities, and humours. For example:

> January is cold and humid by nature; its conformity is the nature of water, and lymph is the reigning humor. In contrast, August is hot and dry, with the nature of fire, and yellow bile the dominant humor...This system provided a framework for dietary and medical considerations, as well as an indication of what crops were favoured by the astrological conjunction.[147]

While this system for categorization might seem overly simplistic to a modern perspective, it constitutes an example of the andalusī agronomists (as well as the long line of Islamic, Greek, or other ancient luminaries who came before them) taking a step back and observing patterns. The question becomes: how does the interplay between the elements, qualities, and humours run through the temporal fabric of a year? How does the land and the human body—both made up of combinations of the same elements—respond to these different changes in elemental constituency? How can we understand the overarching pattern to better be able to treat and attend to the microcosm? This holistic panoramic approach can be fruitfully applied in conjunction with the modern approach to knowledge whose *fuerte* is found in its extreme specialization and close examination of particulars in isolation rather than in relationship.

The Calendar

To create a calendar, you will assemble twelve leaves of paper. Thick is best as thin paper will wear down over the course of the year. You will have ready several sharp pencils, a ruler, and a compass. With these you will draw a pattern to represent the days, one pattern per month. You can elect the grid pattern common to most commercial calendars or experiment with circles, spirals, fractals, three-dimensions, or free drawn lines if these feel a more comfortable or accurate way to transcribe your image of time. While

147 Adapted from Glick, T.F. (1978). *Islamic and Christian Spain in the Early Middle Ages*, 267. Cited by Fitzwilliam-Hall, *Filāḥa*, www.filaha.org.

this process can be done digitally, it is important to keep in mind that the creation of the calendar should be undertaken with the same level of ritual focus as you would have when creating any magical implement. Using a computer to create your calendar does not engage the body in the same way, and is therefore less effective in literally incorporating and internalizing the coming year—and all the astrological phenomena that this entails—into your body.

On each day, record the following: the date, times for the moon's phases, signs and mansions, sunrise and sunset times, hours of daylight, when the sun changes sign, eclipses, the rising of decans, moon void-of-course, lunar apogee and perigee, and on full moon days record moonrise, and, if applicable, estimated times for phases of the menstrual cycle. Religious festivals from your own traditions can also be recorded, and it can be useful to also record the religious festivals or saints' days of the other cultures who live around you.

Title each leaf of paper with the name of the month it corresponds to. This can be done in several languages. Beside or near the name of the month, indicate its average or range of temperatures, record predictions or local knowledge about the onset and end of rains, the falling of frosts, level of fire risk, storms and strong winds, as well as the month's elemental, qualitative, and humoural constituency. Naturally, the constituencies of months will differ depending on where you live. As we have mentioned, in Córdoba, the month we call January is cold, humid, and corresponds to the element of water. However, for someone living in Australia, this constituency would be very different.

Beside the pattern you have elected to represent the month, or on the reverse of the leaf of paper, leave space to record (in point form) the stars and constellations visible during that month, the wild herbs, roots, and fungi that are in season, the species of birds and other migratory animals present, the type of fruits, nuts, vegetables or field crops in season (focusing more on what you have in the garden or on the land you tend), as well as the tasks and chores pertinent to that month.

These twelve leaves will form the bones of your calendar. Once you have drawn them, assemble twelve more upon which you can flesh out your calendar by writing a few paragraphs for each month to act as that month's summary and/or to include any additional information that might not have fit on the other pages. We can look to this extract from the *Calendar of*

Córdoba for inspiration:

> April: The month when...rose water, rose oil, rose syrup and rose preserves are made; violets are picked for the making of syrup, conserve and oil; syrup is made from fumitory; there are cucumbers. The palms are artificially pollinated and the palm leaves are cut. The early grapes begin to form, the olive trees blossom, and the figs come out; the Valencian falcons hatch out their young ones; it takes thirty days for them to grow their feathers. Fawns are born. Supports are made for the citron trees and jasmine cuttings are planted in the ground. The wild carrots are ripe and harvested for the making of jam; and then there are poppies, pomegranates, ox-tongues and the leaves and petals of the dyer's weed from which juice is extracted. It is also the month when henna, basil, cauliflower, rice and beans are sown; the green gourds and aubergines are dug out of their forcing beds; small melons are sown, and also cucumber. Peafowl, storks, and many other birds lay their eggs and begin to brood.[148]

Alongside this more overt "agricultural summary," it is also useful to incorporate artistic and cultural aspects into your calendar. Poetry pertinent to each month, recipes, medicinal and dietary considerations, exercise regimes, as well as paintings or drawings can all be included here. Whether or not you decide to create or paste images in your calendar, it goes without saying that the calendars should be accented by colour, calligraphy, borders, and other types of typographic ornaments to the best of your ability and to the extent of your inspiration. Even if this means just a few highlights, colour and image stimulate clairvoyance and are therefore useful when using the calendar as a compliment to divination work. As permaculture affirms, aesthetics are to be cultivated and appreciated in and of themselves; beauty and the effects of beauty fulfill practical functions.

When writing these paragraphs it can be useful to remember not to gloss over the senses of smell and hearing. In this regard, we are reminded of the "calendar" Federico García Lorca wrote for Granada in the form of smells, sounds, poetry and song: "Cómo cantar a una ciudad de noviembre a noviembre" ["How to sing to a city from November to November"]. For

148 Extract of the English translation by John Brogden retrieved from www.filaha.org.

Lorca, seasonal songs were the true physiognomy of his city, a physiognomy that could reveal its essential rhythms and temperatures:

> Why must one always employ sight and never smell or taste to study a city? [Traditional sweets like] the alfajor, the torta alajú and the mantecado de Laujar say as much about Granada as the delicate Moorish arch; and the marzipan of Toledo with its monstrous garb of plums and pearls of anise, invented by one of Carlos V's cooks, expresses the Germanism of that emperor with more acuteness than his red beard. While a cathedral remains nailed to its epoch, with its profile crumbling, eternal, yet unable to step into the next day, a song leaps suddenly from its epoch into ours, live and trembling like a frog, with its joy or melancholy still fresh, verifying a marvel identical to the seed that flowers after falling out of Pharaoh's tomb. Therefore, we are going to hear the city of Granada...These songs are the physiognomy of the city and in them we are going to behold its rhythm and temperature...We approach with our ears and sense of smell and the first sensation we get is a smell of sedge, spearmint, of the vegetal world softly crushed by the legs of mules, horses, and oxen that come and go over the Vega in all directions. And then, suddenly, the rhythm of the water. But not a goose-water that goes where it wills. Water with rhythm yet without murmur, measured water, just, following a geometric course and accentuated by works of irrigation. Water that irrigates and sings down here below and water that suffers and cries full of tiny white violins up there in the Generalife...[149]

---

149 "¿Por qué se ha de emplear siempre la vista y no el olfato o el gusto para estudiar una ciudad? El alfajor y la torta alajú y el mantecado de Laujar dicen tanto de Granada como el alicatado o el arco morisco; y el mazapán de Toledo con su monstruoso ropaje de ciruelas y perlas de anís, inventado por un cocinero de Carlos V, expresa el germanismo del emperador con más agudeza que su roja barbilla. Mientras que una catedral permanece clavada en su época, desmoronando su perfil, eterna sin poder dar un paso al día próximo, una canción salta de pronto de su época a la nuestra, viva y temblorosa como una rana, con su alegría o su melancolía recientes, verificando idéntico prodigio que la semilla que florece al salir de la tumba del Faraón. Así pues, vamos a oír la ciudad de Granada... Estos cantos son la fisionomía de la ciudad y en ellos vamos a ver su ritmo y su temperatura... Nos vamos acercando con los oídos y el olfato y la primera sensación que tenemos es un olor a juncia, hierbabuena, a mundo vegetal suavemente aplastado por las patas de mulos y caballos y bueyes

Lorca originally performed this "sung calendar" with his piano. For each month, in addition to occasionally describing or mentioning agricultural activities—the smell of burnt olive prunings or the rotting mulch of broad bean plants—he follows the thread of the seasons through Granada throughout the year, with a particular focus on the songs one hears in the streets—which he sang to the audience as he went along—as well as the tastes and smells of the types of sweets being prepared and sold by street vendors. The auditory and olfactory senses, while often neglected, can also help trigger altered states and therefore can be very useful when applying the calendar in a divinatory context. Interacting with the sounds, smells, and tastes of a place can only help the designer (or diviner) know it all the more intimately.

To these twenty-four leaves of paper, it can be helpful to add an appendix outlining your standard daily and weekly schedules, as well as indexes as needed. For example, one index could outline the signs of the zodiac, the decans, or the lunar mansions in shorthand. Add a title page and bind it all together with whatever material you like or is convenient. Make a simple consecration with incense and water and it is ready for use.

While this is a solid and practical frame-work for creating a calendar, remember the knowledge a calendar encapsulates is built up, compost-like, over time. With each passing year, you will be able to revise, reflect and make more accurate predictions.

The Map

A map is essentially a tool that helps one comprehend the tensions and interplay of the elements in a given place. I advise you create at least two maps. One will show the design in its entirety, the other will be more focused on the garden(s) where food is grown. You will make multiple versions of each map, so that each version can highlight a particular element or aspect of the design.

The first version you make will correspond to the element of earth. This version will clearly show all material objects, buildings, slopes, or plants

---

que van y vienen en todas las direcciones por la vega. En seguida el ritmo del agua. Pero no un agua oca que va donde quiere. Agua con ritmo y no con rumor, agua medida, justa, siguiendo un cauce geométrico y acompasada en una obra de regadío. Agua que riega y canta aquí abajo y agua que sufre y gime llena de diminutos violines blancos allá en el Generalife." Translation mine.

in the area being mapped, as well as provide a map of the kinds of soils. Clearly showing the distribution of soils is perhaps needless to say a more important attribute of the "zoomed-in" map of your food garden, and does not necessarily have to be a feature of the version that shows your land or place of operation as a whole.

The second version will correspond to the element of fire, and will focus on mapping the light and shadows. Shadow lengths should be recorded and estimates given for different times of day in different seasons.

The third version will correspond to the element of water. It will clearly show any network of swales you may have dug, water lines (both above and below ground), the flow of rainwater, springs, wells, rivers, streams, or any other body of water that interacts with the system.

The fourth version will correspond to the element of air. Here you will depict the paths of the winds and breezes through the system, taking into account the different effects (whether beneficial or harmful) that each wind or breeze might have on your plants, or on trellises and other structures. Finally, it is on this version of the map that you will record all other vectors. In permaculture, vectors refer to *things that flow across your design*, and include anything from the wind, to birds, to humans, insects or to animals like deer or wild boar that like to get into gardens and often cause damage. While the word vector has negative connotations, as mentioned above, the wise permaculture designer will attempt to also view them as potential sectors (inputs) and devise ways in which their impact can be redirected, neutralized, or harnessed in a positive way, in the same way we catch vectors like sunlight and rainwater.[150] In addition to recording a list of the vectors, this version of the map will include a flow diagram that represents their projected paths through the design.

The fifth version will clearly indicate the zones that make up the design. In permaculture, zones are usually numbered from 1 to 5 (sometimes 0 to 5). Zone 1 refers to the area of the design whose components are subject to the most frequent human use or manipulation, with the other zones descending in frequency of use or manipulation until Zone 5 which refers to a wilderness. Using zones helps a designer arrange the components of the system in a way that minimizes the need for energy input. For example, it is wise to keep your culinary herb garden close to a door, or close to the

150 These are sectors because they constitute input, but can also be considered vectors because they flow across the design.

kitchen, where it is frequently used. This way, the designer need not waste time and energy walking all the way across their site to get the herbs each time they need them for cooking.[151]

On a local or "micro" level, Zone 1 (sometimes Zone 0) typically refers to the house or place of dwelling, or to the area immediately around it. It is the focal point of the site. This is the area that the designer frequents the most, and has the most direct power or influence over. Intensive gardens, and plants such as salad greens, herbs, or berries; greenhouses, small compost for kitchen waste, or raised beds are all found in Zone 1. When Zone 1 refers to the dwelling place itself, actions would include things like installing grey-water systems, solar panels, painting or adorning, or any other action that contributes to creating a self-sufficient healthy place to live.

Zone 2 refers to the area immediately beyond Zone 1, and includes things like orchards, small livestock, larger compost bins, extensive (rather than intensive) gardens or perennial plants that require less attention or are used less than those found in Zone 1.

Field crops—whether for commercial or domestic use—and larger livestock are found in Zone 3. This zone requires little maintenance once crops are established.

Zone 4 refers to the hedgerows, edges of forests, and other spaces where the site begins to change into wilderness. It can also refer to managed forest or rangeland. Things like wildcrafting or gathering kindling occur in this zone.

Zone 5 refers to a wilderness proper, where no human intervention takes place, other than thoughtful observation.

The "zone" concept is also applied on a "macro" level, in which Zone 0 refers to the Permaculture Principles that guide our decisions; Zone 1 refers to the Personal or to the Homestead; Zone 2 to Business and/or Community; Zone 3 to your bioregion; Zone 4 to your country or continent; and Zone 5 refers to the global.

Principles for Revolution

Thinking with zones also helps calibrate our actions with regard to power. Zone 1 is generally considered the place where we have the most direct pow-

151 I have heard different permaculture designers say that if your socks get wet when going out from the kitchen to get herbs, your herb garden is too far away from the house!

er or influence, and therefore the place where the effects of our actions are multiplied, and much more significant than the effects of actions taken, say, in Zone 5. Therefore, this conceptual framework can also provide us with a potential guide for where and how to act in a political or revolutionary context. Sometimes, these results can turn out to be the exact opposite of those originally intended. Overly rash top-down action has caused enough destruction, and there have been enough revolutions gone awry over the course of human history to eschew the need to provide examples here.

Permaculture advocates *Top-down thinking, bottom-up action* and encourages activists to apply their political, ethical, and environmental beliefs first in their own lives, at their own homes, and then expand from there. This is not the narcissism or escapism of New Age "self-help," nor is it a passive "dropping out." It is a practical way of applying and managing your power that can actively and effectively combat capitalism or ecocide. David Holmgren—one of the originators of the permaculture concept itself—writes:

> Taking personal responsibility naturally moves us to be more self-reliant and less dependent on centralised sources of needs and responsibility. In the process, we discover that governments and corporations, while preaching self-reliance, actually need our dependence. This need at the centres of power has become so great that a slackening in the frenzy of consumption is called a "consumer strike"... Self reliance tends to work as a more generalised and invisible consumer boycott, undermining the market share and psychosocial dominance of the centralised and large-scale economies that support and maintain addictive and dysfunctional behaviour. At the same time, it tends to foster and stimulate new local forms of economic activity. For example, I have argued that home food production has tended to foster, rather than compete with, small commercial organic growers serving local markets.[152]

Holmgren then goes on to reflect on how the amorphous and informal nature of self-reliance makes it difficult for the media, corporations, or government to crack down on or to foil this type of action in attempts to protect their interests. Becoming self-reliant comprises a potent albeit invisible revolution.

---

152 See Holmgren, *Permaculture: Pathways Beyond Sustainability*, 87.

These concepts resonate with the philosophy of Ibn Bājja (c. 1085–1138). Ibn Bājja was a poet, philosopher, composer, musician, botanist, physician, astrologer, astronomer, and mathematician. He made several important scientific breakthroughs: he is considered the first to posit that the force that makes a fruit fall from a tree is the same that moves the celestial bodies, and he was the first to define the sex of plants in his botanical work *Kitāb an-Nabāt* [Book of Plants]. Ironically, some believe he wrote the melody that would later be used for the Spanish national anthem, or that that melody was at least based on one of his compositions. A generation before the better known Ibn Rushd (Averroes), he became the first occidental scholar (whether Christian, Muslim, or Jew) to comment the works of Aristotle. The Western world knows him by his Latin name, Avempace.

Ibn Bājja (or Avempace) also made breakthroughs in literature and music. Although it has not survived, it is known he wrote a short work on the relations between the humours of the body, the strings of the lute, and the melodies of the spheres. Some consider him the creator of the *muwashshaḥ* form of strophic poetry. While this may not be the case, he was undoubtedly a master of the genre. Like his contemporaries, he wrote poems on wine and love, and participated in the nocturnal garden soirées with the Hūdī (and later Almoravid) court in Zaragoza where both of these substances were consumed. He was at times derided as a heretic by critics. This is probably due to his philosophical work but also due to him seeming to at times lead the life-style of a wine drinking bon-vivant. He infamously had an affair with a black slave, as well as fell in love with his Christian jailer while imprisoned.

The *Tadbīr al-Mutawaḥḥid* or *The Regimen of the Solitary* is generally considered his most important work, in which he combines aspects of his philosophical, political, and medicinal/botanical expertise. The word "regimen" in the title refers to a "health regimen"—in the same way we refer to dietary or exercise regimens today—for the soul, the body and society. In it, Ibn Bājja applies his medicinal knowledge to the health of a political body in which health is based on a dynamic equilibrium and the proper balance of the elements and humours in the body. He reflects on how if a political body is sick, it will adversely affect the health of the souls and bodies of its subjects. Observing the connections between souls and bodies—from the personal/physical to the political—finds its permaculture parallel in the dynamics between zones, and the effects of health (or its absence) from microcosm to macrocosm and back again.

For Ibn Bājja, revolution starts with the individual. In stark contrast to Plato and many of his intellectual descendants, he believed that the obsession with defining and creating a perfect city headed by a philosopher king who rules by coercion was itself a source of tyranny. A perfect city is the product of fully realized human beings, not the other way around. He distrusted and criticized just about every type of authority, whether jurists and legalists, politicians, moralists, or Sufi brotherhoods. Indeed, Ibn Bājja was fiercely anti-orthodox.

Therefore, some contemporary researchers such as Abdennur Prado read a strong anarchic current running through the philosopher's thought. According to Prado, the rationale behind Ibn Bājja's antinomian conclusions can be found in one of his simple yet seductive premises: *all pleasure is the shadow of something else*. For Ibn Bājja, the ultimate goal of a human being—propelled by the motor of the intellect but without becoming its prisoner—is to transcend material forms (vegetal, animal, etc.), and ascend through the spiritual forms until achieving union with the Agent Intellect. He equates this ultimate goal with something quintessentially human, with human nature. To achieve union with the Agent Intellect is to realize our divine nature, is to become more who we are. We may feel our "partial goals" are ends unto themselves—such as eating to satiate hunger, drinking to quench thirst, or having sex to slake carnal desire—but all of these goals are incomplete, they are passing stations on the path to union with the divine. All pleasure is the shadow of something else. All desire is desire for God.

Just as Ibn Bājja equates this "ultimate goal" with what is human, he equates mistaking "partial goals" for ends unto themselves with what is "animal." Prado asserts:

> Doing things without connecting them to the ultimate goal of man is a waste of time. Salesmen know a lot about this. They sell us illusions, lies, and the dream of being someone through possession. The entire capitalist system is based on maintaining the individual in a state that Avempace classifies as animality.[153]

153 "Hacer cosas sin conectarlas al fin último del hombre es perder el tiempo. Los vendedores saben mucho de esto. Nos venden ilusiones, mentiras, el sueño de ser alguien a través de la posesión. Todo el sistema capitalista se basa en mantener al individuo en este estado que Avempace calificaría como de animalidad." Translation mine. See Prado, "Una lectura anarca de Avempace,"

While it might be inaccurate or unfairly debasing for animals and their nature to be equated with the capitalist consumer daze, whether or not we use the word "animality" to define this state, the connotations of impulsiveness, frenzied consumption, unchecked appetites, greed, or squabbling over scraps all come through with clarity.

Legalists, jurists, moralists, or politicians, then, are tyrannical because they are not conscious of the ultimate goal of a human being. Their laws, morals, and the brute force with which these are attempted to be upheld are mistaken for ends unto themselves instead of means. These ends are partial, for they usually involve using laws and morals to achieve personal material wealth and social status instead of working toward the freedom, realization, and happiness of all. Unlike Plato, Ibn Bājja asserts people are never to be in service of the State, the State is in service of the people. The obsession with partial goals makes society sick.

And if society is sick, the only thing left for the sage to do is unchain themselves from it. Get their mind free. Get their spirit free. Free from the chains of oppressive politicians or manipulative religious moralists. That is why his political work is titled *The Regimen of the Solitary*, as the sage or solitary is one who has detached themselves from the infirm pressures of society.[154]

This solitariness refers more to an inner state than to physical isolation, and detachment more to mystical awareness than asceticism. In Prado's words, it's not so much that the solitary drops out of society; rather, they do not let themselves become its slave. Indeed, Ibn Bājja criticized Sufi brotherhoods for having what he saw as overly rigid hierarchical structures and for confusing practices such as prayer, chanting, or fasting with ends unto themselves. He did not advocate abstinence; rather, he upheld that only once one is capable to comprehend passing pleasures in their greater context are they able to be fully enjoyed, tasted, and savoured. Though couched in philosophical language, union with the Agent Intellect entails a state of ineffable bliss, limitless ecstasy, and mystical rapture. Once this state is achieved, physical pleasures can be fully enjoyed in a conscious healthy manner. Not only that, he asserts that they will even have an *added flavour*.

According to Ibn Bājja , a "perfect" society can only be made up of humans in this exalted state. He dreamed of a spiritual communion of

retrieved from abdennurprado.wordpress.com

154 One can't help but come to the conclusion that if Ibn Bājja were alive today he would defiantly choose not to have a Facebook account or similar.

free, fully realized humans on earth—in which the notion of individuality was greatly transformed—before fully achieving union with the divine in the afterlife. This communion is not achieved by coercion but by leading through presence and example; the solitary philosopher-sage of Ibn Bājja does not seek to exalt themselves above their peers on any hierarchy.

During the course of detaching themselves from society and becoming solitary it is common for the sage to feel some estrangement, or to feel like they are "swimming upstream." Yet, dissidence is not only encouraged, it is considered necessary. For Ibn Bājja, heterodox ideas conceived in an unfettered state are of the utmost importance for effectuating positive change. He defends the right, and even the need, to profess ideas that challenge the status quo. In a stunning inversion of al-Fārābī, Ibn Bājja refers to the dissident solitary sage as a *nābīt,* or "weed." A fitting translation for readers today might be *bad seed*. For al-Fārābī, these weeds refer to the unsavoury or uncooperative individuals that must be ripped out of the manicured garden of a "perfect" society. Prado opines that the term "weed" is "a name that casts light on the transgressive character of Avempace's solitary [sage]. "It isn't the palace gardener that unifies the garden and gives it an external appearance of harmony, but the weeds, impossible to rip out, that ruin the belle utopias of the moralists of any stripe."[155]

In the context of permaculture and guerrilla gardening, the terms "weed" or "bad seed" take on a literal meaning. In some ways, guerrilla gardeners resemble Ibn Bājja's dissident sages, hurling seed balls into empty lots and marginal land, ripping up manicured lawns and modern urban ornamental gardens (gardens that almost always require an unjustifiable amount of energy to maintain and yield precisely nothing, not even beauty), celebrating the resilience and enormous medicinal, edible, and cosmetic value of so many weeds, and planting and nurturing the tough, recalcitrant trees and herbs that can thrive in the ruins of industrial civilization. And indeed actively encouraging them to break through the concrete causeways of capitalism, of "progress," of the new millennium—causeways that glitter as falsely as a costly orthopaedic smile, arranged in square grids designed to

155 "...creo que es un nombre clarificador del carácter transgresor del Solitario de ibn Baÿÿa [sic]. No es el jardinero palaciego que unifica el jardín y le da una apariencia externa de armonía, sino el hierbajo imposible de arrancar que arruina las bellas utopías de los moralistas de todos los pelajes." See Prado, "Una lectura anarca de Avempace," www.webislam.com.

dominate movement and its easy natural flow, suffocate common spaces, and placate the automobile industry (the grid—a pattern almost entirely foreign to nature and first applied by the Romans in order to facilitate the movement of armies through towns and cities), dull concrete, imperial concrete, concrete at once poisonous and sanitized *ad nauseum*.

Towards a Green Necromancy

We opened this epistle with a meditation on the underworld as the birthplace of true wealth, where seeds germinate and begin their ascent toward the light. But the underworld is also the abode of the Dead, and how similar the seed to the human soul!

The permaculture designer or guerilla gardener that, through their love, nurturing, and cunning balance of the elements, guides the souls of plants from the underworld to the surface is, in a sense, a goetic agent of Hermes Chthonios, that oft invisible fleet-footed one who leads human souls there and back again.

This observation is made all the more poignant when we realize that to grow a plant is literally to dialogue with death—with the stuff of long dead plants, animals, and occasionally humans, melting into the soil, making it fertile. And when flowers grow around graves or on burial mounds, is it a human soul or vegetal soul that rises towards the sun?

Naturally, the inverse is also true. To perform a green burial is to plant a seed. To care for plants and watch them grow, die, and rise again is to contemplate the mysteries of necromancy, alchemy, and theurgy.[156] To behold the transmigration of souls on the kabbalistic Tree of Life that rise along its trunk, coil along its branches, and fall again with its fruit....

Baruch Spinoza proclaimed that God is Nature. God is both *nature naturata*, natured Nature, the material world as receptacle, and perhaps more specifically, God is the active principle of nature, *nature naturans*, or in other words, Nature naturing, Nature nurturing, Nature doing what Nature does. The force that makes things grow, and makes them die to grow again. For is not death itself but a *mode* of a single *substance*?[157]

156 Cf. Heliophilus, *Alchemy Rising*, 69.

157 Some have interpreted the philosopher's views as denying any transcendental or "immaterial" aspect to God, and that what we are referring to here as God is the physical, material, universe, and nothing more. Witches and magicians can attest

Slowly, these meditations begin to reveal a present yet unspoken of mystical dimension to *filāḥa* or permaculture as husbandry. Who natures, nurtures, and lovingly helps things grow, merges with God as *nature naturans.*

And with that, friend, we conclude this epistle and wish that you be entirely awash with blessings, success, and salvation, *for in all times and places a green fire burning.*

that this is only part of the story. However, this question depends on how we define matter and whether or not we choose to view spirits and other fluid or airy entities as "material" or "immaterial."

7

Risāla fī jannat al-janān

[Risāla of the Closed Garden]

☿

The blooming of your cheek is the height of pleasure;
Against it is the amber of the hair of your temples, shaped like lams.[158]

The fire of your abandon is to the lover like the flames of hell,
but union with you if you come, is like the garden of paradise.

It is as though a full moon carries the wine and breezes,
and the two hands of the drinker are a halo...

With a sigh, we allowed the water to dilute the wine;
do we not maintain our threads of life by this process?...
You have litigated a pact: Faith built, and desires are not fulfilled.
Fantasy draws near to the desired one, far away from daily concerns;
and the fantasies burst forth into leafy greenery.

The phantom serves drink for a second time—the heart of a destiny of permanent
bewitchment by him—and the soul is left with longing.

Perhaps if the anguish of the night returns to my reproach,
the culmination of desire will be achieved,

Until the excellence of the spectre flees with it, and perhaps
You believed in these fantasies...[159]
—Abū al-Faḍl ibn Ḥasdāy, eleventh century

---

158 A "lam" is an Arabic letter that makes a sound similar to that of the English "L." When written on its own, at the beginning of a word, or at the end of a word, it looks like this: ل

159 Translation by Robinson, "Return from Exile," 66–67.

Philosophy and mysticism coalesce in the verdant gardens of the *majlis al-uns*—the nocturnal wine and poetry party. In al-Andalus, most famously in the *taifa* period, nighttime gatherings in gardens or in the salons of ornate palaces, in which poetry was sung and wine drunk, were celebrated by the poet-courtiers and sovereigns of different courts. These nocturnal garden soirées and the dream-like literature that arose around them sought to conjure a fantastic (no-)space and time-out-of-time, in which paradise could be invoked in the here and now. At these gatherings, cultural and gender identities were blurred, social and political hierarchies subverted, courtly love was born, and art and dissident thought fomented and were even given space to flourish. Radical *badīʿ* poetics as well as the *muʿtazilī* heresy in vogue at the time both shaped the thought and aesthetic of the *taifa majlis,* which was performed to provide pleasure to the intellect [*ʿaql*], the heart [*qalb*], as well as to the five senses of the body. Wine, poetry, song, and overwhelming natural beauty were approached as the vehicles through which the participant might arrive at philosophical epiphany or mystical annihilation. The perfume of the garden, the ruby charms of the cupbearer, and the bewitching melody of a *muwashshaḥ* or a *ghazal* were all considered capable of provoking or inspiring *the night-flight of souls.*

A significant number of these *topoi* are also features in the lyric topography of another semi-mythical nocturnal revelry: the Witches' Sabbat. Exploring this shared topography alongside the philosophical and mystical aspects of the *majlis al-uns* in al-Andalus has the potential to inspire and invigorate celebrations of the Witches' Sabbat today. Whether a mystical session of great depth and discipline, or a more casual wine and poetry soirée, the *majlis al-uns* shows how these and similar gatherings can be celebrated for their emancipatory effect on the heart, mind, and spirit.

The word *majlis* is derived from the root j-l-s [ج ل س] which, in form I, simply means "to sit." *Majlis* can mean a gathering space, or refer to the group of people that gather in that space. Therefore it is often translated as "council," "session," "sitting," "court," and so on. The word *majlis* can also signify a small group with a steady membership, a study group, or a circle, such as a circle of religious scholars that gather around a master, or "mystical sessions" as in Ibn al-ʿArīf's *Maḥasīn al-Majālis* [The Attraction of Mystical Sessions]. *Majlis ash-sharāb* refers to a drinking party or drinking session, and *majlis al-uns* to a soirée of intimate friendship.[160]

160 See *A Dictionary of Modern Standard Arabic*, 154–55.

The beginning of the eleventh century saw the collapse of the Umayyad caliphate in al-Andalus, and the emergence of independent *taifa* kingdoms in its wake. This period of strife and civil war, known as the *fitna*, was instigated by members of the elite belonging to or loyal to the Umayyad dynasty launching a coup after the 'Amirids had essentially turned caliph Hishām II into their puppet. The 'Amirids, unable to legitimize their claim to the throne through dynastic ties or kinship with the Prophet, had to find an alternative rhetoric. For that reason, they cultivated the persona of the learned, wise, poet-courtier as loving-subject, and the sovereign as courtly beloved, dispenser of riches and marvellous pleasures.[161] And so courtly love was invented and shaped through architecture, art, and literature to be displayed as an alternative rhetoric to that of dynastic legitimacy.

The courtly model would prove so effective it was adopted by all the other *taifa* courts and eventually spread to the Languedoc through relations that some *taifa* courts (especially the Banū Hūd of Zaragoza, of whom more anon) had with their Christian counterparts around and to the north of the Pyrenees. Sovereigns in the *taifa* period are renowned for being patrons of art and science; they actively sought to surround themselves with poets and other luminaries. Some poets were associated with a specific court and others went from court to court composing panegyrics upon request. Courtly love served as an adhesive, weapon, or ornament in the politically fractured though culturally fertile landscape of al-Andalus during the *taifa* period.

The *taifa* period spans much of the eleventh century. While the period was marked by conflicts between different kingdoms—especially during the first half of the eleventh century—it is generally renowned as a golden age of literature, science, philosophy, and art. It was the *taifa* period that produced several *Books of Filāḥa* as well as Arabic poets like the poet-king al-Mu'tamid, his courtier Ibn Ḥamdīs, and poet-philosophers like Ibn as-Sīd or Ibn Bājja, or Hebrew poets and philosophers like Shmuel ha-Nagid, Shlomo ibn Gabirol, and Moshe ibn Ezra. Heterodoxy greatly shaped the intellectual landscape of the time. Cynthia Robinson describes how the sundering of the Umayyad caliphate in al-Andalus played a role in the spread of unorthodox ideas:[162]

161 See Robinson, *In Praise of Song*, 48–64.

162 Robinson's book *In Praise of Song* is the best study I have ever read on the majlis and consequently the study upon which I base the majority of the historical and

> Heresy, in the lyrical form of the mu'tazila, and even the shī'a, entered port cities such as Málaga and, once the detaining hand of Empire had been banished, spread northward on lazy waves of economic prosperity and the surprised ease of running things on a regional, rather than a peninsular, scope.[163]

This *mu'tazilī* influence took part in an intellectual ferment that also included *badī'* poetics—a poetics, as Robinson puts it, "based on a hermetic assumption of the transformational powers of metaphor and firmly associated with sundry heresies"—alongside a number of other esoteric influences.[164] The Banū Hūd of Zaragoza, like other *taifa* sovereigns such as al-Mu'tamid, were renowned as patrons of learning. They had an extensive library full of books on magic, astrology, alchemy, and divination. Two Hūdī sovereigns, Aḥmad I al-Muqtadir ibn Hūd, and Yūsuf al-Mu'taman ibn Hūd, were both celebrated mathematicians; Yūsuf al-Mu'taman ibn Hūd wrote a treatise on geometry called *al-Istikmāl* [The Perfection]. From Arabic texts such as those of the Banū Hūd, Latin translators were able to import many divinatory techniques, divination by each of the four elements, earth, air, fire, and water, and *'ilm ar-raml* [science of the sand], the divination system that would come to be known in the "West" as geomancy. It is known that the *Rasā'il Ikhwān aṣ-Ṣafā'* [Epistles of the Brethren of Purity], a collection of texts shot through with neoplatonic and Hermetic religio-philosophical ideas, made up part of the Hūdī library, and it is highly likely *Kitāb Sirr al-Asrār* [Book of the Secret of Secrets]—the text that contained the document known as *The Emerald Tablet*, from which that text made its first appearance into Latin by way of a translator from neighbouring Aragon, Hugo de Santalla—was also part of the Hūdī collection.[165]

One can become intimate with the bewitching world of the *majlis* through the more prominent characteristics of its lyrical topography. These *topoi* include the *locus amoenus* (whether in garden, palace, or a combina-

philological research that went into this epistle. I hope, in a small way, to pay homage to Robinson and her outstanding work, while at the same time making it accessible to a wider audience.

163 Robinson, "Return from Exile" 69.

164 Ibid, 69.

165 See, Burnett, "The Translating Activity in Medieval Spain," *The Legacy of Muslim Spain*, 1036–1059.

tion of the two), the spring, the night, the wine, the lover, and the cup-bearer (or beloved). The religious, literary, philosophical, and mythological origins of these *topoi* can be traced in the Qur'ān, *Shir ha-Shirim* [The Song of Songs], Plato's *Symposium,* as well as the rituals and mythologies of pre-Abrahamic religions of the Mediterranean and ancient Near East.

The Garden

The garden wears a coloured coat,
The lawn has on embroidered robes,
The trees are wearing their wonders to every eye,
And every bud renewed by spring
Comes smiling forth to greet his lord.
See! Before them marches a rose,
Kingly, his throne above them borne,
Freed of the leaves that had guarded him,
No more to wear his prison clothes.
Who will refuse to toast him there?
Such a man his sin will bear.[166]

—Moshe ibn Ezra, eleventh century

As we have mentioned above, the *taifa* period is generally considered to be the literary apogee of al-Andalus. This can be said of both the Arabic as well as Hebrew poetry.[167] Much of the poetry composed in both languages during this golden age takes place in the Spring. Likewise, the physical setting of the *majlis* was almost invariably a garden within some special salon of the palace or mansion reserved for this purpose. From their sofas, or cushions on the floor, *taifa* courtiers could recline and view the rich vegetation, as well as the intricately ornamented carvings and calligraphy on the walls, statues and sculptures at times meant to resemble flora and fauna.

166 Translation by Scheindlin, *Wine*, 35.

167 Andalusī Jews were all but indistinguishable from their Muslim counterparts (except in religious affiliation) and belonged to the same milieu, hence my decision to present poetry by both Hebrew and Arabic poets side by side. See Brann, "The Arabized Jews."

Though many of the poems are set in spring, even if the party was held in some other season, the wine, incense, display of jewels and riches, and the liminal nocturnal setting between waking and sleeping would have been enough to create a world of splendour. Stone animals, stucco-work resembling abstract animal forms, and carved vegetal ornamentation on the walls could appear to become animated and shiver into life. Adherents of this "religion of love" [*dīn al-hawā*] would have felt caught in a perpetual spring, in an endless night.

The *majlis* was shaped by visual and linguistic metaphor, which in turn influenced and reinforced the poetry and art that produced those metaphors in the first place. The oldest extant andalusī treatise of poetics that preludes the *taifa majlis al-uns* in this way is al-Himyarī's *Al-badīʿ fī waṣf al-rabīʿ* [The Most Ingenious Descriptions of Spring].[168] The word *badīʿ* can be translated loosely as "strange," "wonderful," or "marvellous." In a literary context, it denotes a style of poetics that has ʿAbbasid precedents, but reached its peak in the *taifa* period. As a poetic style, it in turn informed the whole courtly ethos and aesthetic characteristic of the *majlis al-uns*. *Badīʿ* as a poetics strays away from the overly concrete, sparse, and literal in favour of ornament and complexity, with a heavy employment of metaphor, simile, and symbol. It largely concerns itself with lyrical themes such as wine and love. The word *badīʿ* is derived from form IV of the root b-d-ʿ [ب دع], which means "to originate" or "to invent." Furthermore, it is related to the derived noun *bidaʿ* which is commonly translated as "heresy," given its denotation of innovation in a religious context. Therefore, the poetics that informed *taifa* court culture can be taken as a garden of the mind, a garden of vision, where paradise is invoked for leisure and to provoke mystical experience.[169] These descriptions of Spring were thought by some to be the most dazzling, marvellous, original, ingenious compositions that heretofore were conceived. A value is placed here on the fresh, the ephemeral, and innovation in the name of Beauty. Just as the spring offers up entirely new flowers every year, the first blooms of love and sexual renewal: a heresy upon the orthodoxy of winter.

---

168 Hereafter referred to as the *Badīʿ*. It is important to note that this work is not really a treatise in sensu stricto but an annotated poetry anthology. See Robinson, *In Praise of Song*, 151.

169 There is a work dated from this time, no longer extant, titled *Rawd al-ʿIlm* [The Garden of Knowledge].

The *Badīʿ* was given as a gift to the then king of the *taifa* of Seville: al-Muʿtaḍid ibn ʿAbbād. It documents the beginnings of *nawrīyāt* [flower poems] coming to be the preferred form of panegyric. Sometimes, these floral lyrics were even offered alongside actual bouquets of flowers.[170] Some decades later, in the late *taifa* period, we continue to see this *topos* used as a crucial ingredient of what makes up the *majlis* anecdote, in which descriptions of allegedly actual *majālis* [s. *majlis*] are given, the lyric verses (typically of the *ghazal* and *khamrīya* genres, lyric poems about wine and love respectively) that were recited and sung at these gatherings, as well as the context in which they were recited and received. These anthologies also at times included rhymed prose and criticism from the part of the anthologist.[171] As these anecdotes are embellished and told through a highly metaphorical and ornate language, they must be approached with caution when trying to extract solid biographical details. Yet, we must also be cautious of being too quick to dismiss them as rootless fantasy.

Among the courtly *topoi* that appear in the *Badīʿ* discussed above is *ẓarf* or elegance. We discover the importance of the *ẓarīf* (or dandified person) well dressed, well mannered, and above all well spoken—which, along with the deliberate display of jewels and riches that festooned the salons where the *majlis* took place would have added to the overall creation of pleasurable and magical (no)space. The codes of behaviour that *ẓarf* encompasses would have dealt with everything from how to speak, act, dress, and which perfumes to wear. Indeed, these boon companions included those whose very shoelaces were inscribed with poetry.[172]

The gardens in these palaces were at times modelled after depictions of Paradise in the Qurʾān. The poems themselves could be considered gardens, and in many instances are referred to as such. Scheindlin posits that the amount of poems that deal with this setting suggest that "the garden in

170 Robinson, *In Praise of Song*, 118–19.

171 An example of one such anthology would be Ibn Khaqān's *Qalāʾid al-ʿIqyān* [Necklace of Rubies].

172 See Robinson, *In Praise of Song*, 70.

spring was a cultural symbol of primary significance."[173]

These interstices between poetry and physical space not only informed the *majlis* itself but at times the very architecture of the palaces where they took place. *Badīʿ*, as a poetics of great metaphorical complexity, is reflected in the rich interlocking designs and vegetal motifs found on the walls of palaces that would have either hosted *majālis* or been influenced by them, both *taifa* and otherwise, as well as physical objects such as the Pamplona Casket depicting the musicians and poet courtiers set in the typical *locus amoenus*—the garden. *Badīʿ* then, as a system for arriving at knowledge, is a garden of verse, the poetry, the guiding aesthetic, and the garden itself.

The Palace

In *majlis* literature, the palace is at times presented as animate, as an entity unto itself, possessing personality. In palace poems or *qaṣrīyāt*, it is often portrayed as a lover or beloved.

The Aljafería—a palace of the Banū Hūd—is one of the best (if not the best) surviving examples of *taifa* architecture and of palatial spaces dedicated to hosting *majālis*. The Aljafería, with its polylobed arcades, rich ornamentation on the walls, vegetal motifs, and limited interior space, is designed to constantly trick the visitor's perception of space. What appears from the outside as a relatively small structure, through its architectural plan, creates the illusion of an infinite paradisiacal world of gardens. The spatiality of the Aljafería is not designed for processions, nor does it contain grand audience halls or mosques typical of buildings constructed with grandiose administrative or political purposes in mind. Rather, it limits movement and induces daydreaming and prolonged contemplation of the filigree on the walls, of the gardens, pools, and ornaments. Furthermore, there are no windows that open up upon outward looking vistas. The Aljafería seems to fold in on itself like two mirrors facing one another.

173 Scheindlin, *Wine*, 4. The importance of flowers and gardens in andalusī society would persist through the centuries. An incredible example can be found in the poetry of Ibn al-Qaysi who, in one of his poems, complains of suffering severe poverty. He states he has no money to buy bread to eat, soap to wash with, or flowers to smell! He regards having flowers to smell as a fundamental human right.

Wine

Your debt to God is righteously to live,
And his to you, your recompense to give.
Do not wear out your days in serving God;
Some time devote to him, some to yourself.
To Him give half your day, to work the rest;
But give the jug no rest throughout the night.
Put out your lamps! Use crystal cups for light.
Away with singers! Bottles are better than lutes.
No song, nor wine, nor friend beneath the sward—
These three, O fools, are all of life's reward.[174]
—Shmuel ha-Nagid

The main activity that took place at the *majlis* was the consumption of wine, accompanied by the singing or recitation of poetry. The *nudamā'* [s. *nadīm*]—or in other words, the participants, or "boon companions"—would recite their poetry to one another while a cupbearer specially trained for the position would ceremonially make their rounds and pour the wine. These poems included panegyrics to their patrons, and poems about wine [*khamrīya*], love [*ghazal*], and beauty in its many forms. If we are to believe the *majlis* anecdotes, improvisational poetic duels, comparable to the rap battles of contemporary times, were also engaged in. These duels included things such as who could improvise the best homonym poem, as well as one poet improvising a line on an object followed by another poet challenged to complete the line.

The *majlis* as socio-cultural institution was identical whether or not the participants were Jews, Muslims, or a mix thereof. Scheindlin writes:

> The practice of wine-drinking—its setting, timing, customary personnel, and entertainment—as described in the Hebrew poetry of the period is identical of that recorded in Arabic sources. It would seem perfectly reasonable to assume that the Hebrew poetry documents a social reality no less than does the Arabic and that the Andalusian Jewish gentry entertained themselves in exactly the same manner as did the Muslim gentry. That some kind of

174 All translations of Hebrew verses in this epistle are by Scheindlin. See Ibid, 47.

> wine-drinking entertainments occurred among the Jews is clear from Maimonides, who speaks of Jewish "elders" and "pious men" attending wine parties at which secular poems in Arabic and Hebrew were sung. It is futile to argue that the language and style of the poetry and the reality they describe are merely a literary fashion copied from Arabic poetry, and that therefore they do not necessarily reflect the experience of the poets.[175]

Indeed, the sheer volume of both the poetry, prose anecdotes and other documents that describe the wine-drinking and other sensual pursuits of the *majlis* are enough to dismiss any arguments that the Jewish courtier-rabbis or their Muslim counterparts were strictly pious and ascetic men dealing in spiritual code words without any layer of literal meaning. As showcased in the poem introducing this section, it appears Shmuel ha-Nagid is advocating that people divide their time in such a way that wine-drinking gets equal if not more precedence to orthodox forms of religious study. In another poem he writes

> If you're like me, and want to pour the wine of joy,
> Hear what I have to say.
> I'll teach you pleasure's way, though you don't want to hear,
> You friend of sighs and pain.
> Five things there are that fill the hearts of men with joy,
> And put my grief to flight:
> A pretty girl, a garden, wine, the water's rush
> In a canal, and song.[176]

I concur with Scheindlin in that the Hebrew wine poems often "seem consciously to defy traditional values by using the language of the synagogue, particularly that of the synagogue preacher in exhorting to the life customarily denounced by the speakers with whom it is traditionally associated."[177] The poem by Moshe ibn Ezra cited above uses language from the Bible giving a further religious feel to this cult of pleasure. "Such a man his sin will bear," as Scheindlin points out, refers to the laws regarding

175 Ibid, 21.

176 Ibid, 51.

177 Ibid, 28.

the Passover offering, and to the fact that he who breaks them will be "cut off from his people" (Cf. Numbers 9:13). Scheindlin observes that "cut off from the community of the service of the rose is our poet's implicit threat to the man who neglects this springtime observance."[178]

Heresy is in the eye of the beholder. While this is true, it does seem evident that the Hebrew and Arabic poets we are discussing were fully aware of the transgressive character of their words and actions. Wine is considered an impure substance and prohibited under traditional Islamic law.[179] The combination of alcohol with music would have been considered even more taboo, due to its prohibition by some Muslim theologians based on the Luqmān and al-Isrā' *suwār* [s. *sūra*] in the Qur'ān. Jewish tradition held similar views. The Iraqi theologian, rabbi, and scholar Hai Gaon wrote:

> As to your question about the legal position of one who, in our time, drinks wine to the accompaniment of music, especially among non-Jews: he is culpable and to be excommunicated, unless he is a courtier and works for the protection of the Jews and trusts himself not to lapse into licentiousness; and unless it is known that at the time of [drinking and listening to music] he is concentrating on the destruction of the Temple, and he is forcing his heart to be sad and not enjoying himself; and unless he listens [to music] only out of deference to the king in order to benefit Israel. For the last hundred years and more there have been in Iraq men in the king's service whom the Rabbis permitted such things.[180]

Courtiers might be excused from such offences, but as we have seen in the poetry of Shmuel ha-Nagid, the wine party is spoken of as something celebratory and joyous, not as lugubrious occasion to bemoan the destroyed Temple while pretending to have fun. The Jews would have had their own *majlis* in their own circles as well, for, if they did not, and the apologists really *are* correct in arguing that the courtier-rabbis only wrote lewd poems about wine and love to please their Muslim patrons, why then did they compose so many of these poems *in Hebrew* when they were perfectly well versed in Arabic? Indeed, as demonstrated above, it is precisely

178 Ibid, 38–39.

179 See the Qur'ān: 4:43. 2:219, 3:90, 5:90–91, 2:219 to give some examples.

180 Scheindlin, *Wine*, 32.

the prolonged contact and intimacy with their Arabic counterparts that gave the courtier-rabbis their literary golden age in the first place.

To provide a few wine-stained examples from some of the Muslim milieu, we have the *fitna* period Ibn Shuhaid, a poet who claimed that one of his compositions made the ghost of infamous Iraqi poet Abū Nuwās cry, and that yet another made him get up and dance.[181] Ibn Shuhaid is also famous for his friendship with Ibn Ḥazm as well as for playing the role of scribe (*kātib*), boon companion (*nadīm*), and minister to *fitna* caliph al-Mustaẓahir. He provides these evocative lines, among many others:

> The most sublime of that which exists among us is suckling at the teat of the glass, with the aroma of the myrtles all 'round us, running along the hem of a breeze's gown as we hunt down drunkenness among the hills, even if they are moments of this world.[182]

Or we could look to Ibn Ḥamdīs, a member of al-Muʿtamid's court in Seville:

> I remember a certain brook that offered the impiety of drunkenness
> to the topers [sitting] along its course, with [its] cups of golden [wine]
> Each silver cup in it filled as though it contained the soul of the sun in the body of the full moon.
> Whenever a glass reached anyone in our company of topers,
> he would grasp it gingerly with his ten fingers.
> Then he drinks out of it a grape-induced intoxication
> which lulls his very sense without his realizing it.
> He sends [the glass] back in the water, thus returning it to the hands of a cupbearer
> at whose will it had [originally] floated [to him].
> Because of the wine bibbing we imagined our song to be melodies which the birds sang without verse,
> While our cupbearer was the water which brought [us wine] without a hand,
> and our drink was a fire that shone without embers,

181 Robinson, *In Praise of Song*, 111.

182 Translation by Ibid, 105.

And which offered us delights of all kinds, while the only reward [of that cupbearer]
for [giving us those delights] was that we offered him to the ocean to drink.
[It is] as if we were cities along the riverbank
while the wine laden ships sailed [the stretch] between us,
For life is excusable only when we walk along the shores of pleasure and abandon all restraint![183]

Or Ibn Bājja, also known as Avempace, a poet famous for his works on astronomy, botany, music, medicine, and philosophy, in this *muwashshaḥ*:[184]

Trail the edge of your robe wherever it pleases,
and add more drunkenness to your intoxication
And light your tinder with a flame
Of silver contained in gold,
Crowned by a string of the pearls of froth,
In the company of a bright-eyed, shining, fresh-lipped one
Whose cup has been filled with wine—a frozen water, a liquid ember.
There the light of dawn has already shone,
While the wind among the flower beds has exuded its fragrance already.
Do not light a lantern in the dark;
Leave it aside and uncover the wine instead
While the tears of the dew flow, and you see the flowers of the garden smiling."[185]

At the root, the *badīʿ* style employed by the *taifa* poet-courtiers is intimately intertwined with the *muʿtazila* heresy. Stetkevych shows how, before it was used to describe a linguistic or literary heresy by its detractors, the "conservative" literary establishment, *badīʿ* was first used to refer to *muʿtazilī* principals of Qurʾānic exegesis. According to *muʿtazilī* thought, God cannot be both man and deity, from which it logically follows that He

183 Translation by Monroe, *Hispano-Arabic Poetry*, (204).

184 Yes, the same Ibn Bājja we met in the *Risāla on Agriculture*.

185 Translation by Monroe, *Hispano-Arabic Poetry*, 284.

cannot be likened to anything in a literal sense. Anthropomorphism in the text should then be interpreted metaphorically or analogically. Therefore, the Qur'ān *cannot* be the eternal Word of God, but is a *created* text, and therefore subject to interpretation.[186]

One commentator, al-Jāḥiẓ, equated the "strange" and "marvellous," qualities of *badīʿ* to the inimitability (*ijāz*) of the Qur'ān, the very attribute used to argue for it being an uncreated text of divine origin. To exponents of the poetics of *badīʿ* the Qur'ān was the perfect example of *badīʿ* in action; Qur'ānic language was therefore thought to be inherently metaphorical, from which meaning could *only* be derived through exegesis. Notably, the time period in which the poetics of *badīʿ* became most developed (late *taifa*) is concurrent with the *bāṭinī* or "hidden" school of exegesis—as opposed to the *ẓāhirī*—becoming popular at *taifa* courts. Not to mention many of the *taifa* poets recorded as regular attendees of various *majālis* were implicated in the *mu'tazilī* heresy. Ibn Bājja, to just give one example, was several times derided as a heretic by al-Fatḥ, compiler of an anthology of *majlis* anecdotes—the *Qalā'id*—as frivolous, silly, and that he "wasted his life drinking and partying and singing frivolous songs." Cynthia Robinson reminds us that Ibn Bājja was a polymath, as mentioned above, with brilliant and influential expertise in philosophy, music, botany, and other subjects, a man who clearly did more than just "pop corks, pinch male bottoms, and sing silly songs."[187]

Nevertheless, the conservative literati loathed the poetic excesses of the *taifa* courtiers. One such reactionist was none other than Ibn Ḥazm, author of the famous work *Ṭawq al-Ḥamāma* [The Necklace of the Dove], a treatise cited by many authors as one of the precursors of the courtly love phenomenon. Courtly love was born in the eleventh century, in *fitna* and *taifa* courts. At least, this is the first time it becomes sponsored in the "official" spheres of court culture, thereby taking on more visibility as well as prestige. Surely the *Ṭawq* would have left some sort of trace among the literature of that period, or in the literature that came afterwards that documented that period. Yet, as Cynthia Robinson notes, nowhere in his anthology does al-Fatḥ mention Ibn Ḥazm or his work, nor does the *Ṭawq* figure in any other anthology of lyric poetry or *ars poetica*. To a staunch

186 See, Robinson, *In Praise of Song*, 150–60.

187 Ibid, 316.

ẓāhirī (in other words, an exponent of the "literalist" school of exegesis) such as Ibn Ḥazm, the lyrical, unreal qualities of *badīʿ* would have likely been anathema. Ibn Ḥazm was, after all, among those who claimed poetry was the language of fiction or lies (*majāz*), and variously lashed out against what he called the "manipulators and torturers of language."[188]

The Cupbearer

In addition to the sovereign, the *nudamāʿ* [boon companions; fellows; participants], and whatever musicians and dancers that may have been present, another key figure associated with the *majlis* was the *sāqī* [the cupbearer]. The *sāqī* was generally an effeminate boy or young man trained in courtly manners to make rounds about the circle and flirtatiously pour the wine for the *nudamāʿ*. He is the loving object, coquettish, gorgeous, intoxicating, and often just beyond reach: *le beau garcon sans merci*. As the beloved, he is often painted by the poets as "the fawn" or "the gazelle." As fresh and sensual as a garden, with a face like the full moon, and eyes two glinting stars beneath heavy lashes, he is a slim branch or willowy trunk, whose saliva is wine and whose glance is devastating. A glance equally provocative of ecstasy and anguish.

Alongside the sovereign, he undoubtedly plays a central role—if not *the* central role—among those that make up the *dramatis personae* of the *majlis*. Wine is a substance that brings enlightenment, that brings knowledge of the unseen, and the cupbearer is the very phantom that broadcasts that divine elixir among the poet-courtiers. Whether consumed in Dionysian revelry, served for the Magi in Zoroastrian paradisiacal lore, glimpsed in Canaanite visions of godly banquets, or indicated in hieroglyphic texts as part of rituals honouring Seth and Horus, wine is an immortal and immortalizing substance. The banquet of immortality and the wine served at it, as Stetkevych illustrates, are liminal in nature and evoke a time out of time, an immortal (no)space. The andalusī *majlis* can certainly fall under the rubric of such a banquet of immortality. The *sāqī*, in serving the wine, takes his place among a long list of liminal figures such as Hermes, Enki, Yūsuf, Thoth, Dionysus, Ganymede, and so on. He is a mediator, the "liminal herm" between clarity and confusion, between meaning and its bastardiza-

188 Ibid, 84.

tion: the hermeneutic tension between text and anti-text.[189]

The poet with his employment of the lyrical "I" was at times cast as the "loving subject" (a role in other instances attributed to the sovereign himself). Through poetry's transformative powers—and the fantastic poetics of *badīʿ* in which the identities of different things melt into each other—the distinction between sovereign and *sāqī*, between lover and beloved, could become (and often did become) quite blurred—as surely as the poet-courtiers dissolved water into their wine. A defining characteristic of the *taifa majlis* is that the sovereign does not watch the festivities, separate from the other celebrants behind some veil or through the window of some chamber. He actively participates alongside the other boon companions and, for the duration of the night, is considered their equal.

Robinson discusses a panegyric composition by Ibn Shuhaid dedicated to one of al-Manṣūr's descendants (ʿAbd al-ʿAzīz al-Muʾtaman) in which a role reversal occurs: the poet assumes the role of the lover and his sovereign is transformed into the "classic full-hipped, delicate waisted and androgynous beloved...accessible to [the poet's] listening pleasure as the tambour sounds, accompaniment to the sweet wine of the king-boy's heavy-lidded, promising glances."[190] Robinson continues:

> Ibn Shuhaid become's the boy's (his patron's?) master, dancing impudently to the notes of his flute before, literally, "jumping him." Proper distance between patron and poet is then, to some degree, restored: the ardent lover does not wrestle the object of his desires to the ground. Then, in line eight, we again find the poet grabbing the silk-clad, perfumed boy with such strength that the latter, in still another rich turning of the tables, obeys, and Ibn Shuhaid becomes his amir, enjoying him in the following line to the limits of licitness.[191]

Additionally, in instances where the sovereign himself is the author of the poem, as in the example below written by al-Mustaẓahir, he himself appears eager to forfeit his power and surrender himself at the feet of the beloved(s), becoming his willing captive:

---

189 See Stetkevych, "Old Wine in a New Bottle."

190 Robinson, *In Praise of Song*, 123–24.

191 Ibid, 123.

> Oh, most wondrous! The lion feared the sharp tip of my spear—
> While I fear the glance from those with languid eyelids.
> So I do battle against (all) terrors, without fear of them,
> Except for (those of) aversion and separation.
> A Trinity [of Graces] has taken over my soul, brilliant faced
> like statues of flesh and blood, tender and went of body!
> Like stars against the darkness they reviled and abused my gaze
> from beneath branches atop dunes.
> This one is the crescent moon, that one, the daughter of Jupiter
> in beauty; and this, the sister of the ban branch.
> With regard to them I summoned insulation to the judge Passion,
> But (Passion) rendered a verdict in favour of a power greater than
> mine.
> So they declared the percent of my heart free for plunder,
> and left me, despite the glory of my kingship, a submissive captive.[192]

Again, I will invoke Robinson's eloquent discussion of these verses:

> Here [al-Mustaẓahir] turns himself into the lovesick lover, slave to languorous glances. His soul is under the absolute dominion of Beauty, as personified by the three classic topoi he names: the crescent moon, the starry heavens, and the slim-waisted ban. He fears no enemy but parting and separation. He is willing (and one would almost say, eager) to be tried and condemned for unnamed and perhaps uncommitted crimes, from within his chosen persona of the lovelorn youth, hoarse with white-hot passion. His kingly glory is freely wasted as he offers up his hands to be tied and bound: the king is captive.[193]

It is also noteworthy that in some instances, the *sāqī* is clearly identified, not just as any boy, but as an *ʿajamī* boy, which is to say, a foreigner. As Robinson shows, through this process, the boy becomes a Boy, the distillation of all Christians into one composite other. He is not only made other, but in his role as the *sāqī* he is a sexually available other. In some instances, due to being cast as unable to speak Arabic, he is mute. His inability to speak robs him of his agency, allowing the Muslim boon companions to

192 Translation by Ibid, 123–24.

193 Ibid, 124.

dominate him as they will. This eroticization of the enemy reduced the threat or danger posed by Christianity into a sexual object. Also it allowed the Muslims to justify their at times intimate and friendly interactions with their neighbours to the North. In another anecdote, Ibn Shahīd from the court at Almería eroticizes Christian *loci* (which, incidentally, is another reoccurring *topos*) describing a certain monastery as a debauched place of orgy, pork-eating, and wine drinking, where the monks, pimped by their own priest (as Robinson puts it), offer themselves up as steeds to be ridden by the Muslim carousers, who happily join in on the pork, wine, and song-singing.[194]

While it is clear that there are politics at play in this literary belittling by the Muslim poets of their Christian neighbours, there also seem to be more layers of meaning to be explored. In one of the anecdotes discussed by Robinson, written by Ibn ʿAmmār, one idyllic paradisiacal day, the Hūdī sovereign al-Mu'taman and his company are out looking for a perfect place to hold a *majlis*. The *sāqī* (who is an *ʿajam*, a foreigner, likely Christian) exclaims, "this is it!" In exchange for his discovery of the ideal *locus amoenus*, al-Mu'taman cedes to him full control over the entire gathering, and declares all should follow the boys orders. Robinson continues: "With the boy... safely confined to his position as scantily clad *sāqī*, scandalously intimate embraces become safe, even licit, ones, and al-Mu'taman and his... company can, as submissive captives before the Boy's deadly beauty, effectively and in a startling twist of collective cultural fantasy, give themselves over into the hands of the enemy."[195]

There are some accounts of the *sāqī* being female, but they are the exception, and this reinforces that as a rule they were male. However, a female playing the role of a boy does put further emphasis on the gender ambiguity that the *sāqī* seems to embody. Although we know of some thirty or forty female poets (some of whom, such as the infamous Umayyad princess Wallāda, were known to have their own literary salons); and although during the *fitna* women appear to have been present at the *majlis* beyond the usual "dancing girls" or "singing girls" mentioned by the poets, the official court-sponsored *majlis* of the *taifa* period appears to have been a largely homosocial institution.

---

194 Ibid, 338–39.

195 Ibid, 385. This anecdote was mentioned earlier in *Risāla on the Inner and the Outer*.

In his examination of dreambooks from the medieval Islamic world, Steven M. Oberhelman shows that the sexual hierarchy was based on penetration, rather than necessarily the "heterosexual" over the "homosexual."[196] Generally, men could penetrate other men, in practice if not in theory, provided the penetratee was of a lower class than the penetrator. In this kind of "phallocracy," the appearance of an erect phallus in dreams embodied power and virility, whereas the limp foretold misfortune. If two men were caught having sex, the penetrator would typically be punished much less than the penetratee (if at all). The reverse was the case for women, in which the penetrator would have been punished more than the penetratee, due to her upsetting of gender expectations. These same politics of penetration featured in heterosexual relations: a man might zealously guard his wives and female family members from other "predatory" men so as not to have his honour tarnished, yet hypocritically, his committing the same predations on women outside of his family made him more of a man, more virile, more powerful. The *taifa* poet courtiers and sovereigns, in offering themselves up to be dominated by their beloveds, at the whim of men lower down on the pecking order than themselves, (young men, and slaves to boot), through poetry, upset the established hierarchies of gender, ideology and power.[197]

While the particulars of laws and punishments have varied throughout time and space, homosexual acts are clearly proscribed in both Jewish and Muslim tradition. As Wright points out, the Qur'ān condemns the people of Lot in 7:80–84; and 26:165–73 reads:

> What, do you come to male beings, leaving your wives that your Lord created for you? Nay, but you are a people of transgressors.' They said, 'If thou gives not over, Lot, thou shalt assuredly be one of the expelled.' He said, 'Truly I am a detester of what you do. My Lord, deliver me and my people from what they do.' So We delivered him and his people all together, save an old woman among those that tarried; then We destroyed the others, and We rained on

196 Likewise, Jame T. Monroe demonstrates that without any word for homosexual in Arabic, the concepts of "heterosexual" and "homosexual" did not exist. See Monroe, "The Striptease that was Blamed..." 115–16.

197 Again, see Oberhelman, "Hierarchies of Gender, Ideology, and Power in Medieval Greek and Arabic Dream Literature."

them a rain; and evil is the rain of them that are warned.

Wright also cites the following two *aḥādīth* [s. *ḥadīth*] which ominously declare:

> "Whenever a male mounts another male the throne of God trembles, the angels look down in loathing and say, 'Lord, why do you not command the earth to punish them, and the heavens to rain stones upon them?' And: "Whomsoever you find committing the act of the people of Lot, kill both the active and the passive partner."[198]

The Hebrew Bible makes similar condemnations: in Leviticus 18:22, "Thou shalt not lie with mankind as with woman kind; it is detestable," and Leviticus 20:13, "And if a man lie with mankind as with womankind: they shall surely be put to death; they have committed a detestable act and their blood shall be upon them."

Despite that, in light of the platonic and neoplatonic thought in vogue for both members of the Muslim and Jewish elite, alongside other various mystical inclinations, we can see the poets appearing to be searching after beauty in diverse forms, and the gender ambiguity of the *sāqī* can suggest a platonic coming together of disparate parts. Reminiscence. The soul made complete. Furthermore the *sāqī*'s reconciliation of gender opposites, and his flirtatious dynamic with the sovereign or patron—when cast as the beloved—can suggest a unified soul in a state of flow and flux from the Source.

The wine itself can also be read in a similar way. The wine the courtiers drank was typically mixed with water, which would have held the double function of allowing them to achieve a milder and more prolonged intoxication in a liminal state between sleep and vigil throughout the course of the night, as well as serving as an apt symbol of two differing substances coming together: the fire of the wine, wedded to the temperance of water. Also, references in the poems to the wine being pressed from the cheeks of the *sāqī* and so on are reminiscent of Dionysus or Jesus. The wine and the youthful vim of the *sāqī* are immortalizing. Wine flows from his lips. The *sāqī* himself can be thought of then as a fountain of youth.

198 Wright, "Masculine Allusion," 1–24.

One might read these motifs subtly expressed by the Hebrew poets as well. Yehuda ha-Levi wrote "Once when I fondled him upon my thighs/ He caught his own reflection in my eyes/ And kissed my eyes, deceitful imp;/ I knew It was his image he kissed and not my eyes!"[199] Moshe ibn Ezra also provides many examples: "All night he made love to me/ At his mouth he suckled me," or, "He offered his lips and I drank of their wine," and, in a clear self-aware blend of the profane and sacred, "Why do they want to discourage me, why?/ What in the world is the sin if I thrill to your beauty/ There's Adonai!"[200]

This line—"There's Adonai!"—as well as the last few verses of Moshe ibn Ezra's poem that opens this section contain Biblical references. As Scheindlin makes clear, "There's Adonai!" is the last line in the book of Ezekiel and refers to the prophet's vision of Jerusalem. In another poem, Moshe ibn Ezra writes:

> Caress a lovely woman's breast by night
> And kiss some beauty's lips by morning light...
>
> Immerse your heart in pleasure and in joy.
> And by the bank a bottle drink of wine,
> Enjoy the swallows chirp and viol's whine.
> Laugh, dance, and stamp your feet upon the floor!
> Get drunk, and knock at dawn on some girl's door.
>
> This is the joy of life, so take your due.
> You too deserve a portion of the Ram Of Consecration, like your people's chiefs.
> To suck the juice of lips do not be shy,
> But take what's rightly yours—the breast and thigh![201]

199 Scheindlin, *Wine*, 122.

200 Ibid, 103, 97.

201 Scheindlin, *Wine*, 91. While, then as now, there were Jewish attitudes towards women that are extremely problematic, the interesting feature of this poem is the way it plays with several direct quotes and *topoi* from the Hebrew Bible, and

The verses including "The Ram of Consecration" and the "breast and thigh" are allusions to the ram that was sacrificed in the ritual in which "Aaron and his sons were consecrated as priests, and because of special rituals involving [the ram's] breast and right thigh, the phrase 'the breast of the wave-offering' and 'thigh of the heave offering' recur with refrain like regularity in the biblical chapters describing the ceremony.'"[202] I will add to Scheindlin's commentary that this can suggest a kind of sexual initiation, as well as the innate holiness of the human body; another heresy. Scheindlin posits that Moshe ibn Ezra "has transformed the biblical account of the consecration of the priests into a secular fantasy of induction into a radically different elite... the courtier class, the privileged devotees of beauty."[203]

Despite the aforementioned condemnations of wine and homosexual acts in both Jewish and Muslim orthodoxies, a seeming paradox arises when in some instances, the Qur'ān seems to maintain the sacrality of wine, and to place a high value on male beauty. In some *aḥādīth* [s. *ḥadīth*], God is depicted as a beautiful male youth. Yūsuf is another figure renowned for his overwhelming beauty. Wright, following Stetkevych's lead, cites the following *ayāt* from the Qur'ān:

> Surrounding them will be (male) youths to serve them in their perpetual freshness, with goblets, shining beakers, and cups filled from flowing fountains. (56:17)
>
> And they (the male cupbearers) will be with beautiful big, and lustrous eyes; like well-guarded pearls. A reward for the deeds of life. (56:22)
>
> Upon them will be green robes of fine silk and they will be adorned with bracelets of silver and their lord will give them to drink wine which is pure and holy. (71:20)

With regard to wine, while the earthly liquor is clearly proscribed as

subverts them along the way.

202 Ibid, 95.

203 Ibid, 95.

demonstrated above, the Qur'ān seems to celebrate its heavenly counterpart with references to "rivers of wine" (47:15), "sealed wine" (83:22), wine served to the Lord (12:41) and "wine that causes no throbbing brows, no intoxication" (56:18). The message is, however lovely the sensual joys on earth may be, they are ephemeral, and to forgo them in favour of the pleasures of the afterlife is the correct choice to make.[204]

Stetkevych draws the interesting link between the immoral and the immortal: what is immoral on earth is immortal and immortalizing in Paradise. Wine, alongside eroticism and poetry, is forbidden due to its association with pagan cultic practices. Let's not forget the Qur'ān was repeatedly at pains to refute the Prophet was a poet (Cf. 21:5, 36:69, 37:36, 52:30, 64:41). Poets are vilified in 26:224–26, considered "those likely to be led into error." Poetry is the anti-text to the Qur'ān's text. The *mu'allaqāt* or "standing odes," with their poetics of ritual, hearken back to the pagan blasphemies and allegedly "barbarous" days before the advent of Islam. Yet, despite its eagerness to disassociate itself from poetry, the Qur'ān references poetry for its own validation. There is a symbiotic relationship between text and anti-text. Wright sums up the paradox: "... when asked to prove that his revelations are sacred, Muhammad recites verse 52:30–34 and challenges the poets to create anything more beautiful; the scripture's authority is both confirmed in its beauty and subverted by its need to compete with poetry."[205]

The *sāqī*, then, is the shadow player whose dancing silhouette is painted upon the veil that separates sacred from profane. He is the "liminal herm," control over whom is sought by both orthodox and heterodox theorists. As Wright asserts,

> Men who associate with, gain control over, or subvert the authority of the "liminal" bearer of the message/liquid... conquer the vicissitudes of time... this gives pursuit of the male sāqī utmost textual importance... the Mu'tazila used this cognitive paradox to escape the anthropomorphism entrapment of literal readings of revelation; the Shī'a used it, albeit only for a short time, to see imaginative rather than dogmatic meaning in Qur'ānic verses, the Isma'ilis used textual ambiguity to justify their militarism; the Sufis

204 See Wright, "Masculine Allusion," 1-24.

205 Ibid, 4.

> used the paradox when forming allegorical and anagogic mystical notions and rituals.[206]

We can add that the *taifa* poet-courtiers used it in planting the first seeds of the rituals and ethos of what would come to be known as "courtly love." The *sāqī* in his Yūsuf-esque role as interpreter, negotiator, clarifier and mystifier between the realms of sleeping and waking, dream and vigil, the fantastic and factual, sober and ecstatic, holds in his cups the liquid key, that *aqua vitae* red as the dawn, between concrete truth and the suggestive "*and if....*"

In conjuring this brief shadow of the *sāqī*, I want to make it clear that I am aware that homoeroticism in Arabic literature, in al-Andalus as well as the wider Islamic world, throughout history, has been subject to both homophobic as well as homophilic sensationalism, often made by Orientalists who take the homoerotic motifs out of context. An example of this would be to take infamous poets such as Abū Nuwās solely at face value without looking at how cleverly he himself was able to take control of the "liminal herm" and use homoerotic motifs to subvert religious and political tyranny, often by subtly exposing the hypocrisies of both. In Arabic literature, the meaning of these *topoi* goes beyond sex, song, and drink, and is more than mere debauched buffoonery.

However, in the *taifa* court context, the poet-courtiers made up the elite, and their sovereigns themselves were among those writing homoerotic poetry, so while the love lyrics they wrote were surely full of political implications (for example, the aforementioned political ties formed through "courtly love" and "noble friendship," as well as the "courtly persona" being adopted as an alternative rhetoric to the typical legitimist claims to the caliphate), the dominant political institutions of the day were tolerant of and even, it seems at times, celebrated homoeroticism.

The subversive element of the poems is not in their satire of the sovereign and his court, but in the way they self-consciously defy the more orthodox and legalist trends in Jewish and Muslim traditions, in al-Andalus and beyond. The sexual preference and love-affairs of many andalusī sovereigns (who kept eunuchs and slave-boys for pleasure), as well as that of many prominent figures, is well documented, further affirming that the homoerotic motifs may record more than mere literary convention or political satire.

Commenting on the sexual preference(s) of the poets is not done to glo-

206 Ibid, 4.

rify or vilify them, nor to judge the artistic merit of their works based upon those preferences, but to weave into the "master narrative" of history those details that often get glossed over. For a historian, and even more so for an Arabist, there is nothing new or out of the ordinary about the wide-spread homoerotic motifs in Arabic literature. However, for most of those with little or no background in these subjects, to learn that illustrious Jewish rabbis or Muslim *kuttāb* sang of wine, death, and men, and were at times each others bedfellows, patrons, protégés, and colleagues, may be a powerful revelation that challenges many commonly held assumptions and biases.

The fact that certain cultural heroes painted by the "master narrative" to be strictly orthodox and exemplary religious role-models wrote markedly heterodox poetry, poetry that could at times be an accurate showcase of their own beliefs, preferences and actions, is something very unsettling for those whose identities and politics are based around the roles these figures play as ancestors, as predecessors to what makes them who they are.

Take Yehuda ha-Levi for example, a cultural hero often depicted as a "proto-zionist," and therefore a hero of Zionist ideology. The fact that he was a devout Jew and went on pilgrimage to Palestine is used to argue for the overly lachrymose telling of andalusī history, that the Jews were always unhappy living alongside Muslims and Christians, and that—if his appropriators even mention it all—it may be true that he wrote songs on love and wine, but that's all fair and well because he later denounced the way of life he led in al-Andalus after setting off on his pilgrimage. Is this really the case, or was his decision to leave related to the restrictions and intolerances imposed by growing Almoravid hegemony? Because he knew that things were taking a turn for the worst and that the lyrical world of the *taifa* kings had reached an omega?

The Flower of the Moon

> Oh how many nights have you ripped
> away the veil of darkness with the
> help of a wine sparkling like a star![207]
>
> —Ibn as-Sīd

Some scholars draw too bold a line between "religious" and "secular" literature. On the one hand, classifying andalusī literature as purely "religious" (i.e. Islamic) has served as justification for excluding it from the canon of "European" literature at large.[208] On the other hand, classifying andalusī literature as purely "secular" has served to trivialize it. As a result of this trivialization, the deeper meanings of many a text have fallen through the cracks of a one-dimensional exegesis.

Despite those studies that have read the *majlis* literature through a purely "secular" lens, it is clear that the *majlis* was at times approached as a medium by which one could reach philosophical epiphany and mystical union.

My approach to the concept of mysticism is formal, rather than historical. Whether or not the *nudamā'* should be classified solely as mystics, philosophers, a mix or a lack thereof, is irrelevant. Many of these men were polymaths and engaged in a number of different grammars in their pursuit of knowledge. To see the mystical truth inherent in one's writing, especially within a larger context of ritual and gesture does not require one to have seen that author explicitly write in some document "I am a Sufi" or "I am a mystic," or to have been described as such by others.

Regardless, in the case of the Jews, we do know that some of the works of the poets we have discussed were instrumental, or at least influential, in the emergence of the Kabbalah a few centuries later. Shlomo ibn Gabirol, for example, was oft cited by Kabbalistic writers of the thirteenth century. In the case of the Muslims, it is highly likely that mystic Ibn al-'Arīf was one of the men who educated poets at the court in Zaragoza we examined, possibly even Ibn Bājja himself. To further connect star to star, the same Ibn al-

---

207 Robinson, *In Praise of Song*, 232.

208 What are the implications for "Europe" if we were to include works of "Islamic" literature as part of its cultural heritage?

ʿArīf is cited several times in the works of that most famous and celebrated of andalusī mystics: Ibn ʿArabī.

As we shall see, in many cases, the thought and divine diction between figures described as philosophers, poets, and mystics only finds its difference in methodology, whether ascetic and/or sensual. Even then, the differences are often slight. The *majlis* poets would, to some extent, have been considered heretics not only by the religious and legal orthodox, but by some of the more ascetically minded mystics as well as some of the more strictly rational philosophers. Scholarship loves the neatly defined categories, loves the smooth narrative: if it is unable to clearly define someone, it will usually, based on its own ideology, categorize them as it sees fit. Lamentably, this is the fate our poet-courtiers have suffered until fairly recently in much of the literature on the subject. This is an injustice: it is to force the voluptuous contours of their song onto painfully rigid examination tables.

Robinson describes how the palace known as the "Aljafería" in Zaragoza—where, as we have mentioned, many a *majlis* likely took place—was probably detailed after the cosmology of poet and philosopher Ibn as-Sīd.[209] The ornamental and architectural program of the Aljaferia has striking similarities with aspects of Ibn as-Sīd's philosophy, with its near omnipresent depictions of "incomplete" or "half" circles, at both the macro and micro levels, where "the pattern of the whole [is] reproduced in the pattern of the parts."[210] An idea applied to the structure of the cosmos, according to *bāṭinī* thinkers.

It is probable that the philosopher, himself one of the poem-singing, wine-drinking *nadīm* that made up the *majlis* of the Hūdī court at Zaragoza, was responsible for or the inspiration behind the palace being designed as it was. Robinson writes about how the salon would have been meant to draw the eye of the *nadīm* [pl. *nudamāʾ*] along certain verses inscribed on the walls, to alight on the vegetation, to then pick up the trail of other verses in other parts of the wall in a particular way, all the while contemplating the geometric complexities of the stucco carvings, in order to convey some

209 For this section, see Ibid, 173–236.

210 Ibid, 207.

kind of message or truth. In this way, as we shall see, the *majlis* becomes "an analogical portal to the seven heavens."[211] Along the intricate ornamentation upon the walls, the eyes of the *nadīm* would come to rest on "flower-points," prominent floral designs which can be considered points of origin, and also points of regression, from which the lines that make up the patterns ascend from and recede to "The Cause of All Causes."

Ibn as-Sīd's philosophy is complex, as is the architecture and ornament that expresses it in the Aljafería. Without going into too much detail, Robinson's paraphrasing of the philosopher's work the *Ḥadā'iq* will be useful here to provide some context:

> For Ibn al-Sīd [sic], creation itself is a potentially endless series of interlocking, imaginary (*wahmīya*) circles which exist in *analogous*, proportional relationships. Man himself exists in the 'image' (*ṣūra*) of a circle, as does his intellect and the larger intellect from which, through emanation, the collective human intellect of which each of us possesses part derives its powers of reason and perception. Each of the imaginary circles, too, like the particular level of creation *analogous* to it, begins at the same point to which it finally returns, having first passed through a process of emanation in which each of the elements or numbers which compose it is derived from the one which precedes it. There are nine concentric circles, each of which corresponds to one of the numerals ranging from one to nine. Each of these circles, though is in fact infinite in the number of numbers it could potentially contain. The second circle corresponds to the number two, and also contains 20, 200, 2000, 20,000, and so on; the third circle corresponds to the number three, and comprises 30, 300, 3000, etc. The sequences, says Ibn al-Sīd, continue to reproduce themselves up to the very end of existence (*wujūd).*
>
> Ibn al-Sīd then states that the analogical system of concentric circles upon which the universe and knowledge of it is constructed is itself analogous to the relationships which exist in the realm of numbers. Their arrangement, in turn, through its illustration of the principles of emanation and *talwīḥ* (metonymy; e.g., the

211 Ibid, 227–36.

> inclusion of 2000 and 200,000 in the concept of the number Two), reflects, or represents in analogical fashion... the process of emanation through which all realms of the universe, from the nine circles of the heavens down to the most insignificant leaf, are brought into being. Between the number One in its perfection and indivisibility, and the number Three, multiple, divided and imperfect, exists Two. By necessity, Three's only path to the perfection of One is through the mediation of the still-imperfect and divided realm of Two, just as Five requires the mediation of Four to reach the relatively greater perfection and unity of Three.
>
> Each level of existence, and each of the bodies or substances it contains, then, is dependent upon the level, body, or thing whose coming into existence... has immediately preceded its own. Each one is the direct cause of that immediately below it, and has in turn been caused by the one above it. All of creation, then, exists in a state of mediation through (*tawassuṭ*, a fundamental concept to Ibn al-Sīd's cosmology) that which is immediately above it and mediates, in its turn, the existence of that which is immediately below it. As Ibn al-Sīd states: "the existence... of the furthest of them [from God] is not possible without the existence... of the closest of them [to Him]..." At the end of this passage, the philosopher clarifies for his reader that all of this has been explained "*lā 'alā-l-ḥaqīqa*," but through analogy, the best way in which the universe may be comprehended.[212]

Robinson proceeds to show how the arcades of the Aljafería also mirror this chain of emanation and mediation; the arcades flow out from the super-structure of the whole palace; each of their arches' multiple lobes mediates the existence of the next lobe, in that the third lobe is impossible without the second, and so on. The Aljafería reconstructs the cosmos through emanation and mediation.

According to the ontology of Ibn as-Sīd (with clear neoplatonic precedents), reality is divided between matter [*mādda*] and that which is free from association with matter [*mujarrada min al-mādda*], or in other words, the Intelligibles, that can only be perceived by the *nafs al-nāṭiqa*, or

212 Ibid, 209–11.

"the rational soul." The world of matter exists within time [*zamān*], whereas the Intelligibles exist beyond time [*dahr*].

Between the celestial and sub-celestial, we encounter the moon. The moon occupies its own heaven, *falak al-qamr*, a heaven it shares with the stars. The position of the moon between the bodies above it that are *'aqlī*, or "of the intellect," and *hayūlī*, "primary material" to be perceived with the "senses" [*maḥsūs*] is exactly that of humanity itself. Like the moon, humans have a foot in each world. They possess a soul, but theirs is (or at least parts of it are) bound to their bodies. Likewise, the moon, is both of matter and divorced from it. The rational intellect of the human soul must rise above the moon and continue in its ascent, contemplating each of the succeeding levels in their turn, until uniting with the Universal Intellect, The One. To Ibn as-Sīd, this is the unique destiny of man below the moon.

The Universal Intellect is analogous to a circle that surrounds the starry net that in turn surrounds the earth. Through the process of emanation and mediation described above, the human intellect—also analogous to a circle—contains something of God's intellect and can therefore aspire to unite with it. However, the soul cannot ascend without an emanation downward and outward of the Universal Intellect's divine light. The human soul is gifted with a further uniqueness in that it is able to look both up and down the ladder of existence, whereas the rest of sub-lunar creation can only look down. These other lower levels would include: animals, plants, pure metals, jewels, and the "four corners" [*al-arkān al-arba'*]: earth, air, fire, and water.

Not only can the human soul look up and down, it *must* look both up and down. If it is unable to comprehend the "natural sciences," ascent is impossible. The soul first journeys down into the heart of matter, (what many have deemed Hell), in order to then rise up, receive the divine light emanating downward from the Universal Intellect, the divine light that transforms and transubstantiates it into a *mu'qūlāt*, an intelligible "capable of comprehending others like it."[213]

Notably it is the "vegetal soul" or *nafs al-nabātīya* that gives the rational intellect its first foothold in its ascent upward, as vegetation is considered the lowest level of matter to have a soul, to have "a basis other than natural." To Ibn as-Sīd, the soul works like this: the vegetal soul acquires attributes of the animal soul that are imprinted [*muṣawwar*] onto it, the animal soul ac-

213 Ibid, 217.

quires attributes of the human soul that are imprinted onto it, the human soul can then acquire attributes of a "philosopher's soul" or "prophet's soul" that are imprinted onto it. One can deduce that the soul of a philosopher, like perhaps the soul of a poet, is a "tattoo" or imprint upon the very soul. Another delightful attribute of the vegetal soul, according to our philosopher, is that it takes pleasure in its own existence.[214]

The visual experience of one of the poet courtiers at the Aljafería mirrors the ascent of his own soul. He begins with a point, a unity, analogous to the number One in Ibn as-Sīd's thought, then proceeds to a line, from a line to a plane, and from a plane to a body. His own soul is rooted in the "vegetal soul," in the luscious vegetation and vegetal motifs that surround him, that cry out for his prolonged contemplation. His gaze climbs along the dense vegetal and geometric designs to contemplate the dome-like forms so suggestive of stars and moons, that accent the Aljaferia's net of lace-like ornament. Between the fractal of the gardens and the unity of the heavens we find the aforementioned flower-points, the rosettes from which lines emerge, and to which they recede. The moon, as touchstone between spirit and matter, can be taken itself as a kind of flower-point. A knot in the warp and weft of destiny; a mystic rose emerging from, and disappearing into, the leafy vine-tendril tangle of the bower of the night sky.[215]

There is a text by one of the Hūdī sovereigns, Aḥmad II al-Mustaʿīn ibn Hūd—which lamentably has not survived—titled *The Book of Perception and Optical Illusions*. For both the Hūdī sovereigns as well as their entourage of poet (and philosopher) courtiers there is an obsession with optics, with perception, and spatiality. The emphasis in the poems and treatises on poetics and philosophy alike is on "*seeing*" things. It is through the visual commands of *imagine*, or *you see*, *you gaze*, *I hallucinated*, and so on, made by various *taifa* poets when dealing with the verdant paradisiacal world of their *majlis* and its borderline illicit similarities with the Qur'ānic equivalent, that paradise is evoked in the here and now. This is also, paradoxically, the nowhere (everywhere) and never (always).

Ultimately for Ibn as-Sīd, the ascent begins with visual contemplation, first with the physical eye, but one must close their eyes in order to divorce their soul from matter and journey through the heavens: one must see with

214 Ibid, 222 n. 89.

215 Ibid, 176–236.

the heart. In this way, while the animating force of the music, wine, and poetry brought stone to life, made the vines of the vegetal ornament shiver, made owls and other night birds appear from out of the abstract geometric shapes, one could complete the semi-circles of the Aljafería—those semi-circles so important to Ibn as-Sīd—made into full circles in the eye of their hearts.

Another common motif that surfaces with some frequency in the *majlis* literature is the association with the creation of poetry and rhymed prose with the working of precious metals such as gold and silver. We find this association clearly drawn in an *ars poetica* contemporaneous to the *Badīʿ* titled *Sirr al-Adab wa-Sabk adh-dhahab* [The Secret of Belle Lettres and Gold Working]. Its author, Ibn Burd al-Asghar, speaks of the "ordering of words" in the "most eloquent [fashion], from which are created interwoven clusters (ta'qīd); we melt down verse into little trickling streams, then we mould (rhymed) prose into jewels of mother-of-pearl. "[216]

In this way, the poet is cast as silversmith. In some cases they actually were silversmiths or the sons of silversmiths such as Ibn Rashīq and Ibn Bājja, who, in many sources is known not as Ibn Bājja, but as Ibn al-Sā'igh, "Son of the Silversmith." It is through this metaphorical collusion between poets and silversmiths, verse as silver working, the creation of the charmed world of the *majlis* both temporal and physical as working silver, that the silver light of the moon is wrought by the poet into a vehicle by which he may fly beyond it.[217] In one of his treatises Ibn as-Sīd himself defended poetry as a worthy medium through which to convey philosophical epiphany. It is as twentieth century Palestinian poet Mahmoud Darwish wrote in his "Phases of Anat,": "poetry is our ladder to the moon."[218]

The *majlis*, that lyric garden of moonlight, that palace of the heart, is both the wings on which the poet-courtiers fly, as well as the point from

---

216 Translation by Ibid, 192.

217 Robinson writes: "Perhaps, if the nadīm in question was Ibn Bājja, when he looked up from his position in the garden, or from the generous shade of the Northern Salon's depths, at the stunning intricacies of the arcade at the southern limit of the patio, he thought of a brooch, an earring or a necklace over which his fingers had once laboured, remembering its knots, its interlace, its melding and moulding, as his eyes followed an arcade on its path back toward its point of origin, as his ears and heart absorbed the intricacies of a well-wrought ghazal." See Ibid, 193.

218 Darwish, *The Adam of Two Edens*, 97.

which they may take flight. In the *majlis* literature, the vines of the language of the frondous garden of the *badīʿ* style interweaves the themes of the *khamrīya* and *ghazal*, of wine and love lyrics, with a wealth of celestial terminology and allusions. The poets situate the *majlis* in the exact level that the moon occupies, both of matter and beyond it. In this way, it is a portal to the seven heavens. The *majlis* lies right below the stars that whirl above, and by metonymy the entire universe is invoked.

Both *sāqī* and sovereign are likened to the moon. Whether halo, cupped hands, or moon-cheek, the string of voluptuous lunar imagery whispers of the *sāqī* as silver bearer of the divine light that flows down from above. At times the *nudamāʾ* are described as constellations or stars, and the rounds that the *sāqī* makes in dispensing the wine, as well as the rounds of poem-singing and rhymed-prose reciting the *nudamāʾ* engage in, suggest the orbits of celestial bodies.

The *majlis* literature is also rife with references to night journeys and allusions to the nocturnal journey of the Prophet through the seven heavens—the *masran* and the *miʿraj*, respectively. The night journey, or night flight through the seven heavens, is also a *topos* employed in Sufi literature. These signal terms, alongside *fanāʾ*, or in other words "annihilation of the soul" (a word derived from the root 'f-n-ā' [ف ن ى] that can be translated as "to perish," "to cease to exist," or "to undergo obliteration" that also shows up with relative frequency in the *majlis* literature) point us toward further possibilities for mystical interpretation of the *taifa majlis* and court culture. Once one achieves that desired-for state—whether philosophical unity or mystical annihilation—the means become unimportant. The poets fly on "the wings of lovesickness," on the rim of their goblets, or on the lute strings: this is courtly love emerging from a mystical and philosophical ferment.

And it is not just the wine, food, drink, perfumes, the voices of the singers, the garden or the palace itself that are vehicles to arrive at, symbols for, or (no)spaces where the mystical experience is enacted. It is language itself. Can we say language really exists if it is not uttered? The breath of the speaker substantiates the words of a language, and thereby the reality that those words entail. In this way we are reminded of part of Ibn ʿArabī's telling of creation, in which the breath of The Compassionate substantiates the many names of God. And not unlike that later mystic, the poetry of the *majlis* can certainly at times fall under the rubric of a "mystical language of unsaying."

Indeed, apophasis is a prominent and striking characteristic of the discourse employed by our poets. The struggles with the duality of language, the bitter-sweet paradoxes, and the negations upon negations that will only ever let us grasp the cloak's hem (yet the mirror is polished none-the-less) are all present in lesser to greater extents throughout the *majlis* literature. The poets of the *taifa majlis* are clearly mystics of language. Not just in the style of the *Sefer Yetzirah* or the later Kabbalah that would emerge in Provenza and Catalonia, or because the Hebrew and Arabic languages are considered holy in and of themselves, but due to their poetics. We can call them mystics of language in the same way Luis de Góngora—that dark angel of the Spanish baroque—has been called a mystic of language.

The way *badīʿ* style poetics is alleged to work (or happen), is strikingly similar to typical accounts of how one is to arrive at mystical experience, and to what happens once one arrives, across many different cultures and time periods. The poet and silversmith Ibn Ra<u>sh</u>īq thoroughly discusses *badīʿ* in his treatise *al-ʿUmdah fi mahāsin a<u>sh</u>-<u>sh</u>iʿr wa-adabih*. He justifies the predilection of *badīʿ* for fantastic untruth by arguing that *majāz* [fiction] can be more appropriate than *ḥaqīqa* [truth] and that it "gives more pleasure to the ears and heart."[219] The *istiʿāra* technique—which can be considered a complex and often outlandish metaphorical comparison—is said to create pleasure in the souls of both the listener and the metaphor's creator.

Another technique, the *i<u>sh</u>āra*, can be considered the *istiʿāra* pushed to the extreme. This truly profound type of metaphor is considered the most noble, for through the superb manner in which the poet has crafted his words, all difference between two very different things or ideas is erased, allowing for the establishment of perfect harmony. In other words, the most noble technique in the arsenal of *badīʿ* is a metaphorical comparison that provokes a polishing of the mirror.

Ibn Rashīq continues to explain how *bayān* (the precise moment in which the meaning of a metaphorical construction is revealed), leads to *idrāk* (deep understanding). A metaphorical comparison combined with *bayān* "brings what is dark and obscure into the light." Ibn Rashīq refers to "an unveiling of meaning," while quoting ar-Rimānī, "so that the soul

219 Ibid, 154.

(*nafs*) comprehends without the aid of the intellect (*ʿaql*)." He specifies that his process takes place in the hearer's heart. Furthermore, the metaphor must not be so complex that it requires exegesis in order to be understood. The affect of an exquisitely wrought metaphor [*ishāra*], is described as "a daring flash of brilliance produced by the instantaneous comprehension of the listener." Ibn al-ʿArīf might have disapproved of the methodology of the *taifa* courtiers based on the grounds that (according to him) a true mystic needs no mediator, not even poetry, to arrive at knowledge. Yet, the way meaning is conveyed in *badīʿ* style poetics, from spoken comparison to the ears of the listener to revelation of meaning to flash of understanding in the heart and soul, as stated above, requires no exegesis, nor does it need to be explained. Indeed, it *shouldn't* be explained. Rather, it is an accident, an inoculation; it happens in the wink of an eye.[220]

While the blurring of the lines between the sacred and the profane has been briefly discussed above in a literary context, the vines of this *topos* also snaked out of the poetry to physically cover the walls of the Aljafería. According to Robinson, the Aljaferia can be divided into two axes. The north-south axis comprises both salons with the patio-garden between them. Its program of meaning, as well as the uses to which its spaces would have been applied, consists of "pleasures, performance, literary and visual ornament." The east-west axis, on the other hand, was much more sparsely ornamented: its architectural design did not employ the same sort of complexities reminiscent of *badīʿ* and Ibn as-Sīd's philosophy to the same extent as did the north-south. This second axis ran from western portal to mosque portal, and included the oratory. Several inscriptions of eschatological verses from the Qur'ān ran along the walls pertaining to this axis: Victory: 1–5, The Cattle: 59–62, and most importantly Sovereignty 1–14. These verses are concerned with *jihād*, and the admittance of believers into paradise. The term revelation appears in Victory: 1–5 and as Robinson reminds us "may carry apocalyptic connotations of God removing the veils between himself and humanity in order to reveal himself."[221] She identifies this, as well as the term "paradise," as key to the program of meaning on this axis.

The east-west axis seems to be at odds with the program of meaning along the north-south axis, but there are several nexus points, and indeed, there is a

220 On this subject see, Ibid, 150–60.

221 Ibid, 251.

symbiotic relationship between them: each is dependent on the other.

First: the *topos* of the garden (allusions to leafy greenery, etc.) is more or less present in all of the verses, linking the immortal gardens of Qur'ānic paradise alluded to in the verses inscribed along the east-west axis to the earthly paradise of the physical gardens, sensual pleasures, and poetry (recited and sung) along the north-south axis.

Second, verses 59–62 from "The Cattle" are repeated twice, both along the east-west axis as well as within the oratory itself, as well as in Ibn as-Sīd's treatise, *Ḥadā'iq*:

> He has the keys to all that is hidden; none knows them but He. He has the knowledge of all that land and sea contain: every leaf that falls is known to Him. There is no grain of soil in the darkest bowels of the earth, nor anything green or sear, but is recorded in His glorious book.

Ibn as-Sīd used this verse to exemplify his assertion that God is present in all of his creation. For example, wine itself contains something of God. The implication is that wine is therefore a viable path toward arriving at knowledge of him.

Third are the verses 30–40 from the sūra 'Yā Sīn.' Like the Northern Salon where they are inscribed, they are perhaps the clearest nexus point between the two axes. When the Northern Salon was used to hold a *majlis al-uns*, as Robinson shows, the participants would have been seated facing the gardens. In this way the eschatological verses would not be visible, but the verses from Yā Sīn could still be seen from the periphery. Likewise, if courtiers were passing through the Northern Salon along the east-west axis on their way to the oratory to pray, views to the gardens and north-south axis are minimized, yet the verses from Yā Sīn are still also peripherally visible:

> Let the once-dead earth be a sign to them. We gave it life, and from it produced grain for their sustenance. We planted it with the palm and the vine and watered it with gushing springs, so that men might feed on its fruit. It was not their hands that made all of this. Should they not give thanks? Glory be to him who made his creatures male and female: the plants of the earth, mankind themselves, and living things they know nothing of. The night is another sign for me. From the night, we lift the day—and they

> are plunged in darkness. The sun hastens to its resting-place: its course is laid for it by the Mighty One, the All-Knowing. We have ordained the phases for the moon, which daily wanes and in the end appears like a bent and withered twig. The sun is not allowed to overtake the moon, nor does the night outpace the day. Each in its own orbit runs.

Rather than getting too caught up in an in depth discussion of these verses, it is sufficient to point out that the references to the different orbits of the sun and moon, of day and night, are suggestive of the two different axes upon which the Aljafería generates meaning. They are at once two different worlds but come together in the nexus, in the flower-point of these verses. When not being read in light of Qur'ānic eschatology, the orbits of celestial bodies can also refer to the sovereign, the rounds of the *sāqī*, and the microcosmos of the *majlis* itself, a microcosmos enveloped by palms, vines, and shot through with gushing springs, where God's creatures feast themselves on the fruits of the earth. Ibn as-Sīd himself states in the *Ḥadā'iq* that his concept of *tawḥīd* or "unity" is equivalent to the *fanā'* of the Sufis: mystical annihilation of the soul.

The fires of Hell, the sensual pleasures of earthly gardens, *jīhād*, the world to come, and revelations can all be interpreted in light of other mystical notions and contexts. Open-ended signifiers are an important part of *badī'* poetics and to Ibn as-Sīd's philosophy, giving room for the visitor to the Aljafería to approach these *topoi* in a variety of ways. Especially when the verses from "Sovereignty" 1–14, inscribed along the east-west axis, with their references to "missiles for pelting devils," the "scourge of the flames," and unbelievers being "flung into the fire" are taken into account. One is reminded of Ibn 'Arabī's garden in flames, and even of mystical notions as far afield as the fires of Marguerite Poirete's Dame Amour, or Blake's marriage of Heaven and Hell, Dante's *Comedia* and the widespread motif across several cultures and traditions that the roots of the empyrean are to be found in the infernal.

Returning to the context of *taifa* court culture, while there was interpenetration between courts it must be clearly stated that each *taifa* court was its own entity, each made up of poets and philosophers whose ideas at times certainly varied. Therefore, the above discussion of the Aljafería should be taken to primarily relate just to the Hūdī court at Zaragoza. Examinations of what little remains of other *taifa* palaces in the same way Robinson has done hers on the Aljaferia could potentially yield more insights into the symbiotic relationships between literary and visual ornament, as well as the making of courtly love. Unfortunately, these have not been preserved nearly as well as the Aljafería has.

We cannot assume that the other palaces played exactly the same role in the *majlis al-uns* of other *taifa* courts as did the Aljafería in the Hūdī court. Though not universally applicable , the relationships between palace, poetry, wine, philosophy, and mysticism, in a context in which the sacred and profane are blurred, represents a tradition of art (both visual and literary). That tradition of art—and the politics and philosophies that inform that art—"went public" in the *fitna* period, reached its apogee in the (late) *taifa* period, and was continued in "unofficial" spheres of society into the Almoravid period and onward. The Aljafería is arguably the best example of the marriage of all these concepts, and while in many respects idiosyncratic to the Hūdī court at Zaragoza, it does further our understanding of *taifa* culture in general.

In our discussion of the Aljafería we have mostly focused on an Islamic perspective. Yet it's important to keep in mind that this discussion bears a relation to the Jewish poet-courtiers as well. The *taifa* kingdom of Zaragoza in all phases of its existence was a thriving centre for Jewish intellectuals.

Even before the Banū Hūd, under the Banū Tujīb, the court was home to poets and philosophers such as Marwān Jonah ben Janah and Yequtiel ben Yitzhak. The latter was the educator of Shlomo ibn Gabirol, who himself grew up in Zaragoza. Later under the Banū Hūd, the court was home to poets such as Yūsuf ibn Ḥasday and Moshe ibn al-Taqanah, the poet, philosopher and mystic Bahya ibn Paquda, the physician and botanist Jonah ibn Yitzhak ibn Buqlaris, and poet Levi ibn at-Tabban. Also, Abū Faḍl ibn Ḥasday (whose verses are cited above, and who was purported to have been a regular at the Hūdī *majlis*) was himself a converted Jew.

Some sources have Shlomo ibn Gabirol as remaining in Zaragoza for the first six years or so of the Hūdī regime, others say that he left for Granada in 1038 or 1039 (the year in which his former mentor was assassinated). In any case, it is said he did return toward the end of his life and therefore would have overlapped with some of the literati we have discussed. Though a late-comer to the party due to his being born toward the end of the eleventh century, Yehuda ha-Levi was from Tudela and would also have grown up under the influence of the court at Zaragoza.

While political relationships between *taifa* courts were sometimes friendly, sometimes hostile, they nevertheless were constantly in a state of communication and artistic and intellectual exchange. Many of the poets we have discussed wrote love letters, panegyrics and poetry to one another. Examples include Yūsuf ibn Ḥasday in Zaragoza dedicating a panegyric to Shmuel ha-Nagid in Granada, and the well known friendship and correspondence between Yehuda ha-Levi and Moshe ibn Ezra. Not to mention many of our poets and philosophers, both Jews and Muslims, travelled a great deal and changed their residencies from court to court depending on patronage and the political climate.

In addition to cross-cultural exchange between Jewish and Muslim luminaries, we can consider some of the mystical and philosophical concepts of the *majlis* that find parallels in Jewish tradition. For example, we find the motif of the seven heavens echoed in the Talmudic concept of the *shamayim*. We also see the ring-within-ring cosmology of Neoplatonism and that of the Muslim seven heavens in some ways paralleled by the *sefirot* of the Kabbalah. Another intriguing parallel, if more poetic than historical, is that of the palace in *majlis* mysticism compared with the Hekhalot literature: stories of ascents to heavenly palaces and the thrones of God. The word *hekhalot* itself means "palaces" in Hebrew.

So let us remember the moon, that pearled flower-point both of matter and divorced from it, through the eyes of Shmuel ha-Nagid, who gives us a look into a Jewish view on this mystery. His depiction of the moon in this poem as a *yod*—something I read as a deliberate choice, as there are other Hebrew letters that also resemble moons (whether crescent or full)—opens up a sublime flash of knowledge given the importance of that letter in Jewish mysticism, as well as being the first letter of YHWH. We have only to drift between waking and sleep, as the Nagid does in this poem, and look to the moon to be given an inkling of what it was he might have been feeling:

How exquisite that fawn who woke at night
To the sound of viol's thrum and tabor's click,
Who saw the goblet in my hand and said,
"The grape's blood flows for you between my lips. Come, drink."
Behind him stood the moon, a letter *yod*
Inscribed on morning's veil in golden ink.[222]

—Shmuel ha-Nagid

The Majlis and the Witches' Sabbat

Almost all of the *topoi* we have discussed above have parallels in the depictions of the Witches' Sabbat.[223] The association with transgressive sexual and sensual activities; the Sabbat wine; music and dancing; the night flight; the interplay between Truth and Lies, between the concrete *indicative* and the shifting *and if*; the blurring of the sacred and the profane, the infernal and the empyrean; the emphasis on the moon, moonlight, and silver; the celebration of the natural world and acknowledgement of it as an inspirer of apotheosis; as well as the subversive political and heretical implications of all of these, are all landmarks that the lyrical topography of the Sabbat shares with the *majlis*. They are both banquets of immortality.

Yet, there are also significant differences between each of these nocturnal revelries. Whereas the attendees of the Sabbat are primarily depicted as women, the *taifa majlis* appears to have been primarily celebrated by men. Whereas the *locus* of the Sabbat is often characterized by stormy nights, blasted heaths, haunted woods, and hell-broth, that of the *majlis* is one of palaces, pleasure gardens, fountains, pools, and perfume. While the Sabbat has the potential to decimate social differences, it is primarily cast as a rural or peasant phenomenon, whereas the *majlis* flowered in the courtly spheres of society.[224]

There are many aspects of the *majlis* that can serve to inspire or be incor-

222 Scheindlin, *Wine*, 69.

223 On the Witches' Sabbat, see Grey, *Apocalyptic Witchcraft*.

224 However, this is not to insinuate that aspects or personages from "popular" classes did not influence the development of the majlis and vice-versa. Cf. *Risāla of the Arrow in the Heart*.

porated into celebrations of the Sabbat amongst witches today. One does not need a whole arsenal of expensive perfumes, jewels, garments, food or drink to celebrate the Sabbat. However, a little rose water or frankincense, a good feast, and maybe the odd jewel or magic ring can go a long way when it comes to inducing mystical ecstasy. Sabbats need not always be held in some lugubrious haunt. In the warmer months of the year especially, Sabbats can be celebrated amongst wildflowers and aromatic plants, or in "pleasure" gardens prepared and tended by the celebrants, circumstances permitting. The physical structure of the covenstead, if any, can incorporate art, emblems, icons, or designs that reflect the Sabbat's mysteries, or that otherwise have meaning to the coven, and whose prolonged contemplation leads to epiphanies and theophanies, in a way similar to the Aljafería in Zaragoza. Coveners can appoint a cupbearer to pour the wine or themselves take turns filling this role.

Perhaps most importantly, the *majlis* provides a useful blueprint for incorporating a more artistic component into celebrations of the Sabbat. This also provides an excellent model for reconciling witchcraft with "bardic" traditions.[225] As the wheel spins round and each covener has their chance to sing, recite, lead a dance or chant, power builds, the world at once melts away yet at the same time feels more intimate and immediate than ever.

However, there are also several problematic aspects of the *majlis* that need to be addressed. As we have discussed, the role of cupbearer of the historical *majlis* was often played by a youth. While perhaps most often than not no actual sexual relations occurred between celebrants and the cupbearer, we do know that many Islamic sovereigns in both the East and West, like the Greeks before them, kept slave-boys (and girls) for sexual pleasure. When I suggest witches can incorporate a cupbearer into their rituals it should by no means be taken as an apology for pederasty, a thing unethical and abhorrent in the extreme.

It is important to remember that sometimes poets wrote love poems to cupbearers in which the alleged objects of their desire were really naught

---

225 Cf. The cupbearer as bestower of sovereignty in north-western European traditions, and also the eroticization of court-poets and their relationship with the king in the Irish poetic tradition. On the former see Enright, *Lady with a Mead Cup: Ritual,* prophecy and lordship in the European warband from La Tene to the Viking Age. Thank you to Erynn Rowan Laurie for bringing this comparison to my attention.

but masks for their sovereigns. More than one bearded (and probably at times elderly) man was praised by *taifa* poets as if he was a youthful androgynous wine-pouring beauty. More than a historical figure, the *sāqī* is a mythical figure, a phantom. His youth and effeminate charms are derived from depictions of the Qur'ānic paradise, of which the poets sung praises to invoke that paradise into their midst.

The cupbearer of a Witches' Sabbat need not be eroticized, nor even flirty, and they certainly should not be cast as sexually available objects. The cupbearer is a mask. Therefore the role of cupbearer can be filled by a man, woman, or by those who identify as both or neither. Nor need they be youthful. Elderly people can play the role of cupbearer if they desire to. Any kind of person—as long as they are consenting adults—can play the role of cupbearer, and either style themselves after the historical cupbearers through the adept application of make up, heavy mascara, silks, masks, cross-dressing, and jewels—or just come as they are. In any case, the gender ambiguity of the cupbearer can give some trans-gendered people a mythological figure with which they might feel an affinity, and some cis-gendered people the opportunity to better explore their own gender identity by temporarily blurring it in a ritual context.

While its revolutionary applications and implications are sometimes overlooked, truly, the Sabbat and similar gatherings are a vital component of any beautiful resistance. They provide the *joi* ever so necessary to prevent burn-out, depression, or *ennui*—and like the Greek Mysteries, they bequeath us with the power and wisdom to live as if we are already dead. In this way, the initiate tastes immortality—they come to live full of *duende* and fear death no longer.

8

Risāla fī l-kawkaba taḥta l-arḍ

[Risāla of the Anti-Court]

☿

> Imp and witch to Malkin gate
> In all strange shapes assemble
> Gather, till with fiendish weight,
> The old walls shriek and tremble!
> Snake from muddy pit, toad from tomb,
> Cat from the cottage ember;
> Hurrah for the hell-broth, banquet, broom,
> Blue fog and black November![226]

Great fires are lit when the members of wealthy and powerful courts convene. Crowns glow brightly, silverware and other riches are aggressively displayed, lords and ladies seek to posture as if they were monarchs, and monarchs seek to posture as if they were the Sun itself. Whether these be the gatherings of the nobility of yore, modern galas held in palaces such as the White House, the Kremlin, or the Moncloa, or the tacky award shows of the celebrity class, blinding dazzling light is perverted into a hegemonic device to assert, legitimize, or advertise power. However, unbeknownst to the ruling class and their shiny puppets, the light they abuse inevitably casts shadows. And these shadows, as if by some magnetic pull, have a tendency to be drawn together into gatherings of their own.

Such was the case on Good Friday in the year 1612. The matriarchs of two rival witch clans—Mother Demdike and Mother Chattox, plus one of Demdike's granddaughters and one of Chattox's daughters (Alison Device and Anne Redfearn, respectively), are imprisoned in Lancaster castle after Alison was accused of using her black dog familiar spirit to lame the pedlar John Law. About a month later, on Good Friday, a meeting was called at

---

226 Henry Spicer, The Witch Wife: A Tale of Malkin Tower, Song of the Witches, Act III, Scene 2, 1849. Cited in Cobban, The Lure of the Lancashire Witches, 1.

Malkin Tower—the derelict residence of the Demdikes—that was later described by Thomas Potts as "a great Assemblie of all the most dangerous, wicked and damnable witches farre and neere [sic]." One would imagine that this would have been no insignificant meeting, for as Jennie Lee Cobban puts it, "in those days, Pendle Forest grew witches rather than trees."[227]

Attended by Demdike's son and daughter, her other two grandchildren, and their family friends, the agenda for the meeting was to discuss how they might be able to free their imprisoned witch-kin before the impending trial that coming summer. While the witches feasted on freshly stolen mutton (James Device, Demdike's grandson, was alleged to have irreverently helped himself to a neighbour's sheep earlier that day), they were said to have "christened" Alison's familiar spirit, and to have hatched a plan to blow up Lancaster castle with gunpowder, free the inmates, and kill the jailer Thomas Covell.

At least that is what Jennet Device, the youngest person present at the gathering, subsequently accused them of doing upon being questioned by the authorities after word of the mysterious meeting had got around to them. Tragically, that accusation led to the execution by hanging of three of her family members (Mother Demdike died in prison before the witches were sent to the gallows), the two accused Chattox women, as well as her family friends Jane and John Bulcock (mother and son), Alice Nutter, and Katherine Hewitt (who was also known by the charming alias of "Mouldheels"). Christopher Holgate—Mother Demdike's son—managed to elude the authorities, a feat he repeated twenty-two years later after again being accused of attending another witch-meeting. Bravely, and in a final *fuck you* to the Crown, judges, and Church, Alice Nutter and the Bulcocks gave no speeches of penitence, remaining defiant till the very end.

Regardless of whether or not Jennet's accusation was true or false, we

227 Pendle Forest was eventually cast in popular imagination as an incurable breeding ground for witches. My stars were such that during Samhaintide of the 400th year anniversary of the Pendle Witches' trial and execution I found myself passing through Lancaster, summiting Pendle Hill, and visiting a healthy number of graveyards in the surrounding area. After spending those few days becoming intimate with Lancashire's ill-reputed and haunted landscape all I can say is the rumours are true...

might choose to view this infamous meeting as the convening of an anti-court. An anti-court is not the opposite of a court. Just as the opposite of belief in God is not belief in the Devil but rather atheism, if a court is an assembly, the opposite of a court would be empty space.[228] The relation of court to anti-court then, is similar to that of God to the Devil, one is the shadow of the other. The anti-court may be orthopraxic in its outward resemblance of a court, but the interpretation of the theory behind that praxis is markedly heterodox. What follows is a casting of the coven as anti-court and a discussion of tradition, identity, and ethics with regard to party politics.

Let us begin by travelling to the first half of the thirteenth century. We are in the city of Girona, a town that at this time in history belonged to the Principality of Catalonia, one of the territories under the hegemony of the Crown of Aragon. Jaime I, "The Conqueror," sits on the throne, and during his reign, the Crown of Aragon establishes itself as the dominant power of the western Mediterranean. The period that history erroneously dubs the Reconquista is in full swing; in a mere number of decades, Mallorca (1230), Menorca (1231), Ibiza and Formentera (1235), Valencia (1239), and Murcia (1265-66) fall from Muslim hands and are brought under the influence of the Aragonese and Catalans. At this time, Catalan-speaking colonies can be found throughout the shores of the Mediterranean in places as far afield as the coast of Egypt.

While efforts were made to repopulate these conquered areas with Christians, this did not imply a full ethnic cleansing until a couple centuries later when the Catholic Monarchs—Isabel and Fernando—outlawed the profession of Islam and the speaking of the Arabic language. Indeed, places like Valencia retained their majority Muslim population until the fifteenth century. The Albigensian crusade in the Languedoc displaced a significant number of the population who sought refuge in the Crown of Aragon, and the relatively recent Almohad conquest of al-Andalus along with their subsequent persecutions of Christians, Jews, and indeed Muslims of other stripes, caused many to flee northwards. This was not a culturally homogenous landscape.[229]

---

228 The word "court" is ultimately derived from the Latin cohors and cohort, linguistic doublets that mean "yard" and "retinue" respectively. The word "court" can refer to a political entity; a sovereign's household, councillors, and entourage; or to a physical gathering space.

229 See Assis, *Golden Age*, 300; and Chaytor, *A History of Aragon and Catalunya*, 94

Due to Jaime I's vexed relationship with the nobility whom he could not trust and upon whom he could not depend on for neither feudal loans nor fighting men (Jaime's armies employed numerous mercenaries, many of them dispossessed Muslims from other parts of the Peninsula), the relative scarcity of natural resources in the territories that comprised the Crown of Aragon, and the constant depletion of the royal coffers that comes with undertaking continuous military campaigns, Jaime I was forced to take a keen interest in (and exert a firm control over) commerce as his principal means of generating liquid capital.[230] There would be no transaction in all the realm that would pass unnoticed and unauthorized by the monarch and his agents; indeed, Jaime I ordered merchants to bring all their transactions to the notary for registration.[231]

This climate favoured the rise of the merchant class. The monarch sought the power that comes with the conquest of new territories; merchants sought the opening of new markets in foreign lands. The natural economy prevalent in previous centuries—where goods where primarily produced to be consumed locally and villages were self-sufficient—was gradually being replaced by a monetary economy where goods were produced to be sold in an international market, in which creditors played an important role.

Therefore, a symbiotic relationship emerged between the monarch and the merchant class. Merchants were willing to fund the monarch's military campaigns in exchange for authorization of their transactions, and for the privilege to have their businesses protected as royal monopolies. An example would be monopolistic rights on flour and baked goods or on salt: the monarch would prohibit the purchase of flour, bread, or salt that did not precede from the royal mill, ovens, or salt mines. The price a merchant had to pay in exchange for these rights was an annual deposit of 30,000 *sueldos* into the royal coffers. Therefore, Jaime I protected merchants as the thriving of their businesses meant an increase to his wealth, and thereby the augmentation of his power.

A similar relationship emerged between the monarch and the Jews that lived in the territories of the Crown of Aragon. Since the days of Alfonso II, the Jews legally belonged to the monarch in both persons and assets. This meant that in addition to any material assets they might own being legally

230 See, Fancy, *The Mercenary Mediterranean.*

231 See Shneidman, "The State and Trade in Thirteenth Century Aragon."

considered the property of the king, they themselves as people were also considered the king's property. This deprecating situation gave the Jews the curious benefit of procuring the king's protection from ecclesiastical hostilities (among others), for naturally he did not want his precious property to incur any damage.[232]

Therefore, the Jewish quarters in the Crown of Aragon were often walled or located within the grounds of a castle. In exchange for this protection, the Jewish communities of the Crown of Aragon were required to pay the king special taxes. Having recently been prohibited by law to own land for cultivation or to engage in a number of other professions, many Jews went into money-lending (though contrary to popular anti-semitic critiques, usury was by no means a Jewish monopoly).[233]

Jaime I greatly encouraged the implantation of new Jewish communities in the Crown, and called for Jews from other parts of the peninsula such as the Crown of Castile or Jews from al-Andalus fleeing Almohad persecution to settle in his domains. He also encouraged Jewish money-lending as a strategy for bypassing Christian taboos on this practice and thereby enforced an additional tax on his populace. For the richer the Jews became—being his property and being required to pay him a large percentage of their earnings—the richer he himself became.

In the midst of these conquests, political tumult, migrations, and economic change, a rabbi from Provenza named Yitzhak the Blind began to receive visitations in dreams of the prophet Elijah, an important figure in mystical Judaism, who began to bequeath him with a series of revelations that Yitzhak would later transmit to his disciples. These revelations coincide with the appearance of the text known as the *Sefer ha-Bahir* [Book of the Bright] in the Languedoc and the emergence (or perhaps reemergence) of the mystical current known as the Kabbalah.[234]

Yitzhak's teachings primarily took root in Girona, whose cobble streets we have been walking in the direction of its Jewish quarter. There, lacking a safety that its walls could never guarantee (and indeed, no wall can ever guarantee), lived a *hevra* or fellowship of Kabbalists that included a few of the most well-known figures in the history of Judaism: Ezra ben Shlomo,

232 See, Riera Sans, "Jaime I y los judíos de Cataluña."

233 See Ibid, 141; Baer, *Historia*, 186–286; and Assis, *Jewish Economy*.

234 See Scholem, *Origins of the Kabbalah*.

Azriel of Girona, the poet Meshullam ben Shlomo de Piera, and the infamous Moshe ben Naḥman, also known as Naḥmanides, or by the acronym RaMbaN. Not many people know that the English word *cabal* is actually a loan word from Hebrew that is derived from the word *kabbalah* [tradition]. The colloquial use of the word *cábala* in Spanish refers to the intrigues or plots that a person might be engaged in, in order to obtain some sort of personal benefit. It is likely that these connotations entered into vernacular speech thanks to the circle of Kabbalists we have just mentioned, for in some senses they did indeed seem to comprise a cabal.

These mystics were implicated in the two great concurrent controversies of their day that rocked Jewish communities not only in Sepharad, but in Ashkenaz as well as in the "East." The first, the Maimonidean Controversy, was a religious and philosophical polemic. The second was a political and economic polemic that resulted in a change in the way the *aljamas*—the legally recognized political entity of a Jewish community—were governed. This change involved the previous Jewish elite—a wealthy oligarchy whose power can be termed "autonomy by default"—being supplanted by a new elite, also wealthy but operating in a more limited economic sphere, who rode the rising crest of the merchant class and whose power can be termed "autonomy by royal intervention."[235] While some researchers have viewed these two controversies as separate issues, they were, in fact, intimately intertwined.

Even toward the end of his life, Maimonides' controversial works attempting to reconcile Jewish tradition with Aristotelian logic were beginning to cause quite a stir, which only intensified with the passing of the decades after his death at the beginning of the thirteenth century. At the same time that some of the more "orthodox" communities banned his works, other communities retaliated by pronouncing anathema on his critics whom they considered public agitators and heretics, and condemned the Kabbalists whose doctrine of the *sefirot* they saw as dangerously close to polytheism and the negation of God's unity, and whose interests in and profession of astrology were viewed as a form of idolatry. Maimonides himself thought the text known as *Shi'ur Qomah*, an important text in mystical Judaism, should be burned.[236]

The association of the Kabbalists with one of the main "agitators" in

235 See Klein, *Royal Power*.

236 See Idel, "We Have No Kabbalistic Tradition on This," 72; Rensoli, "La escuela de Kabbalah de Gerona: una introducción," 249.

the Maimonidean Controversy (Jonah Gerundi, who was Naḥmanides cousin), as well as scholarship's obsession with delineating intellectual and religious currents and individuals in black and white terms, has resulted in the Kabbalists being cast as the nemeses of the Maimonidean "rationalists." Researchers taking Meshullam de Piera's biting polemical poetry that at times satirizes Maimonides and his followers without recognizing or acknowledging the complexities and inherent paradoxes in the poet's work have not helped paint a more nuanced picture of the conflict.[237]

This categorization is overly simplistic and quite frankly not true. It is unclear whether or not Jonah Gerundi or Shlomo ben Abraham (two of the most famous "agitators" who railed against Maimonides' works) were Kabbalists, and the attitude of the Kabbalists themselves regarding Maimonides and philosophy in general is at times one of praise, at others one of criticism, but mostly somewhat ambiguous. Naḥmanides himself was not an anti-maimonidean; he instead attempted to play the role of mediator in the conflict.[238] In some poems even fiery Meshullam praises Maimonides, referring to him as "the greatest of this generation" and in one poem states:

> My heart harbours great fear and respect for him
> for he has illuminated the eye's pupil
> and sweetened language to gift blind eyes with light
> despite weak-minded reasoning finding blunders in his work
> he has brought forth innovations to the end of awakening the sleepers.[239]

Indeed, contrary to popular belief, the Kabbalists of Girona were not anti-philosophical, nor were they anti-rational. The Kabbalah itself emerged under the shadow of philosophy. The influence of Neoplatonism on the work of our mystics was great, and is perhaps most notable in that of Azriel of Girona.[240] Sometimes the Kabbalists assimilated philosophical terms

237 See Faur, "Anti-Maimonidean Demons," 46–50, who casts Nahmanides and Kabbbalists as "spiritists" and apologists for witchcraft.

238 See for example, *Caputo, Nahmanides in Medieval Catalonia*, 9–12.

239 See the poem »בהזות בובואה/לבב חזום ראה« Brody, Shire, vv. 62–65, 53–57. All English translations of Meshullam's poetry that appear in this epistle are my own, though I am indebted to Ribera Florit's versions in Catalan and Bartolomé Pons' versions in Castilian.

240 See the famous statement made by Azriel: "The words of the Torah and the words of the philosophers are as one." Cited in Dauber, "Competing Approaches to

or concepts, and other times they presented their own original concepts as reactions to the ones elaborated by the philosophers. The complex relationship between philosophy and the Kabbalah was at once one of dependancy and subversion. This relationship is summed up by an enigmatic declaration made by Naḥmanides about Abraham ben Ezra, another Jewish andalusī philosopher like Maimonides (though he differed with Maimonides significantly on numerous points) associated with philosophical "rationalism": "For Abraham ben Ezra we will have open rebuke and concealed love."[241]

What does this mean? Why would Naḥmanides and his circle at times openly criticize philosophers but harbour a different attitude behind closed doors? These, and other enigmatic statements reveal that the true axis of the Maimonidean Controversy was not a religious debate but a political conflict. On the one hand, Maimonides had made the controversial claim that his *Mishnah Torah* was the only book one would need to interpret the Law. This statement was seen as greatly problematic to talmudists (Kabbalists among them), who took it as a threat to their office: for if all one needed was to read the *Mishnah Torah*, the role of the talmudist in interpreting the Torah would be rendered redundant and eventually defunct. Furthermore, the Kabbalists appear to have been implicated in "overthrowing" the old Jewish elite, an elite often associated with philosophical rationalism, who used what the Kabbalists thought to be twisted interpretations of Maimonides' work to justify their greedy accumulation of wealth, immoral governing, moral laxity, ruthless tax-farming, and their maintaining of unjustifiable and undesirable ties with the Christian overlords.[242]

Maimonides in Early Kabbalah," 69.

241 See, Septimus, "Open Rebuke and Concealed Love."

242 This is to speak in general terms, as things were not quite so clear-cut. Without getting into excessive detail, it is useful to note that Meshullam served as head of his community for a while, which implies a degree of contact or even cooperation with the Christian authorities per obligation. Naḥmanides maintained a fruitful relationship with Jaime I until after the Barcelona Dispute when the ecclesiastical and political authorities turned on him, resulting in him being outcast to the Land of Israel, from whence he wrote letters home to his son that are still extant today. Neither of the two were impoverished; Naḥmanides' cousin in Barcelona was granted monopolistic rights to a flour mill and Naḥmanides himself controlled Girona's oven—an oven used by both Jews and Christians—and in the year 1258 Jaime I advanced him a payment of 40 golden maravedis.

What do we do with this information? Was Naḥmanides a "proto-capitalist,"

In any case, it's clear that much can be gleaned from the poetry of the aforementioned Meshullam de Piera. Indeed the poets of our own beautiful resistance can learn a lot from the sharp arrows of Meshullam's verses, for it was Meshullam who cast his kabbalistic circle as an "anti-court." He achieved this by appropriating the imagery, poetics, and language of courtly love employed by the Hebrew poets of *taifa* al-Andalus to his own ends. Sometimes Meshullam is faithful to the poetic tradition, other times he uses it in surprising new ways. His goal however was not to break away from his illustrious predecessors or the tradition that they belonged to, but to apply that tradition in a new socio-political context. His poems are subversive in their employment of the language of courtly love to undermine the power of the Christian nobility and its Jewish equivalent, and in their redefinition of lineage and value against the backdrop of the shift to a monetary economy and the rise of the merchant class.

Meshullam's poetry was written at the interstice between two poetic traditions from two different cultures and seems to have absorbed aspects of both of these worlds with ease: one was the andalusī Arabic poetic tradition, and the other was that of troubadour poetry. The majority of Meshullam's Hebrew poems are written in the Arabic *qaṣīda* form, one of the oldest, most emblematic and enduring forms in all of Arabic literature. He mostly uses Arabic metres first adopted into Hebrew by his andalusī Jewish predecessors. At the same time, he also employed metrical systems never before seen in Hebrew poetry that closely resembled some of those employed by troubadours writing in Occitan or Catalan.[243]

---

or were these negotiations made in the interest of his coreligionists? Bread in any case was an extremely important aspect of the medieval diet, and of course holds an important role in the celebration of the Jewish Sabbat as well as in several religious holidays. Ovens were communal; people made the dough at home and brought it to their nearest oven to be made. Being handed control of the oven in Girona would have constituted a great seizure of power for the Jews in those days. It would have enabled them to prepare bread in a kosher manner, and avoid potentially being harassed by their Christian neighbours each time they needed to bake bread. I am not interested in claiming the Girona circle of Kabbalists as "proto-leftist" heroes, which they most certainly were not. Rather, I am interested in looking at the relationship between language, power, praise, and satire in Meshullam's poetry, and what can be learned from it and applied today. On Naḥmanides, the oven, and the gift of the golden maravedis, see Assis, *Golden Age*, 282 and 314.

243 See Vernet, "Mètriça i estròfica en la poesia de Meixul·lam ben Xelomó de Piera."

The Albigensian Crusade and the economic changes of the time period had begun to mark the beginning of the end of troubadour poetry, but Jaime I was known to have employed troubadours in his entourage. Several Provenzal troubadours fled to the Crown of Aragon seeking asylum (such as Peire Cardenal o Aimeric de Belenoi, for example) and toward the end of his life Meshullam would have overlapped in his home town with Cerverí de Girona.[244] As much as Meshullam was averse to keeping close relations with his Christian neighbours, there would have been plenty of opportunities for contacts to be made, as when Jaime I toured his domains with his court (there was no fixed capital; the court moved from town to town) they were lodged in the Jewish quarters, whose buildings, furniture, food, and even inhabitants, were literally the king's own property.[245]

There was no Jewish nobility in the sense of a social class with a special legal status, but the "old elite" of Aragonese and Catalan Jewry that we have alluded to in some ways resembled an aristocratic class in them adopting the titles *nasi*, which means prince in Hebrew. It appears that the andalusī Hebrew poet, courtier, and man of letters Ḥasday ibn Shaprut was the first Jew to bear the title without any direct relation to the exilarchate or gaonate of the Jewish East.[246] The title was bestowed upon him not due to any alleged royal lineage or belonging to the House of David (as all the exilarchs claimed they did), but due to the contributions he made to andalusī Jewry as patron of the arts and protector of their interests at the Umayyad court in Córdoba before the caliphate splintered in the *fitna*. It was not a title that he passed down to his descendants.

The *nesi'im* [s. *nasi*] of the Crown of Aragon, however, seemed to refer to themselves as such based on their wealth, social power, and connections with Christian courts upon which they sought to legitimize their entitlement to power within the Jewish communities. And they did, in fact, pass this title down to their sons, in an attempt, or so it seems, to establish some sort of aristocratic lineage. Many (but not all) were staunch followers of Maimonides, such as members of the Alconstantini family, for example, and were employed by Jaime I as responsible not only for the collection of taxes in Jewish communities but in Christian communities too. Indeed,

244 See Egan, Vidas; Cabré, Cerverí de Girona, 2.

245 Assis, *Jewish Economy*, 25.

246 See "Court Jews" in Stillman, N. A. (ed.), *Encyclopedia of Jews in the Islamic World*. Leiden, Brill.

at different times, members of the Alconstantini family were the chief tax collectors for the entire Crown, including its Christian subjects. While Maimonides may have written his works with the more honest intention of facilitating the interpretation of scripture for any Jew, the *nesi'im* took advantage of his works as an excuse to supersede talmudic and halakhic authorities in what appears to be an attempt at further consolidating their already immense power.

Meshullam seized control of the language of courtly love and aristocratic titles in his praise poems dedicated to members of his kabbalistic circle and other friends (some of whom were possibly also patrons).[247] It seems this was an attempt at undermining the social power of these terms by applying them out of their typical context, in a way that was not based on noble lineage, wealth, or on affiliation with any royal court. Both he and Naḥmanides rejected the notion that the title *nasi* was something that could be inherited, or that it was something that gave an individual a right to govern. The thing that makes Meshullam's fellow initiates princes and kings, according to him, is their "flawless" moral conduct, generosity, and level of achievement in the esoteric practicing of Judaism. He famously wrote the following verses (among others) in praise of Naḥmanides:

> I have a friend, of this time
> but whom I will love forever,
> as for a significant time
> I have enthroned the lovers.
> There is but one whom I call eternal friend:
> ben Naḥman, whom I have anointed as my king.[248]

He also offers heartfelt praises to other members of his circle on numerous occasions, such as Ezra and Azriel, whom he describes as pouring wisdom and Kabbalah over his hands, and as having suckled him on the breasts of faith.[249] To Abraham ben Ḥasday he writes "Ben Ḥasday, my leader/is

247 Examples of these terms used by the poet include *my lord* [עדי], *prince* [שר or at other times, נשיא], *king* [מלך], *friend* [ידיד], *my kinsman* [עמיתי]. *hero* [גביר] among others.

248 See the poem that begins «לולי למחול מספדי הפחתי/קדר עדי המותה הלכתי» Brody, Šire, vv. 21–22, 34–36.

249 See the poem that begins «ירבו מזמותי ולא נגמרו/כי אחקר סודות ולא נחקרו» ibid, vv. 89–90, 99. On the Kabbalistic doctrine of "suckling wisdom," see Haskell, *God as*

the light of my eyes/for he is flower, diadem, and ornament," and to one Yitzhak, a member of his circle whose exact identity has yet to be identified, he writes:

> My heart of perishing beauty
> Will go unto you
> Surpassing the norm
> Like the love of nuptials[250]

By describing himself and his companions in these terms, Meshullam not only pulls the rug of power out from under the feet of the *nesi'im*, he attempts to use them to empower and extol his own circle.

Meshullam also distrusted the "new elite" who, while they did not sport princely titles, justified their power in Jewish communities through interventions made by the king on their behalf in the internal affairs of those communities. Most members of the new elite made their living through usury, hence the king's willingness to go to bat for them when conflict arose in their home communities.

Meshullam's appropriation of the language of courtly love, like the troubadours and the *taifa* poets before him, was made with the additional intention of fortifying alliances and political ties between individuals that did not depend on aristocratic lineage on the one hand or commercial relationships on the other. A recurring *topos* in his poems is the praise of generosity and the satire of avarice, a *topos* that often goes hand-in-hand with the *topos* of "good lineage," in which Mehullam asserts that good lineage is not based on titles or wealth but on generosity and ethics.

He makes his intentions to use courtly love in this way explicit when he writes lines such as "who trusts you is extolled in the bindings of your love

---

Suckling Mother.

250 For the verse praising Abraham ben Ḥasday, see the poem that begins «בפשע הזמן כי-לא בשלי/יכחש בי ולא יכיר פתילי» Brody, Šire, v. 18. Abraham ben Ḥasday and his brother Yehuda were among the last members of the Barcelona elite that bore the title of nasi. Contrary to some of the other nesi'im, however, they seemed to be on friendly terms with Meshullam and the Kabbalists, and do not seem to have been involved in the taxation system to the same extent that others such as the Alconstantinis were in Zaragoza or the family of Makhir ben Sheshet was in Barcelona. For the verse praising Yitzhak, see the poem that begins «באזני יתנו קול כמחלות/יתנו על-מדעי גדלות» Brody, Šire, v. 4, 39–42.

[בחבלי חשקך]" or "I summon the brothers, the allies/... all lovers to relations are connected/they have been implicated,/in my heart's most intimate reaches and in the rules of love"[251] or "We will pour our perfumes over you/ and a generous wind will transport our aroma to your nostrils./Form an alliance [ברית] with the linkages of our love [עם-קשרים לך אהבה] and intertwine it with our members and our souls."[252] These links are also compared to the love between God and Israel, who is ultimately the only legitimate king in the eyes of a somewhat anarchic Kabbalist such as Meshullam: "Between me and my creator there exists an alliance of love [ברית עם-אחוה]/they are amorous ties [קשרי אהבים] that will not be unwoven."[253]

Lastly, Meshullam used his poetry to propose a redefinition of value. He makes frequent allusions to pearls, precious incenses, perfumes, jewels, gold, and other treasures, but these all serve as metaphors for wisdom (including esoteric wisdom), generosity, and good moral conduct. The message is clear: value and riches emerge from transcendental truths and cannot be measured in coin.

Meshullam as a poet is little known and has not garnered much attention outside of the context of his involvement in the Maimonidean Controversy. Israeli researchers such as Ezra Fleischer have tended to view the innovations made in his poems as the poet deliberately breaking with the Hebrew poetic tradition of al-Andalus, and claim that he did so to disassociate Hebrew poetry from its Arabic influences, in an attempt to bolster their own identity politics. Catalan researchers such as Ribera i Florit, on the other hand, have also argued that he breaks from the tradition of al-Andalus, but that his innovations are not uniquely Jewish, but come from influence of the troubadours, also, it seems, in an attempt to claim him as one of their own.

Neither are correct, however, as Meshullam himself states in the context of poetry and tradition: "I do not seek to abort the famous notables."[254] And in another poem, "Call for Meshullam ben Shlomo/whose flute sings his own praises./Behold... the attractive poetry he has renewed in his times/

251 See the poem that begins «צפים נתיבות בערב ישאלו/מתי אלי האהבים תיצהלו» ibid, vv. 9-10, 36-39.

252 See the poem that begins «עבים רכובו שם נזיר אחינו/או יהלך אט על-כנף רוחנו» ibid, v. 14-15, 26-28.

253 See the poem that begins «קי קי בארך הזמן נוכחו/יהמו לאחריתם וישתוחחו» ibid, v. 38, 29-31.

254 See the poem that begins «לולי למחול מספדי הפחתי/קדר עדי המותה הלכתי» ibid, vv. 12–18, 34–36.

as a sign and testimony for a glorious future."[255]

In the same way, leftists can follow Meshullam's lead in using poetry to undermine capitalism (or in his day, what we might call "proto-capitalism") and take a similar approach to tradition as something mutable and alive, and while perhaps reinterpreting some of its outworn premises, employ its forms to great effect.

This might strike some as a controversial claim. leftists are typically seen as being, and indeed often are, fundamentally averse to tradition. But before taking this point further, let us take a step back and examine the core differences between left and right-wing politics.

Many of us will know the terms left and right are derived from the seating arrangement in the French Estates General during the French Revolution, with those who sat on the left supporting the revolution and the creation of a secular republic, and those who sat on the right supporting the *Ancien Régime*. It is important to note that from the get-go the dividing line is couched in temporal terms: one group wants to cling to the "old" while another group wants to usher in the "new." One considers itself "Conservative" and the other "Progressive."

The other fundamental difference between both factions, it seems, revolves around the question of hierarchy: in right-wing rhetoric, hierarchy and social inequality are inevitable, even desirable, whereas the left rejects social hierarchy in favour of egalitarianism. The central premises not always spoken of but implicit in these conclusions are that, 1) according to the right, hierarchy and inequality are rooted in Nature; and 2) according to the left, hierarchy is essentially anti-egalitarian. But are either of these premises even true?

Let's begin with the first premise. According to right-wing theorists, Nature is fundamentally unequal in its ways. This cynical way of being in the world views Nature as essentially cold, unforgiving, excessively violent, opportunistic, self-serving, and merciless; and the acceptance of this fact allegedly gives humans the right to behave the same way. The law of the

255 See the poem that begins, »בפשע הזמן כי-לא בשלי/יכחש בי ולא יכיר פתילי« ibid, vv. 34–36, 42–44.

jungle is "survival of the fittest." Plants and animals do not aid each other nor show solidarity for their sick or wounded, there is no cooperation or collaboration across members of different species or across members of the same species for that matter. Well-being, and thereby evolutionary success, is measured in material terms: access to the best food sources, the best hunting grounds, the ripest fruit or the most fertile soil. This access is achieved through brute force or other special adaptations that make one species "more fit" than another. Humans are considered the most advanced species, and therefore are perfectly justified in dominating all the rest. Likewise, some humans are "more fit" than others, and this gives them the right to dominate, oppress, exploit or otherwise consume their "weaker" fellows.

First there was religion (Abrahamic religion in particular) to legitimize "Man's" claim to superiority over the rest of the natural world, and then there was Darwin's theory of evolution. However, what many people are unaware of, is that Darwin based his scientific conclusions on the prevalent (capitalist) economic theories of his day and not the other way around.

Furthermore, more and more studies are emerging that demonstrate that natural selection and the ability for a species to thrive is not based on competition, but on *cooperation*.

A marvellous example of this can be found by examining trees and the mycelial fungal networks that connect them. Trees communicate with one another through chemical signals, and exchange resources through their roots and mycelium. They warn each other of impending pests and they practice what we might call "mutual aid," as they know they are stronger and healthier when they are growing together as a forest rather than in isolation. I will now quote extensively from the work of Peter Wohlleben, itself based in part on the work of Dr. Suzanne Simard, to illustrate these points for readers becoming acquainted with them for the first time:

> What and how much information is exchanged [between trees] are subjects we have only just begun to research. For instance, Simard discovered that different tree species are in contact with one another, even when they regard each other as competitors. And the fungi are pursuing their own agendas and appear to be very much in favour of conciliation and equitable distribution of information. If trees are weakened, it could be that they lose their conversational skills along with their ability to defend themselves. Otherwise,

it's difficult to explain why insect pests specifically seek out trees whose health is already compromised. It's conceivable that to do this, insects listen to trees' urgent chemical warnings and then test trees that don't pass the message on by taking a bite out of their leaves or bark. A tree's silence could be because of a serious illness or, perhaps, the loss of its fungal network, which would leave the tree completely cut off from the latest news. The tree no longer registers approaching disaster, and the doors are open for the caterpillar and beetle buffet. The loners I just mentioned are similarly susceptible—they might look healthy, but they have no idea what is going on around them. In the symbiotic community of the forest, not only trees, but also shrubs and grasses—and possibly all plant species—exchange information in this way. However, when we step into farm fields, the vegetation becomes very quiet. Thanks to selective breeding, our cultivated plants have, for the most part, lost their ability to communicate above or below ground. Isolated by their silence, they are easy prey for insect pests.[256]

On its own, a tree cannot establish a consistent local climate. It is at the mercy of wind and weather. But together, many trees create an ecosystem that moderates extremes of heat and cold, stores a great deal of water, and generates a great deal of humidity. And in this protected environment, trees can live to be very old. To get to this point, the community must remain intact no matter what. If every tree were looking out only for itself, then quite a few of them would never reach old age. Regular fatalities would result in many large gaps in the tree canopy, which would make it easier for storms to get inside the forest and uproot more trees. The heat of summer would reach the forest floor and dry it out. Every tree would suffer. Every tree, therefore, is valuable to the community and worth keeping around for as long as possible. And that is why even sick individuals are supported and nourished until they recover. Next time, perhaps it will be the other way round, and the supporting tree might be the one in need of assistance. When thick silver-gray beeches behave like this, they remind me of a herd

256 Wohlleben, Hidden Life, 11.

> of elephants. Like the herd, they, too, look after their own, and they help their sick and weak back onto their feet. They are even reluctant to abandon their dead.[257]
>
> This equalization [of resources] is taking place underground through the roots. There's obviously a lively exchange going on down there. Whoever has an abundance of sugar hands some over; whoever is running short gets help. Once again, fungi are involved. Their enormous networks act as gigantic redistribution mechanisms. It's a bit like the way social security systems operate to ensure individual members of society don't fall too far behind."[258]

These observations are backed up by the work of Dr. Suzanne Simard, a professor of forest ecology at the University of British Columbia. One famous experiment of hers involved completely shading one tree in the vicinity of several others. One would imagine that tree would die due to light-deprivation, but die it did not: its neighbour trees kept it going by supplying it with some of their own sugars through their roots systems. By using radioactive carbon to measure the flow and sharing of carbon between trees and between tree species, Dr. Simard discovered a symbiotic relationship between birch and fir trees: the latter provides extra carbon to the firs when they lose their leaves and through their roots when the firs are in the shade, and the firs provide the birches with sugar and nutrients (also through roots and mycelial networks) especially in the seasons when the birches are experiencing their annual sugar deficit.

These and countless other examples demonstrate that the right's theories about Nature are unfounded and false. Nature is not "savage," nor lacking an essential goodness. And despite what we hear on the news, or have personally endured, I thoroughly reject that Nature or humanity can be anything other than essentially Good. God—a codeword for something we might also describe with such names or terms such as Nzambi, Olodùmarè, The One, The Gods, The Agent Intellect, The Divine, or the Star Goddess, among countless others—is essentially Good. If God is equated wholly or in part with *nature naturans*—Nature doing what nature does, bearing forth, living, thriving, dying, and bearing forth again—then Nature is

257 Ibid, 4.

258 Ibid,16.

Good. If humanity is part of Nature, then humanity must also be Good. Take one look at a newborn baby and you will see there is nothing sinful (original or otherwise) about them. Having spent time among numerous infants and children, including my own son, I have found them to gravitate intrinsically toward caring and sharing, and many scientific studies being carried out today are yielding the same results.

So what about all the atrocious acts and injustices that humans commit against the planet and each other? These acts are not natural. How can they be anything other than natural if humanity is a part of Nature? Because the humans that commit these and other acts are no longer part of Nature, or when committing them are attempting to act outside of it. Humanity—in particular *civilized* humanity—in its extreme hubris and blindness, perceives itself as something separate from Nature, and incidentally superior to it. Therefore, *humanity is separate from Nature insofar as it perceives it to be separate from the same.* And so a toxic perception creates a toxic reality. The root of evil, then, is the failure of humans (or any other part of Nature for that matter, though humans are the only part that have been known to do this) to recognize that they are a part of, and have a role to play in, an infinitely complex, interconnected, and divine whole.

So what about hierarchy? Is Nature hierarchical? Hierarchy is a tricky word. Like other words and terms such as "social justice" or "well-being," it has become completely void of meaning, with different factions imposing their own meanings onto it in order to fill the void. If we take hierarchy at its most basic meaning, to simply mean an arrangement of items in which some are above and others below, then indeed hierarchies can be observed in Nature in things like hierarchies of age or hierarchies of physical size. However, hierarchy is a very inadequate concept to apply to Nature as it implies a fixed bottom and a fixed top; that items on the hierarchical chain are mere isolated parts and not wholes unto themselves; and it does not accurately demonstrate how a change in one part of the hierarchy can effect all the others. A more accurate term might be *holarchy*, as each *holon* or item in the holarchy is a whole unto itself (i.e.; a cell within a tree within a forest), and the arrangement has no fixed top or bottom.

Which brings us to our second question: are hierarchies (or holarchies) essentially anti-egalitarian? Before proceeding I request that readers bear with me as I am aware that, for some leftists, to suggest anything but would be to commit sacrilege. A hierarchy is only anti-egalitarian insofar as its parts act as if they are in isolation to each other. The notion that either the bottom level or the top level of a hierarchical ladder is somehow superior to the others arises from this misunderstanding of how hierarchies (or holarchies) work in Nature. For example, there is nothing anti-egalitarian about organizing the seating arrangement in a room in accordance with age from oldest to youngest out of respect for the elders present, as is common in many traditional African cultures and religions. However, if the young were to forget, dismiss, or were unaware of their connection to the elders (the ones who reared them, taught them, and cared for them) they might view this arrangement as oppressive to them or anti-egalitarian. Likewise, if the elders used this seating arrangement as an excuse to lord themselves over the young, they are forgetting that it is upon the young that they will depend once the limitations of old age begin to set in.

If we accept the famous Hermetic axiom *As Above so Below,* the alleged hierarchies present in Nature do not and could never imply anti-egalitarianism. Nature, God, is a single substance.[259] *The Centre is the Circumference of All,* a cherished dictum of the Feri tradition that reads the same in reverse, sums this up nicely. It is as Victor Anderson wrote in one of his English language haiku: "Pine tree bows to Wind/Unseen Wind bows to Pine tree/ Respect without words."

It is extremely arrogant of the "atheist left" (or atheist right for that matter) to assume *there is no higher power* than humans. Anyone who has experienced an earthquake or hurricane, or has been tossed around by the ocean's waves, or even looked through a telescope, has had the humbling realization of just how small, insignificant—and dare I say, powerless—we really are in the grand scheme of things. Any natural mystic knows that at least a degree of "conceptual" if not "actual" hierarchy (and its subsequent subversion) plays a part in the mystic experience: to be awed by Nature, to forfeit one's agency, even ones individuality—if only temporarily—are acts that paradoxically lead to the marriage of their heart with the heart(s) of all things, and to all the infinite forms and ways in which that black heart

259 The monism of Spinoza, which some have described as pantheistic, purports spirit and matter to be one. They are a single substance, and this substance is Nature. Spinoza's monism can be read as compatible with animism, or an expression of animism couched in philosophical language. Paradoxically, it might not be incompatible with polytheism. It is similar to the Lakota phrase "all my relations," and to the axiom "energy cannot be created or destroyed." There are mysteries here that bloom out of the cracks of Language and its limitations.

beats. In addition to some (most?) interpretations of the God of Abrahamic religions, it is precisely the thought that there is no higher power that has at times given humans the alleged right to rape, pillage, and destroy the rest of the natural world with impunity.

The hubris of some leftist thought in this regard leads us to another of its arrogant blindspots: that leftist politics are "progressive," what is new is fundamentally superior to what is old. The premise that this conclusion rests on is an assumption that time is linear. If this is not the case, as we have hoped to demonstrate throughout this volume, where does that leave "progressive" politics? It has been a grave and recurring error in the (mostly white) factions of the left to apply this line of thinking in order to discredit, dismiss, silence, or otherwise oppress indigenous and other pre-modern or pre-industrial peoples.

Conversely, it is high time that leftists drop the erroneous term "conservative" when referring to our right-wing opponents, and expose the hypocrisy inherent in them referring to themselves as such. Truly, the right does not care about "conserving" the environment, culture, history, or even the health of their own children and descendants, as scores of examples all around the world have demonstrated. The Conservative Party of Canada's exploitation of the tar sands and construction of oil pipelines that are harmful to (primarily, but not exclusively) indigenous communities as well as the environment is a fitting example. Stephen Harper's appeal to (white) "old stock Canadians" (as if First Nations were not the true "old stock!") and call for a return to "traditional" (i.e.; colonial) Canadian "values" in the style of right-wing ideologues all over the world, makes clear beyond the shadow of a doubt that the only thing that "Conservatives" really care about conserving is their own power and privilege. Even at the inception of right-wing politics the term *Ancien Régime* is a misnomer: the repugnant Valois and Bourbon dynasties only date from the late medieval period, a brief moment when one considers the hundreds of thousands (if not millions) of years that make up human history. The right is anything but traditional.

These comments have been made in the hopes of overcoming the ossification of political thought into dogma, duality, and the confrontational sectarianism inherent in party politics. Some critique contemporary identity politics by exclaiming it merely "passes for politics." However, a graver and perhaps far more widespread problem is that affiliation in party politics passes for identity. When this occurs, people become more concerned with looking, acting, and dressing the part, talking all the right talk and citing all the right material that corresponds to their political affiliation, rather than fostering a free-thinking dissident attitude or actually taking steps to put their political beliefs into practice in the offline world.

Mystics, poets, philosophers and other practitioners of esoteric arts have long been wary of the dangers of religion or politics as identity. Take, for example, the *Ikhwān aṣ-Ṣafā'*, or the *The Brethren of Purity*. This clandestine society admitted Muslims, Christians, and Jews of all stripes, as well as philosophers and alchemists. Initiation was open to men and women. Indeed, one of their purposes in coming together as a group was to overcome the sectarian divides of tenth-century Iraq. They write the following in their epistle known as "The Call to God:"

> Know this, my Brother, we are not opposed to any science, we do not cling fanatically to any doctrine, and we do not keep ourselves away from any of the books that the sages and the philosophers have written or composed on the various sciences and the subtle meanings which they have extracted by their intellects and observations. As for the support, assistance, and foundation of our cause, they are the books of the prophets, God bless them all, the revelation which they have set forth, as well as the information, inspiration, and revelation passed to them by the angels.[260]

Similarly, I am also rather averse to flag-waving. However, the current political climate is such that if you do not come out and openly declare your political affiliation you will have it declared for you. Furthermore, vagueness when it comes to such things is a known characteristic of crypto-fascists. Therefore, I want to make it clearer than moonlight on snow that I am an anarchist and my loyalties lie with the egalitarian dissident free-thinking left. When it comes to human politics, to paraphrase a quote attributed to Federico García Lorca, "I will always be on the side of whose who have nothing, and who aren't even allowed to enjoy the nothing they have in peace."

This should be taken as a statement of ethics, not of ideological dogma. For example, if a truly humble, wise, and clement king, queen, or monarch suddenly appeared out of thin-air and with a snap of their fingers created a

260 From Epistle 48 "On the Call to God." Cited in Catallay, *On Magic*, 123 n. 127.

truly healthy society I would not oppose it just because they wore crowns. However, no such king or queen has ever existed, except in the imaginations of people like Plato. Since its inception, the State, in all of its manifestations, has never been anything other than a corrupt, sick entity created by a few to exploit the many per force. Likewise, my anti-capitalism does not stem from some blind devotion to communism or any zealous faith in being admitted to a classless workers paradise in the post-dictatorship afterlife. Rather, it comes from a simple premise: capitalism is harmful to all living things (whether they realize it or not), and indeed for one living thing to lord itself over another is to commit "anti-natural" acts that stem from a perceived (yet false) separation from and superiority over, the rest of the natural world. Therefore, for me, anti-capitalism and anarchic politics are professions of ethics, not dogma.

Spinoza wrote his *Ethics* as a response to the dualism of Descartes—a wretched man who thought animals were but soulless machines and from whom many of the worst premises underpinning modernity and industrial civilization originate. For me, ethics will always supersede dogma, identity, or religious affiliation. I have no issue with having friends or neighbours that do not share my beliefs. I will share food with them, joke with them, debate with them, sometimes even learn from them, as long as they don't cross any certain unethical lines that should never be crossed. Of course, there is no universal code in this regard; exactly what is to be considered ethical is up to each person to decide for themselves. I do not have all the answers and indeed am learning all the time. This attitude is not one of niceties or compromise; rather, it is to prevent intellectual ossification—and far more important still—it is to recognize that in a post-industrial future our very survival might depend on adopting a similar attitude, on being able to search for the Good in our neighbours regardless of what their dogma might be, on sharing, looking out for another, and lending a hand in times of need. We are stronger together.

Nationalists claim that *good fences make good neighbours*. This is utter nonsense. Anyone who has lived in close proximity to someone who has erected a fence where there previously was none knows that their act of construction is really an act of aggression. A "good fence" will make far worse neighbours than it can ever make good ones, and indeed will likely have the effect of souring the good ones. Stefan Zweig famously remembered how before WWI, passports did not exist. Asylum or entry into a country was never denied unless that country was at war. A quick look at borders the world over reveals we are living in a state of perpetual war. *Good fences don't make good neighbours; good ethics do.* Good ethics, and a healthy dose of gift-giving, sharing, lending a hand, and, amazingly, remembering seemingly insignificant things like people's birthdays.

Ethics are the barometer by which the contemporary left can reappraise its relationship with tradition. (Let me make it clear that by left I am not referring to mainstream liberals who, while thumping their ethical chests all the live-long day, are only ethical or liberal insofar as they are able to continue making a profit at the expense of people and the planet). If a tradition or an aspect to a tradition is found to be unethical it is to be discarded. Sometimes, when there are aspects of traditions that are unethical, the unethical component can be discarded allowing for the tradition to still be preserved albeit in a heretical way.

For example, marriage is typically considered a traditional practice. There have been (and still are in many cases) many unethical aspects to the way marriage has been practiced, including it being considered the exclusive purview of heterosexual cisgendered couples; the woman becoming the man's property upon taking her vow; and divorce being prohibited in order to lock her into a state of objectification forever more. However, these aspects can be discarded; there is nothing unethical about people choosing to publicly declare their love and commitment to one another in a ritualistic context. When love is truly present, the ties of marriage do not represent the chains or burden of the conjugates but the very key to their freedom.

Many contributing writers to Gods&Radicals Press, alongside other exponents of the pagan anti-capitalist movement at large, have made a consistent effort to reconcile traditional world views, cultures, customs, religions and traditional ecological knowledge with leftist thought, in an effort to protect those traditions from appropriation by the fascist enemy. Fascists use traditional symbols in a thaumaturgic manner that appeals to peoples' irrational, unconscious, and emotional faculties in an attempt to bolster their own ranks. As more than one contributor has made explicit, if we steal back tradition from their hands, or indeed don't let them make offwith it in the first place, they are rendered powerless.[261]

This is similar to wars described in the Bible in which the Philistines and

261 For example, see Rhyd Wildermuth, "Saving What We Love," retrieved from https://paganarch.com/2018/02/08/saving-what-we-love/

the Israelites alternately steal the Ark of the Covenant from each other in order to undermine each other's power. If the left was less dogmatically opposed to tradition, fascism would lose whatever appeal it might have. One wonders how many artists and intellectuals in the 1920s who were duped into admiring figures like Mussolini would have instead thrown in their lot with a motley crew of anti-capitalist pagans had we been around back then.

Furthermore, an additional goal of many anti-capitalist pagan activists is to heal the gaping disconnect between us and our pre-colonial, pre-industrial, and pre-modern ancestors. Therefore, we should always walk gently and with much cunning when it comes to iconoclasm. True to the non-linear nature of time, the ancestors—and the descendants—are all around us, supporting us, teaching us, intervening on our behalf. To do away with tradition all together would be to do them a profound disservice.

And with that we return to the coven as anti-court.

Traditional forms of ritual and magic can and should be preserved, provided the initiates deem them ethical, and the spirit behind the letter can be reinterpreted if it came with some unethical baggage. Indeed, traditional magical practices might sometimes appear simpler but are often far more potent and practical than their modern equivalents. This is likely due to them having been developed over the course of thousands of years if for no other reason.

All coven members are equal in worth and status. However, elders in age should be respected and their mileage acknowledged. Roles should be determined by the unique abilities and skill sets of each member, but never be let to ossify or to become set in stone. In other words, if a covener wants to take on the role of drummer in a given ritual yet has no experience or prior skills in drumming, she should be given the opportunity to learn from a member who does, and have the humility to respect that member as her teacher. The teacher should be perceptive enough to realize that she will never fully learn unless she tries, and undoubtedly will lose the beat a few times when starting out.

Courtly language can be employed in the poetry and invocations of the coven for reasons expressed above, and members can refer to themselves as kings, queens, lords, ladies (or gender-neutral/gender-blurring courtly *senhals* like the titles Beautiful Vision or My Magnet as employed by troubadours) as a way to subvert social hierarchy and reclaim personal dignity, pride and self-worth. These titles should by no means, however, be perverted into status symbols or excuses for some members to lord themselves over other ones. The subversive roots of courtly love can be looked to as a source of inspiration when cultivating new codes for strong and infallible sexual ethics. Needless to say, the development of these codes should not be gender-exclusive and should never attempt to put any gender in a box, nor exalt any one or two genders over any other. The structure of the coven is not hierarchical, it is a constellation, an asterism, a cluster of stars.

So feast, witches, dance and make merry. Convene with your coven and celebrate your rites on Black Friday—which is the infamous Good Friday meeting of the Pendle witches and never the capitalist holy day of nauseating unfettered consumerism:

> What joy like ours can mortals find?
> We control the Sea and Wind:
> All elements our Charms obey,
> And all good things become our prey;
> The daintiest Meat, the lustiest Wine,
> We for our Sabbaths still design.
> 'Mongst all the great Princes the sun shall e'er see,
> None can be so great, or so happy as we.[262]

262 Thomas Shadwell, *The Lancashire Witches*, Act II, Song of Demdike and her witches, 1691. Cited in Cobban, *The Lure of the Lancashire Witches*, 148.

9

Risālat al-kahf

[Risāla of the Cave]

☿

Behold! Human beings living in an underground den, which has a mouth open towards the light and reaching all along the den; here they have been from their childhood, and have their necks and legs chained so that they cannot move, and can only see before them, being prevented from the chains from turning round their heads. Above and behind them a fire is blazing at a distance, and between the fire and the prisoners there is a raised way; and you will see, if you look, a low wall built along the way, like the screen which marionette players have in front of them, over which they show the puppets.[263]
—Plato, The Republic, Book VII.

The method must be purest meat
　　and no symbolic dressing,
actual visions & actual prisons
　　as seen then and now.

Prisons and visions presented
　　with rare descriptions
corresponding exactly to those
　　of Alcatraz and Rose.

263 Translation by Benjamin Jowett in Buchanan (ed.), *The Portable Plato*, 546.

> A naked lunch is natural to us,
> we eat reality sandwiches.
> But allegories are so much lettuce.
> Don't hide the madness.
>
> —Allen Ginsberg, in his poem "On Burroughs' Work"[264]

There was once a time when I made my home in a cave on a holy mountain. Disgusted with the state of the world and mourning the sudden death of a dear friend, it seemed like the most sensible thing for me to do at the time.

The cave would become my home for the better part of the following two years. Upon waking in the morning I would descend the mountain and walk to town to sell Arab and Mediterranean-style honey cakes and to peddle my poetry in the streets. In the evening, I would fill my carafe with water and make the climb back up to my *chthonic* home.

Of course, there's much more to the story than just water, honey, or poetry and in this epistle I will tell part of that story. As much as I can anyway. Thus, what follows is part of the story of my own *katabasis*, my own *allegory of the cave*. Except it's not an allegory at all. It's a true story, *and* it really happened.

There was once a mountain above the old road to Guadix that went by the name of Valparaíso. At the end of the sixteenth-century, however, the name was changed to Sacromonte [holy mountain] after a startling discovery was made there: a series of texts inscribed on circular lead leaves, written in a combination of Arabic and Latin found secreted in the depths of a cave. These texts claimed to be a lost but integral part of Christian holy scripture that told the story of a mysterious and hitherto unknown saint: San Cecilio. The discovery rocked the Christian world at the time. Sacromonte became a site of pilgrimage famous for having more crosses on its mountainous slope than any other holy site in Europe; there were even some who considered these *Lead Books* or *Libros Plúmbeos* to be a lost "fifth gospel."

264 See Ginsberg, *Reality Sandwiches*, 40.

However, in the seventeenth century, the *Lead Books* were proven to be naught but the work of three master forgers. The three men who are thought to have forged them were *moriscos* [Muslim converts to Christianity], and they had forged the books in Arabic and planted them in a cave on Valparaíso intending for them to be found in an attempt to fight the omnipresent persecution of their culture of origin and thereby overcome the sectarian divides prevalent in Spanish society.

Today, Sacromonte is possibly one of the most famous traditional neighbourhoods of the Spanish Roma, known colloquially as the *gitanos,* or *el pueblo calé (*the *calé* people), after the name of their traditional language, *caló.* Some believe the Roma settled in Sacromonte due to it being riddled with caves. Others acknowledge this but point out that they would have also settled there for professional reasons. The crossroads where the Cuesta del Chapiz meets the Camino del Sacromonte—a crossroads presided over today by a statue of the so-called "*rey gitano*" Chorrojumo—previously functioned as one of the principal gates into the walled city of Granada.

The Roma made their home outside those walls because there the city gate opened onto the aforementioned road to Guadix. Many readers will know that historically the Roma were skilled horsemen and metalworkers and were said to have travelled southward to Andalucía in the wake of the conquering Christian armies, for whom they did work as blacksmiths. Therefore, upon arriving in Granada, they are thought to have settled in Sacromonte in order to provide horses, horseshoes and other supplies for travellers making preparations to embark on journeys, or for those newly arriving. Sacromonte is also famous around the world for being one of the neighbourhoods in which flamenco was born.

There is an old story re-told in Washington Irving's *Tales of the Alhambra* about a Moorish astrologer. This mysterious figure was said to have wandered the world learning ancient and half-forgotten arts and sciences, in particular those of the pagan magicians of ancient Egypt. Upon arriving in Granada he quickly gained favour at the Nasrid court for providing them with various magical talismans that subsequently assured them victory in their wars against the Christians. In exchange for his help, the Nasrid sultan offered to give the astrologer any lavish mansion he chose, but the astrologer preferred to live in a cave across the valley from the Alhambra—on the same side of the valley where Sacromonte can be found today—so he could look down on the city below and keep an eye on the activities of its inhabitants. He was said to have decorated his cave lavishly in any case. Indeed, the interior of the cave was said to have been covered with rich tapestries, carpets, and lanterns of a thousand colours.

One day the sultan became quite enamoured of a dark-haired, pale-skinned Visigothic princess whom he had captured in war, after the astrologer had yet again used his arts to bring the Muslim armies to victory. The Christian princess mysteriously wore a chain with a silver pendant in the shape of a lyre around her neck. This was a magical talisman said to possess the power to induce sleep. The sultan made her his wife, though (unsurprisingly) she was unhappy at his side, and longed to escape.

Years went by, and the sultan, always amazed by the capacities of the magical arts of the astrologer, in a fit of ambition eventually asked him if he could create him a palace unlike any other, whose gardens would rival those of paradise. The astrologer accepted, but requested that upon completion of the palace, the sultan was to give him the first thing that crossed through its glittering gate. And so a bargain was struck.

The astrologer conjured spirits at the appropriate times, and lo! a stunning palace appeared out of the very air, a palace more dazzling and beautiful than anyone had ever seen. Thus, in a clear mirroring of the construction of Solomon's temple, the Alhambra came into being.

The sultan was delighted, and could not believe his good fortune. He decided to dedicate the newly built palace to the Visigothic princess. Therefore, he decided she herself should lead the procession into the palace mounted on horseback. Alas, in his hasty excitement, he had forgotten the pact he had made with the astrologer. The princess had hardly crossed through the palace gates when a great cave opened up into which she descended without looking back. The sultan cried out and tried to follow after her, but it immediately closed up again. The astrologer had come to "take his due."

Legend has it, the magical couple is still happily living together in their underground dwelling, and that on nights of the full moon one can still hear the music of an otherworldly silver lyre rising up from the depths of the earth...

My own ears caught this lyrical lullaby music and I followed them down into the earth. In a way, my story mirrors that of the Seven Sleepers or of Plato's famous allegory—but in reverse. For Plato, the cave is a prison where illusion dances on the wall, and if the prisoners were able to break free, they would find illumination only by emerging into the light of the sun. For me, it was precisely the opposite. I left the surface-world daylight illusions and horrors of capitalism, industrialization, and cyber-society—and found truth within the earth.

My cave was not located in Sacromonte proper, but further up the mountain in wilder, rougher reaches. I did have a view of the Alhambra and the Albayzín though, and often wondered what sort of characters would have made their home there in times gone by. As much as I would have liked to imagine I was living in the cave of some wise astrologer, the truth was probably a trifle more prosaic. There was a trough in the cave next-door to mine—a cave that previously had a tunnel that connected it to mine, but was later sealed over—and my neighbours and I heard from an old Roma man from the neighbourhood down below that the caves we were living in were once used to keep horses.

Down in Sacromonte proper there are still caves; many of them look like houses from the outside. These caves are furnished and equipped with water and electricity; my own had neither. Some of the neighbours pinched from the nearest streetlights, but I was unable to do so for fear of using too much energy and raising an alarm. To be honest, I kind of liked it without electricity anyway. At night I would set up recycled mirrors around the cave's interior to amplify the light of my candles. There was also an open area in the ceiling (if you could call it that). This made it a little unnerving at times given the ease with which unsavoury characters (and alas, there were no shortage of these) could enter, but I loved how I could see the stars from inside my cave, and when the moon waxed from new to full there would be moments when the whole interior of my underground home would become flooded with moonlight.

Granada, located in the foothills of the snowy Sierra Nevada, is notorious for its deathly cold winters. I remember coming home some nights, soaked, and due to the aforementioned hole in the ceiling, would have to curl up in a wet cave. I'd often light a small fire and make broth to warm up. One time I even remember waking up to snow falling on my sleeping bag.

Though I had some neighbours who lived nearby, I was the sole human occupant of my cave. Despite this, I was never really alone. Sometimes at dawn birds would fly in and I'd wake up to wingbeats. There were a few insect roommates and sometimes the odd snake. We got along fine. It was ok, maybe even necessary, for me to distance myself to an extent from other people, in a way not unlike the solitary sages or "weeds" described by Ibn Bājja. In any case, at all times I could feel my ancestors surrounding me and lending me their light. I do admit there were some lonely episodes, and at those times I would stubbornly quote Emily Dickinson and wonder whether "It might be lonelier/Without the loneliness."[265]

Most of the neighbours unfortunately were either unsavoury people (drugs or no drugs) and others were savoury but were also (for example) recovering addicts, and unlike yours truly, weren't necessarily living there by choice. They came from all over the world and for one (often unfortunate) reason or another had come to make their home in caves. However, I was fortunate to find two people that became dear friends. We banded together, shared food, and looked out for each other when some of the more hostile individuals in our proximity would start acting up.

One of them had set up an ingenious system for tapping potable water through a network of partially underground hoses. This involved running a hose underground and over a nearby roof to finally connect to a nearby drinking fountain. This was often a Sunday night activity, as we needed to be discreet. Through this system, we were able to fill up hundreds of litres of water right from within the comfort of his cave, eschewing the need to haul that heavy liquid up the mountain ourselves.

I was teaching a bit of English at the time, and that plus selling the sweets and poetry, and work I was doing at a flamenco venue, earned me about €25–50 a week (sometimes more, sometimes less, depending on the week), so I was often in charge of buying things we couldn't otherwise come by. My two friends collaborated in their own ways. For example, one of them would collect most of the firewood and dumpster-dive regularly for vegetables. We would make all kinds of things, meat, dairy, anything we could get our hands on. I remember lentils with recycled vegetables seemed to be an almost weekly favourite.

Some uninhabited caves close to ours (also outside Sacromonte) were once the hideouts of *bandoleros*, or in other words, political bandits. These outlaws were famous for sticking up carriages carrying goods, aristocrats,

---

265 Dickinson, *The Selected Poems*, vi.

and political enemies (La Guardia Civil, high-ranking military men, etc.) who were travelling along the road to Guadix. Later on, they were the hideouts of *maquis*—Republicans and other anti-fascist partisans who kept up the fight in the years following the disastrous outcome of the Spanish Civil War.

I remember one night in town with one of my two neighbours, at one of our friends' houses. There was a young liberal "activist" there who was harping at us about all the organizations he was a part of and about all the social change he was trying to bring about. My cave-friend who I'd come with looked at me, raised an eyebrow, and whispered *"Que venga al monte... a ver lo que aguanta."* (Let him come up to the mountain...we'll see how long he lasts.)[266]

Over the years there have been many attempts made by the police, acting on behalf of their capitalist overlords, to evict all the caves in order to claim the mountaintop (with its beautiful views) as choice land for the construction of mansions and apartments. Time and time again they have arrived with excavators, clashed with the occupants, and caved-in the latters' homes with all of their belongings still inside. Time and time again, the cave-dwellers of Sacromonte have returned to dig out their caves and re-occupy them once more.I learned an immense amount from this experience. I learned I had power and could live almost entirely independent of the State. Though I was mourning my friend who had died, it was still one of the best times in my life. This doesn't mean it wasn't also hard at times, or that I wasn't cold in winter, or that there weren't some nights when I experienced a degree of hunger, or that there weren't some nights in which confrontations arose and I had to stand my ground. However, I don't regret a single minute of it and probably would still be living there were it not for another fateful twist in the plot.

If it was mourning a death that in a way, got me into that cave, it was falling in love that got me out of it.

Although I didn't know it at first, in another cave, down in Sacromonte, not too far away from my own, lived a woman who—after we found one another—would later become my accomplice and creative partner, wife, and co-parent. While we both decided that the mountains outside Sacromonte were no place to raise a child (due mainly to the hostile environment alluded

266 While I think my friend had a point, I don't mean for this to be taken as a judgmental dismissal of more conventional forms of activism.

to above), had we wanted to we would not have been able to anyway, as it is now prohibited to raise children in caves that don't meet certain government regulations. So we left. Fortunately, we still live entirely "off the grid" and each year are learning more and growing as much food as we can.

Many people have heard of the bombing of Guernica, but less people have heard of the Sauceda, a town that was also bombed (a few months prior to the more famous attack immortalized by Picasso) and entirely wiped off the map. At first, it might seem strange that Franco would have decided, with the help of Nazi aircraft, to obliterate this tiny silvicultural town with a population of a little over 1000 people. This strangeness evaporates, however, upon learning that the Sauceda has been seen as symbol of freedom for centuries.

The Sauceda was said to have been originally populated by refugees fleeing Nasrid Granada once the Catholic Monarchs finally had that kingdom signed over to them by the last Nasrid monarch, who history remembers primarily by the name "Boabdil." There they were said to have founded a religiously tolerant "free republic," where both Christians and Muslims, *payos* and *gitanos*, lived together in harmony, raising animals and sustaining themselves by working the thick, near impenetrable, oak forests. Even Cervantes made mention of the Sauceda in his *Coloquio de los perros*, a place that seemed to have somewhat of an anarchic reputation even in his day. Vicente Espinel, a writer almost exactly contemporary with Cervantes, wrote the following: "I went to the Sauceda, where there are places and solitudes so remote that a man can live many years neither seen nor found should he so desire."[267]

In the following centuries, the Sauceda became known as a notorious hideout for *bandoleros* and other outlaws. During the Spanish Civil War, there was a moment in which its population greatly increased as more and more refugees fleeing the fascist advance northwards fled into that forest with the hope that its difficult terrain and remote location would keep them safe. Alas, Franco was determined to destroy the Sauceda and everything it stood for. Men, women, and children were slaughtered. Some

267 Translation mine. The original reads: "Fuíme a La Sauceda donde hay lugares y soledades tan remotas, que puede un hombre vivir muchos años sin ser visto ni encontrado si él no quiere."

women who were spared were given a special payment by the fascist government to tell people their husbands had died in accidents. The "Marrufo" cottage close by was the site of one of Spain's most notorious death camps, where hundreds of people were tortured, killed, and thrown into mass graves. Volunteers have only recently begun to dig them up, and dig up the history that was buried there with them.

It was in the middle of this haunted wood, in the central square in what today is a ghost town whose remains have been all but reclaimed by nature, in front of the ruins of a bombed-out church, where my wife and I were wed. Together we danced *El fuego fatuo* from Manuel de Falla's *Amor Brujo* [Witch Love], clasped hands, and in a ritual mirroring its Sfaxian counterpart—jumped the fish of destiny.

The rangers who live near the site told us that they had seen wedding parties visit there to take pictures in nature, but never a full wedding ceremony take place. We wondered if ours was the first wedding to take place since before the town was bombed and its population massacred.

There were times during our wedding when just touching a tree trunk or the stone of some blown-up cottage would provoke an analeptic vision, and I could see smoke and hear planes, and screams, and centuries old trees crashing to the ground. We only chose to invite our immediate families and a few close friends. But hundreds of others showed up uninvited. The ghosts of the forest-town's long dead inhabitants watched from the twain shadows between the tree-trunks, and fluttered about us like so many moths and so many stars.

This is the necromantic power of love, revealed to us at last by Dead Hermes. And by raising the ghosts of the past we are given visions of the future, a future that for better or for worse might look all too similar to the way the Sauceda does today, bearing the semblance of a landscape destroyed by human folly and later retaken by the greenwood once more.

There's something I would like to make clear: my experiences are in no way exceptional, nor are they special in any regard. In fact, they're quite normal. And that's what gives me hope. All over the world there are people who have lived or, truly, are caught in the thick of experiences similar to or far more fantastic than the ones I describe. I know, friend, that you too have experienced some of the same things, endured similar hardships, and dream of a day after the smoke clears, a day marked by birdsong, the sun through oak leaves, and the music of silver lyres rising from the underworld. Work to usher in that day. Work swiftly, but above all—work with grace, for it won't come in time and it won't come too late.

Bibliography

☿

Abram, D. (1996), *The Spell of the Sensuous: Perception and Language in a More-than-human World*. New York: Pantheon Books.

Abu l-Jayr al-Ishbili. (1991), *Kitab al-Filaha*. J. M. Carabaza Bravo (Ed.) (trans.) Madrid, Spain: Instituto de Cooperación con el Mundo Árabe.

Abu-Haidar, J. A. (2001), *Hispano-arabic Literature and the early Provençal Lyrics*. Richmond. Surrey: Carzon Press.

Adonis, Darwish, M., Al-Qasim, S. In al-Udhari, A. (Ed.) (trans.) (1984) *Victims of a Map: A Bilingual Anthology of Arabic Poetry*. London: Saqi Books.

Agrippa, H. C., Tyson, D. (Ed.), Freake, J. (Trans.) (1992), *Three Books of Occult Philosophy*. Woodbury, MN: Llewellyn.

Akbari, S. C., Mallette, K. (2013), *A Sea of Languages: Rethinking the Arabic Role in Medieval Literary History*. Toronto: University of Toronto Press.

Assis, Y. T. (2008), *The Golden Age of Aragonese Jewry*. Liverpool: Liverpool University Press.

— (1997), *Jewish Economy in the Medieval Crown of Aragon*. Leiden: Brill.

Baer, Y. (1985), *La Historia de los Judíos en la Corona de Aragón*. Zaragoza: Diputación General de Aragón, Departamento de Cultura y Educación.

Baffioni, C. (2010) (Ed.) (Trans.), *The Epistles of the Brethren of Purity, On Logic: An Arabic Critical Edition and English Translation of Epistles 10–14*. Oxford: Oxford University Press.

— (2013) (Ed.) (Trans.), *The Epistles of the Brethren of Purity, On The Natural Sciences: An Arabic Critical Edition and English Translation of Epistles 15–21*. Oxford: Oxford Univserity Press.

Blasco Martinez, A (2009), Jaime I y los judíos de Aragón. In Sarasa Sánchez, E. (Ed.) *La sociedad en Aragón y Cataluña en el reinado de Jaime I 1213–1276*. Zaragoza: Institución Fernando el Católico, 97–134.

Borges, J. L. (2010), *On Mysticism*. M. Kodama, S. J. Levine (Eds.) New York: Penguin Books.

Bourdieu, P. (1986), "The forms of capital" in Richardson, J. (Ed.) *Handbook of Theory and Research for the Sociology of Education*. New York: Greenwood, 241–58.

Brann, R. (2000), "The Arabized Jews" in Menocal, M. R., Scheindlin, R. P. - Sells, M. (eds.) *The Literature of Al-Andalus*. Cambridge: Cambridge University Press, 435–54.

Brener, A. (2003), *Isaac ibn Khalfun*. Leiden: Brill.

Brody, H. (1938), "Šire Mešulam ben Šelomoh de Piera" in *Studies of the Research Institute of Hebrew Poetry in Jerusalem*. Jerusalem: Hebrew Books. [Hebrew].

Burgwinkle, W. E. (1997), *Love for Sale: Materialist Readings of the Troubadour Razo Corpus*. New York: Garland Publishing.

Burnett, C. (1992) "The Translating Activity in Medieval Spain in," in Jayussi, S. K., Marín, M. (Eds.) *The Legacy of Muslim Spain*. Leiden: Brill, 1036–59.

Cabré, M. (1999), *Cerverí de Girona*. London: Tamesis.

Caputo, N. (2007), *Nahmanides in Medieval Catalonia: History, Community, Messianism.Notre Dame*. Indiana: University of Notre Dame Press.

Carabaza Bravo, J. M. (1994), "El agua en los tratados agronómicos al-Andalus," in *Anaquel de Estudios Arabes* 5, 19–38.

Chaytor, H. J. (1933), *A History of Aragon and Catalunya*. Londres: Methuen & Co., Ltd.

Cobban, J. L. (2011), *The Lure of the Lancashire Witches*. Lancaster, UK: Palatine Books.

Cohen, M. Z. (2000), "Moses ibn Ezra vs. Maimonides: Argument for a poetic definition of metaphor (isti'āra)" in *Edebiyat: Journal of Middle Eastern and Comparative Literature*. 11: 1–28.

Copenhaver, B. P. (Ed.) (trans.) (1992) *Hermetica: the Greek Corpus Hermeticum and the Latin Asclepius in a new English Translation*. Cambridge, NY: Cambridge University Press.

Corriente Córdoba, F. (1999), *Diccionario de arabismos y voces afines en iberroromance*. Barcelona: Editorial Gredos.

Darwish, M. (2000), *The Adam of Two Edens: Poems*. M. Akash, D. Moore (Eds.) Syracuse, NY: Syracuse University Press.

Dauber, J. (2009), "Competing Approaches to Maimonides in Early Kabbalah" in Robinson, J. T. (ed.), *The Cultures of Maimonideanism: New Approaches to the History of Jewish Thought*. Leiden: Brill, 57–88.

De Callatay, G. - Halflants, B (Eds.) (Trans.) (2011), *The Epistles of the Brethren of Purity On Magic: An Arabic Critical Edition and English Translation of Epistle 52a*. Oxford: Oxford University Press.

Dickinson, E. (1994), *The Selected Poems of Emily Dickinson*. E. Hartnoll (Ed.) Ware, Hertfordshire: Wordsworth Editions Ltd.

Dimech, A., Grey, P. (Eds.) (2010), *XVI*. Scarlet Imprint.

Dorón, A. (2005), "La posición del poeta en tiempos de Alfonso X: Reflejos literarios" in Martines, J. (ed.) *Actes del X Congrés Internacional de l'Associació Hispánica de Literatura Medieval*. Alicante: Institut Interuniversitari de Filología Valenciana, 689–94.

Egan, M. (Ed.) (trad.) (1984), *The Vidas of the Troubadours*. Nueva York: Garland.

Enright, M. J. (1996) *Lady with a Mead Cup: Ritual, Prophecy, and Lordship in the European Warband from La Tène to the Viking Age*. Dublin, Ireland: Four Courts Press.

Fancy, H. (2016), *The Mercenary Mediterranean: Sovereignty, Religion and Violence in the medieval Crown of Aragon*. Chicago. Illinois: University of Chicago Press.

Faur, J. (2003), "Anti-Maimonidean Demons," in *Review of Rabbinic Judaism*. 6.1. Leiden: Brill, 3–52.

Ferlinghetti, L (2007), *Poetry as Insurgent Art*. New York, NY: New Directions, 12.

Fierro Bello, M. I. (1991), "La emigración en el islam: conceptos antiguos, nuevos problemas" in *Awraq* Vol. XII: 11–41.

Filios, D. K. (2005) *Performing Women in the Middle Ages: Sex, Gender, and the Medieval Iberian Lyric*. New York, NY: Palgrave Macmillan.

Fitzwilliam-Hall, S. (2012), "A Introductory Survey of the Arabic Books of Filāḥa and Farming Almanacs," retrieved from www.filaha.org.

Fleischer, E. (1983), "The Gerona School of Hebrew Poetry" in Twersky, I (Ed.) *Ramban: Explorations in his Religious and Literary Virtuosity*. Cambridge. Massachusetts: Harvard University Press, 35–49.

Forcano, M. (2003), *La lletra apologètica de Rabí Iedaia ha-Penini: Un episodi de la controvèrsia maimonidiana a Catalunya i Provenca*. Barcelona: Universitat de Barcelona, 56-59.

— (1991), "Nova aportació a la poesia polèmica de Meshul-lam ben Shelomó de Piera." in *Anuari de Filologia*. 14: 73–86.

García Sanjuán, A. (2013), *La conquista islámica de la Península Ibérica y la tergiversación del pasado*. Madrid: Marcial Pons.

Gillman, N. (2000), *The Death of Death: Resurrection and Immortality in Jewish Thought*. Nashville. Tennesse: Jewish Lights, 170.

González Alcantud, J. A. (2014), *El mito de Al-Andalus: Orígenes y actualidad de un ideal cultural*. Córdoba: Editorial Almuzara.

González Ferrín, E. (2006), *Historia general de Al-Andalus: Europa entre occidente y oriente*. Córdoba: Editorial Almuzara.

Greer, J. M. (2011), *The Wealth of Nature: Economics as if Survival Mattered*. Gabriola, BC: New Society Publishers.

— (2012), *The Blood of the Earth: An Essay on Magic and Peak Oil*. Scarlet Imprint.

Grey, P. (2015), *Lucifer Princeps*. Scarlet Imprint.

— (2007), *The Red Goddess*. Scarlet Imprint.

— (2013), *Apocalyptic Witchcraft*. Scarlet Imprint.

Holmgren, D. (2002), *Permaculture: Pathways Beyond Sustainability*. Hepburn, Australia: Holmgren Design Services.

Ibn al-'Awwam. (1802) *Kitab al-Filaha*. J. Antonio Banqueri (Ed.) (trans.) Madrid, Spain: Imprenta Real.

Ibn Bajja. (1997), *El régimen del solitario* [*Tadhīr al-mutawaḥḥid*]. J. Lomba (Ed.) (trans.) Madrid: Editorial Trotta.

Idel, M. (1983), "We Have No Kabbalistic Tradition on This" in Twersky, I (ed.) *Ramban: Explorations in his Religious and Literary Virtuosity*. Cambridge. Massachusetts: Harvard University Press, 51–73.

Jayussi, S. K. - Marín, M. (Eds.) (1992) *The Legacy of Muslim Spain*. Leiden: Brill.

Jiménez, E. (2005), "Un poema laudatorio de Mešullam ben Šelomoh de Piera (s. XIII): A Yishaq (Reflexiones sobre el lenguaje)" in *Anuari de Filología*. 26: 55–68.

Johnston, K. R. (1998), *The Hidden Wordsworth: Poet, Lover, Rebel, Spy*. New York: W. W. Norton and Company.

Kaufman, B. (1981), *The Ancient Rain: Poems 1956–1978*. New York, NY: New Directions, 55-56.

Kaufman, M. D. (2011), "The Hermeneutics of Recruitment: The Case of Wordsworth." In *Biography*, Vol 34, 2: 277–97

Klein, E. (2006), *Jews, Christian Society, and Royal Power in Medieval Barcelona*. Ann Arbor. Michigan: University of Michigan Press.

Kruse, J. P. (2014), *The Blue Spark: A Philosophical Treatise on the Reality of Ideas and how to Access this Reality*. Granada: Swamp Lantern Books.

Lehman, J. H. (1981), "Polemic and Satire in the Poetry of the Maimonidean Controversy" in Prooftexts. 1.2: 133–51.

Mazo Karras, R. (2017), *Sexuality in Medieval Europe: Doing Unto Others*. Milton Park, Oxfordshire: Routledge.

Menocal, M. R. (1994), *Shards of Love: Exile and the Origins of the Lyric*. North Carolina: Duke University Press.

— (1987) *The Arabic Role in Medieval Literary History: A Forgotten Heritage*. Pennsylvania: University of Pennsylvania Press.

Metcalf, A. C. (2005), *Go-Betweens and the Colonization of Brazil: 1500–1600*. Austin, TX: University of Texas Press, 12.

Monroe, J. T. - Pettigrew, M. F. (2003), "The Decline of Courtly Patronage and the Appearance of New Genres in Arabic Literature: The case of the Zajal, the Maqāma, and the Shadow Play." In *Journal of Arabic Literature*. 34.1. Leiden: Brill, 138–77.

— (1997), "The Striptease That Was Blamed on Abu Bakr's Naughty Son: Was Father Being Shamed or Was the Poet Having Fun? (Ibn Quzmān's Zajal no. 133)" In Wright J. W., Rowson E. K. (Eds.), *Homoeroticism in Classical Arabic Literature*. New York: Columbia University Press, 94–140.

— (2004) *Hispano-Arabic Poetry: A Student Anthology*. Piscataway, NJ: Gorgias Press.

Monroe, J. T. (2013), "Why was Ibn Quzmān Not Awarded the Title of "Abū Nuwās of the West?" ('Zajal 96', the Poet, and His Critics). In *Journal of Arabic Literature*, 44, Leiden: Brill, 293–334.

Nielson, R. P. (2014), "The Unmappable Sertão" in *Portuguese Studies*, 30:1, Cambridge: Modern Humanities Research Association.

Nirenberg, D. (2009), "Love and Capitalism." In *The New Republic*: 39-42.

— (1996), *Communities of Violence: Persecution of Minorities in the Middle Ages*. New Jersey: Princeton University Press.

Nogueras, M. A. (1994), "Un poema de benvinguda de Meixullam ben Xelomó de Piera," *Anuari de Filologia*. 17: 83–90.

Oberhelmen, S. M. (1997) "Hierarchies of Gender, Ideology, and Power in Medieval Greek and Arabic Dream Literature." In Wright J. W., Rowson E. K. (Eds.), *Homoeroticism in Classical Arabic Literature*. New York: Columbia University Press, 55-94.

Park, K (2013), "Medicine and Natural Philosophy: Naturalistic Traditions" in Bennett, J., Mazo Karras, R. (Eds.) *Oxford Handbook of Women and Gender in Medieval Europe*. Oxford: Oxford University Press.

Patterson, L. M. (1993), *The World of the Troubadours: Medieval Occitan Society*, C.1100–c.1300. Cambridge: Cambridge University Press.

Paz, O. (1993) *La llama doble: amor y erotismo*. Barcelona: Seix Barral.

Prado, A. (2011) "Una lectura anarca de Avempace," retrieved from https://abdennurprado.wordpress.com.

Rensoli Laliga, L. D. (2010), "La escuela de Kabbalah de Gerona: una introducción," in *eHumanista*.14. Santa Barbara. California: UC Santa Barbara, 239–70.

Rexroth, K. (Ed.) (trans.) (1956), *Thirty Spanish Poems of Love and Exile*. San Francisco, CA: City Lights Books.

Ribera Florit, J., Bartolomé-Pons E. (Eds.) (trad.) (2008), *Poemes de Meix-ul-lam de Piera (Girona, s. XIII).* Gerona: Patronat Call de Girona.

— (1982), "La polèmica contra Maimònides reflectida en la poesia de Me-shul-lam ben Shelomó de Piera," *Anuario de Filología*. 8: 177–88.

— (1983), "Una poesia polèmica del jueu català Meshul•lam Shelomó de Piera," *Anuario de Filología*. 9: 187–93.

— (1984), "Un poema laudatori dedicat al rabí Jonà ben Abraham Gerundí," *Anuario de Filologia*. 10: 147–53.

— (1987), "Com mantenir un secret. Segons el poeta Meshul-lam ben She-lomó de Piera" in *Calls*. 1: 7–9.

— (1987), "El poeta polemista Meshullam ben Shelomó de Piera" in *Calls*. 2: 17–25.

Riera Sans, J. (2009), "Jaime I y los judíos de Cataluña," in Sarasa Sánchez, E. (ed.) *La sociedad en Aragón y Cataluña en el reinado de Jaime I 1213–1276.* Zaragoza: Institución Fernando el Católico, 135–55.

Riquer, M. de. (1975), *Los trovadores: Historia literaria y textos*. Barcelona: Editorial Planeta.

Rivera Garretas, M. M. (1995) "La construcción de lo femenino entre musulmanes, judíos y cristianos (Al-Andalus y reinos cristianos, siglos XI-XIII)" in *Acta historica et archaeologica mediaevalia*. vol. 16–17, Barcelona: Universitat de Barcelona, 167–79.

Roach, A. P. (2005), *The Devil's World: Heresy and Society 1100–1300.* New York, NY: Pearson Education.

Robinson, C. (2007)," Love in Times of the Fitna: 'Courtliness' and the 'Pamplona Casket'." in Anderson, G., Rosser-Owen, M. (eds.) *Revisit-ing Al-Andalus*. Leiden: Brill, 99–112.

— (1999) "Return from Exile," SCRIPTA MEDITERRANEA, Vols XIX-XX 1998-1999, 66-70.

— (2002), *In Praise of Song: The Making of Courtly Culture in Al-Andalus and Provence, 1005–1134 A.D.* Leiden: Brill.

Said, E. (1978) *Orientalism*. New York, NY: Pantheon Books.

Scheindlin, R. P. (2000), "Moshe ibn Ezra" in Menocal, M. R., Scheindlin, R. P., Sells, M. (eds.) *The Literature of Al-Andalus*. Cambridge: Cambridge University Press, 252–64.

— (1999a), *Wine, Women, Death: Medieval Hebrew Poems on the Good Life.* Oxford: Oxford University Press.

— (1999b), *The Gazelle: Medieval Hebrew Poems on God, Israel, and the Soul*. Oxford: Oxford University Press.

Schippers, A. (1994), *Spanish Hebrew Poetry and the Arabic Literary Tradition: Arabic Themes in Hebrew Andalusian Poetry*. Leiden: Brill.

Schirmann, J. (1954-1960), *Ha-Shira ha-'Ibrit bi-Sefarad u-bi-Provence.* Jerusalem: Mosad Bialik. [Hebrew]

— (1954), "The Function of the Hebrew Poet in Medieval Spain" in *Jewish Social Studies*.16.3. Bloomington. Indiana: Indiana University Press, 235–52.

Scholem, G., Zwi Werblosky, R. J. (Ed.), Arkush, A. (trad.) (1987), *The Origins of the Kabbalah*. Princeton. New Jersey: Princeton University Press.

Sells, M. (1994), *Mystical Languages of Unsaying*. Chicago. Illinois: University of Chicago Press.

Septimus, B. (1983), "Open Rebuke and Concealed Love: Nahmanides and the Andalusian Tradition" in Twersky, I (ed.) *Ramban: Explorations in his Religious and Literary Virtuosity*. Cambridge, Massachusetts: Harvard University Press, 11–34.

— (2008), "Isaac de Castellón: Poet, Kabbalist, Communal Combatant," In *Jewish History*. 22.1. New York: Springer, 53–80.

Shneidman, J. L. (1959), "The State and Trade in Thirteenth Century Aragon" in *Hispania*.19.76: 366–77.

Silver, D. J. (1965), *Maimonidean Criticism and the Maimonidean Controversy*, 1180–1240. Leiden: Brill.

Snyder, G. (2005), *Axe Handles: Poems*. New York, NY: Shoemaker & Hoard, 51.

Spinoza, B. (2000), *Ethics*. G. H. R. Parkinson (Ed.) (Trans.) Oxford: Oxford University Press.

Stamets, P. (2005), *Mycelium Running: How Mushrooms Can Help Save the World*. New York: Peguin Random House.

Starhawk. (2004), *The Earth Path*. New York: HarperCollins.

Stetkevych, S. (1997), "Intoxication and Immortality: Wine and Associated Imagery in al-Maʿarrī's Garden." In Wright J. W., Rowson E. K. (Eds.), *Homoeroticism in Classical Arabic Literature*. New York: Columbia University Press, 210–33.

— (1981), "Toward a Redefinition of badīʿ Poetry" in *Journal of Arabic Literature*, 12, Leiden, Brill: 3–29.

— (1993), *The Mute Immortals Speak: Pre-Islamic Poetry and the Poetics of Ritual*. Ithaca, New York: Cornell University Press.

Stillman, N. A. (1979), *Jews of Arab Lands: History and Sources*. Pennsylvania: The Jewish Publication Society.

Stratton-Kent, J. (2010), *Geosophia*, vols 1–2, Scarlet Imprint.

Taylor, J. (1988) "Robin Hood." in *Dictionary of the Middle Ages*. New York, NY: Charles Scribner's Sons.

Twersky, I. (1983), "Introduction" in ed. Twersky, I. *Ramban: Explorations in his Religious and Literary Virtuosity*. Cambridge. Massachusetts: Harvard University Press, 1–11.

Valabregue, S. (2006), "Philosophy, Heresy, and Kabbalah's Counter-Theology" in *Harvard Theological Review*, 109.2: 233–56.

Vernet Pons, E. (2005), "Mètriça i estròfica en la poesia de Meixul•lam ben Xelomó de Piera: parallelismes hebreus, àrabs i occitans" in *Actes del II Congres per l'estudi dels Jueus en territoris de llengua catalana*. Barcelona: 37–58.

Viguera, M. J. (1992) *Aṣluḥu li 'l ma'ālī: On the Social Status of Andalusi Women*. In Jayussi, S. K. - Marín, M. (Eds.) (1992) The Legacy of Muslim Spain. Leiden: Brill, 709–725.

Webster, J. R. (1985), "Patronage and Piety" In Burns, R. I. (ed) *The worlds of Alfonso the Learned and James the Conquerer*. Princeton. Nueva Jersey: Princeton University Press, 76–77.

Wehr, H. (1979), *A Dictionary of Modern Written Arabic*, Cowan, J. M (Ed.), Urbana, IL: Spoken Language Services.

Wildermuth, R. (2018), "Saving What We Love," retrieved from https://paganarch.com/2018/02/08/saving-what-we-love/.

Wohlleben, P. (2015), *The Hidden Life of Trees: What they Feel, How They Communicate*. Vancouver, BC: Greystone Books.

Wood, A. (2008), *Of Wings and Wheels: A Synthetic Study of the Biblical Cherubim*. Berlin: De Gruyter, Inc., 1–4.

Wright Jr., J. W. (1997), "Masculine Allusion and the Structure of Satire in Early 'Abbāsid Poetry." In Wright J. W., Rowson E. K. (Eds.), *Homoeroticism in Classical Arabic Literature*. New York: Columbia University Press, 1–24.

Zwartjes, O. (1997), *Love Songs from Al-Andalus: History, Structure, and Meaning of the Kharja*. Leiden: Brill.

Index

☿

A

ʿAbbasid, ʿAbbasids 150

ʿAbd al-ʿAzīz al-Muʿtaman 160

Abū al-Faḍl ibn Ḥasdāy 145

Abū l-Khayr 109, 111–12, 117, 122, 124

Abū Nuwās 50, 156, 168

agriculture 22, 69, 101–5, 107–10, 112–15, 117,–18, 127

Aḥmad I al-Muqtadir ibn Hūd 148

Aḥmad II al-Mustaʿīn ibn Hūd 175

ʿajam, ʿajamī 162

al-Andalus 21, 22, 37, 39, 45, 50, 52–56, 93–94, 106, 108, 110–11, 115, 128, 146–47, 149, 168–69, 189, 191, 195, 199

Al-badīʿ fī waṣf al-rabīʿ (see Badīʿ) 150

Alberti, Rafael 34

alchemy 22, 142, 148

al-Filāḥa an-Nabaṭīya (see also Nabatean Agriculture) 113

al-jabr (etymon) 22

Al-Jabr (treatise) 22

Aljafería, the 152, 171–73, 175–76, 179, 181–82, 185

aljama 192

al-khīmiyāʾ 22

al-Khwārizmī 22

almanac 126–28
Almohad, Almohads 189, 191
Almoravid, Almoravids 49, 52–53, 138, 169, 182
al-Mustaẓahir 156, 160–61
al-Muʿtaḍid ibn ʿAbbād 151
al-Mūʿtaman (see Yūsuf al-Mūʿtaman ibn Hūd) 60
al-Muʿtamid 147–48, 156
ʿAmirid, ʿAmirids 147
ʿandalīb 33, 40
andalusī 49, 52, 56, 61, 94, 102, 108, 111–12, 114–19, 123, 126, 130, 150, 159, 168–71, 194–96
anti-court 187, 189, 195, 210
ʿaql 146, 174, 179
Arab, Arabic 12, 22, 27, 36, 39–40, 45, 48–50, 52–54, 59, 65–66, 71, 95, 101, 111–12, 107, 126–28, 128, 129, 147–49, 153–56, 161, 168–69, 178, 189, 195, 199, 214–15
Aragon, Aragonese 45, 95, 148, 189–91, 196
aristocratic, aristocracy 93–94, 196–98
Aristotle 23, 113, 115, 138
Aṭ-Ṭighnarī 122
Avempace (see Ibn Bājja) 139
Azriel of Girona 192, 193

B

badīʿ (poetics) 37, 146, 148, 150, 157, 158, 159, 160, 177, 178, 179, 181
Badīʿ (poetry anthology/treatise) 150, 151, 152, 176
Banū Hūd of Zaragoza, Hūdī 39, 147, 148
Banū Tujīb 182
baroque 37, 178
bāṭin, bāṭinī 49, 60–61, 158, 171
Bahya ibn Paquda 182
Beatriz de Día 86
Bernart de Ventadorn 87
Bolos Democritos of Mendes 113
Books of Filāḥa 103–4, 106, 108, 111, 113, 116–18, 120–21, 147
Burgwinkle, William E. 89, 94

C

calendar (permaculture) 106, 125–26, 131–32, 134
Capitalism 68, 82, 84, 95–96
Cassianus Bassus 113
Catalan 44–45, 110, 189, 195–96, 199
Cathars, catharism 39, 90
Catholic 44–45, 47, 56, 189, 220
Cerverí de Girona 86, 92, 196
Christian, Christianity 21, 40, 44, 46–47, 52–53, 56–57, 60, 73, 110, 127–28, 138, 147, 161–62, 169, 189, 191, 194–97, 207, 214–16, 220
Church 85, 87–90, 95, 188
civilization 10, 21–23, 27–28, 31, 36–37, 41–43, 50, 53–55, 57, 89, 103–5, 117, 141, 208
Classical 21–23, 36–37, 50, 54, 111, 126, 130
Clement IV 85
cosmogony 19, 20
courtly 56, 82, 84, 86–87, 93–96, 147, 150–51, 159, 168, 184, 210–11
courtly love 85, 87–90, 93–96, 146–47, 158, 168, 177, 182, 195, 197–98, 211
coven 77, 185, 189, 210, 211
cupbearer 40, 60, 94, 146, 149, 153, 156–57, 159, 166, 185–86

D

dār al-ḥarb 23
dār al-islām 23, 107
dār al-kufr 23–26
dār aṣ-ṣulḥ 25
Darwish, Mahmoud 35, 176
Davis, Wade 67, 71
Demdike, Mother 187–88
Descarte, René 68, 208
duende 35, 42, 186
dynastic legitimacy 93, 147

E

East and West 19–21, 27, 185
ecology, ecological 73, 203, 209

elements, classical 48, 117, 123, 130, 138, 142, 148, 172
empire 29–30, 34–36, 45, 48, 60, 70, 82, 84, 93, 95, 108, 148
epistle 10–12, 16–17, 50, 69, 104, 106, 142–43, 148, 207, 214
ethics 11, 85, 98, 189, 198, 207–9, 211
Ezra ben Shlomo 191

F
fairy, fairies 10, 17, 30, 36, 42, 59, 77, 84, 99
fanāʾ 177, 181
fascism 12–13, 210
fatwā 26
filāḥa 101–2, 106–9, 112, 114–17, 126, 143
fin'amor 90, 91, 97–98
fitna 147, 156, 158, 162, 182, 196
Fitzwilliam-Hall 106, 108, 116, 126
flamenco 35, 42, 215, 218
Folquet de Marselha 85

G
García Lorca, Federico 42, 132, 207
ghazal 146, 151, 153, 177
Giraut de Bornelh 87
go-between 14–15
golden age 16, 36, 147, 149, 156
Góngora 35, 71–72, 178
Gui Fouqueis 85
Guilhèm de Peitieus 84

H
Hai Gaon 155
Ḥasday ibn Shaprut 196
Hebrew 11–12, 36, 45, 48, 56, 65, 95, 128, 147, 149, 153–55, 164–65, 178, 183, 192, 195–96, 199
heretic, heresy 21, 28, 37, 39, 60, 90, 138, 146, 148, 150, 155, 157–58, 166, 171, 184, 192, 209
Hermes 15, 17, 63, 68, 70, 78–79, 159, 221
Hermes Chthonios 10, 13, 17, 79, 142

Hermetic 65, 81, 115, 126, 148, 205
hevra 191
hijra 24–26, 28, 30
hinterland 27–28, 30–31
homoerotic, homoeroticism 40, 54, 57, 94, 168–69
homosexual 57, 89, 163, 166
Hūdī 60, 138, 148, 162, 171, 175, 182
Hugo de Santalla 148
husbandry 102–7, 111–12, 116, 127, 143

I

Ibn al-ʿArīf 146, 170, 179
Ibn al-ʿAwwām 102, 111–12, 115, 118–21, 128
Ibn as-Sīd 147, 170–76, 179–81
Ibn Bājja 22, 138–41, 147, 157–58, 170, 176, 218
Ibn Baṣṣāl 111
Ibn Burd al-Asghar 176
Ibn Ḥamdīs 147, 156
Ibn Ḥazm 156, 158–59
Ibn Khaldūn 22
Ibn Luyūn 111–12
Ibn Quzmān 49–50, 52–53, 55–58, 60
Ibn Rashīq 176, 178
Ibn Rushd 138
Ibn Shahīd 162
Ibn Shuhaid 156, 160
Ibn Wāfid 111
Ibn Waḥshīya 113
Ibn ʿAmmār 162
Ibn ʿArabī 11, 61, 171, 177, 181
identity 11–13, 26, 61, 68, 71–72, 186, 189, 198–99, 206–8
iggeret 11
ishāra 178–79
Islam, Islamic 21, 23–25, 36, 44, 46–47, 50, 54–55, 57, 59, 70, 102–3, 105, 107–9, 113, 116–17, 127, 130, 155, 163, 167–68, 182, 185, 189
istiʿāra 178

J

Jābir ibn Ḥayyān 22
jāhilīya 59
Jaime I 189–91, 196
Jew, Jewish 45, 46, 53, 56, 127–28, 138, 153–55, 163–64 , 168–70, 182–83, 189–92, 194–97, 198–99 , 207
jinn 59
joglar 86, 100
joglaressa 86
joi 35, 38, 91, 98, 186
Jonah Gerundi 193
Jonah ibn Yitzhak ibn Buqlaris 182

K

Kabbalah, Kabbalist, Kabbalistic 48, 142, 170, 178, 183, 191–95, 197, 199
kātib, kuttāb 156, 169
k͟hamrīya 151, 153, 177
kitāb al-anwāʾ 128
Kitāb al-Filāḥa 102, 109, 111–12, 115, 117–18
Kruse, J. P. 68

L

Lambarda 86
land, the 10, 13, 27, 42, 63, 65, 85, 101–2, 107, 109, 114, 124, 126, 130–31
language 10, 12–14, 26–27, 30, 34, 36–40, 42, 45, 53, 63–74, 76–77, 79, 81, 90–94, 111–12, 126, 128, 131, 140, 149, 151, 154, 158–59, 177–78, 189, 193, 195, 197–98, 205, 210, 215
Language 48, 63, 67–71
Lawrence Ferlinghetti 14, 43
Lead Books 214, 215
Levi ibn at-Tabban 182
locus amoenus 148, 152, 162
Logos 10
lyric 31, 34–42, 45, 47–48, 58, 66, 82, 84–85, 87–89, 91, 94, 146, 151, 158, 168, 176–77

M

Maimonidean controversy 11, 192–94, 199
Maimonides 154, 192–94, 196–97
majlis, majālis 148–55, 158–60, 162, 170–72, 175–78, 180–85
map (permaculture) 134, 135
Marcabrú 86
Marwān Jonah ben Janah 182
masran 177
medieval 11, 16, 21–22, 36–37, 41, 45–46, 82–84, 86–87, 89, 109–10, 126, 163, 206
Menocal, María Rosa 34, 45
Meshullam (Meshullam ben Shlomo de Piera) 192–93, 195–99
midons 92–93, 97, 99
miʿraj 177
modern, modernity 14, 21–22, 29, 36–37, 41–43, 45, 48, 79, 82, 84, 103–4, 110, 117, 122, 124, 130, 141, 187, 206, 208, 210
modernism, modernist 41–42
Monroe, James T. 46, 52, 57, 58
moon, moonlight 9, 17, 20, 22, 49, 81, 120, 127, 131, 145, 156, 159, 161, 170, 174–77, 181, 183–84, 207, 216–17
morisco 25, 110, 215
Moshe ibn al-Taqanah 182
Moshe ibn Ezra 147, 149, 154, 165–66, 183
mozarab 53
Mudéjar 22
Muslim 22, 24–26, 46, 53, 56, 103, 112, 128, 138, 153–56, 161–64, 166, 168–70, 183, 189–90, 207, 215–16, 220
muwallad 53
muwashshaḥ 49, 138, 146, 157
muʿtazila , muʿtazilī 146, 148, 157–58, 167
mystic 61, 84, 170–71, 175, 178–79, 182, 192–93, 205, 207
mysticism 12, 146, 170, 182–83

N

nadīm, nudamāʾ 153, 156, 170–72, 177
Naḥmanides 192–94, 197
nasi, nesi'im 196–98

Nation-State 36–37, 45, 82
nature 12, 27–29, 31,35, 38, 41, 48, 63, 67, 69, 76, 79, 82, 85, 91, 96–97, 117, 120, 126–30, 137, 139, 140, 142–43, 159, 200, 203–5, 210, 221
nature naturans 142–43, 203
nature naturata 142
nawrīyāt 151
neoplatonic 148, 164, 173
nightingale 34–36, 40, 43, 81
noble, nobility 49, 82–83, 85–87, 93–94, 168, 178, 187, 190, 195–97

O

Occitan 39–40, 83, 85, 92, 195
ʿOmar Khayyām 22
ontology 173

P

Peire Vidal 86
permaculture, permacultural 27, 64, 104–6, 109, 113, 114–16, 118–19, 121–23, 125–26, 132, 135–38, 141–43
Permaculture Principles 114, 136
philology 12–13, 47, 52, 84
philosophy, anti-fascist 12, 219
Pistoleta 86
poetics 59, 146, 148, 150, 152, 158, 160, 167, 175, 178–79, 181, 195
poetry 19, 22, 35, 37–39, 41–43, 50, 53–54, 56, 58–60, 66–67, 69–70, 72, 82, 84–96, 126, 132, 138, 146, 149, 150–55, 158–60, 163, 167–69, 176, 178–80, 182–83, 193, 195–96, 199–200, 210, 214, 218
poetry, Arabic 154
poetry, Hebrew 149, 153, 195, 199
poetry, lyric 35, 39, 84, 87–88, 158
poetry, modern 41–43
poetry, troubadour 22, 85, 87–91, 94–95, 195–96
popular 38, 49, 84, 86–87, 158, 191, 193
progress 27, 36, 45, 70, 113, 116, 141

Q

qaṣīda 59, 95, 195

qaṣrīyāt 152
Qur'ān, Qur'ānic 24, 27, 57–61, 149, 151, 155, 157–58, 163, 166–67, 175, 179, 180–81, 186

R

Raimbaut de Vaqueiras 86
Raimon de Miraval 86
Rasā'il al-Ḥikma 11
Rasā'il Ikhwān aṣ-Ṣafā' 11, 148
Regimen of the Solitary (see Tadbīr al-Mutawaḥḥid) 138
Renaissance 23, 36–37
rewilding 27
Riquer 87
risāla 11, 16, 59, 66, 93–94, 106
Risālat al-Anwār 11
Robin Hood 82–84, 97
Robinson, Cynthia 39, 147–48, 158, 160–62, 171–73, 179–80, 182
Romantic poets, Romanticism 37–42, 84
rosinhols 40

S

sabbat, witches' 146, 184–86
sāqī 94, 159–62, 164, 167–68, 177, 181, 186
Scheindlin 151, 153–55, 165–66
sector (permaculture) 121, 123–24, 135
sefirot 183, 192
senhal 92, 97, 211
sertão 27–31
Shelley, Percy Bysshe 38, 40–41
Shlomo ibn Gabirol 147, 170, 182
Shmuel ha-Nagid 147, 153–55, 183–84
Simard, Suzanne 201, 203
Spanish 15, 37, 42, 44–47, 52, 71, 73, 122, 138, 178, 192, 215, 219–20
Spinoza, Baruch 142, 208
State, the 30, 31, 34–35, 45, 48, 104, 106, 140, 208, 219
story and discourse 11, 19
Sufi 90–91, 139–40, 167, 170, 177, 181

T

Tadbīr al-Mutawaḥḥid (see Regimen of the Solitary) 138
taifa 37, 39–40, 52–53, 60, 94, 146–52, 157–58, 160, 162–63, 168–69, 175, 177–79, 181–84, 186, 195, 198
tawḥīd 181
Tibors de Sarenom 86
time and space 32, 125, 163
topos, topoi 60, 91, 146, 148–49, 151, 161–62, 168, 177, 179–81, 184, 198
tradition, traditional 11–14, 17, 22–23, 25, 30, 38, 42, 64–65, 68–70, 73–75, 84, 93–94, 103, 105, 107, 113, 115–16, 127, 131, 133, 154–55, 163, 168, 181–83, 185, 189, 192, 195, 199–200, 205–6, 209–10, 215
trobairitz 39, 86, 89
trobar clus 81
trobar ric 81
troubadour 22, 35, 39, 84–95, 97–98, 195–96, 198–99, 211
true wealth 101, 142

U

Umayyad 37, 52, 147, 162, 196

V

Varro 113
vassal, vassilic 92–93
vector (permaculture) 123–24, 135

W

wine 35, 38, 49–51, 53–54, 56, 58, 60–61, 138, 145–46, 149–51, 153–57, 159–60, 162, 164–67, 169–71, 176–77, 180, 182, 184–86, 211
witch 14, 19, 30, 34, 36–37, 61, 78, 86, 95, 146, 184–85, 187–88, 211, 221
witchcraft 10–11, 58, 98, 185

Y

Yeats, William Butler 42
Yehuda ha-Levi 56, 165, 169, 183
Yequtiel ben Yitzhak 182
Yitzhak the Blind 191

Yūsuf al-Mu'taman ibn Hūd, (see al-Mū'taman) 148
Yūsuf ibn Ḥasday 182–83

Z

ẓāhir, ẓāhirī 60–61, 158–59
zajal 49–50, 57–58
ẓarf 151
ẓarīf 151
zones (permaculture) 64, 135–36

www.ingramcontent.com/pod-product-compliance
Lightning Source LLC
Chambersburg PA
CBHW071156070526
44584CB00019B/2810
9781732552357